# DAILY PRAYER
## The Worship of God

## Supplemental Liturgical Resource 5

*Prepared by*

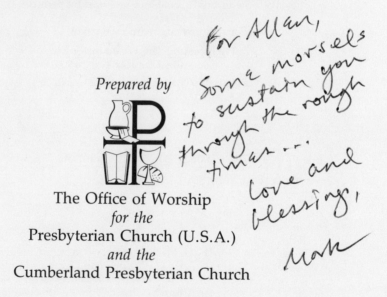

The Office of Worship
*for the*
Presbyterian Church (U.S.A.)
*and the*
Cumberland Presbyterian Church

*Published by*
The Westminster Press
LOUISVILLE

For Acknowledgments, see pages 430–432

Published by The Westminster Press®
**Louisville, Kentucky 40202-1396**

PRINTED IN THE UNITED STATES OF AMERICA
6  8  9  7  5

**Library of Congress Cataloging-in-Publication Data**

Presbyterian Church (U.S.A.)
   Daily prayer.

   (Supplemental liturgical resource ; 5)
   Bibliography: p.
   Includes index.
   1. Presbyterian Church (U.S.A.)—Liturgy—Texts. 2. Cumberland Presbyterian Church—Liturgy—Texts. 3. Presbyterian Church—Liturgy—Texts. 4. Presbyterian Church (U.S.A.)—Prayer-books and devotions—English. 5. Cumberland Presbyterian Church—Prayer-books and devotions—English. 6. Presbyterian Church—Prayer-books and devotions—English. I. Office of Worship for the Presbyterian Church (U.S.A.) and the Cumberland Presbyterian Church. II. Cumberland Presbyterian Church. III. Title. IV. Series: Presbyterian Church (U.S.A.). Supplemental liturgical resource ; 5.
BX9185.P73 1987    242.805137    87-14781
ISBN 0-664-24089-5 (pbk.)

# CONTENTS

# PREFACE

A significant aspect of the contemporary liturgical movement is the rediscovery of the discipline of daily prayer, centering upon praying the psalms. Daily prayer has ancient roots and across the centuries has been important in shaping Christian piety. In sixteenth-century Genevan Protestantism, daily services in the church were the custom. Daily prayer was also an important part of family life. Unfortunately, in Protestantism daily prayer eventually lost its relationship with the psalms. Even more tragically, daily prayer itself is a lost discipline for many. Nevertheless, today there is a widespread thirst for a spiritual discipline that will sustain Christians in the midst of the tests of daily life. Daily prayer is integral to the fulfillment of this need.

In 1980, the antecedent denominations of the Presbyterian Church (U.S.A.), and subsequently the Cumberland Presbyterian Church, took action to begin the process of developing a "new book of services for corporate worship, including a Psalter, hymns and other worship aids." Hope was expressed that this would be an "instrument for the renewal of the church at its life-giving center." The process called for a series of volumes for trial use before the finalization of the book of services.

To those charting the process, it seemed appropriate that among the volumes to be developed, a resource for daily prayer be included. Such a resource would provide for the growing interest that is emerging in daily prayer. It was furthermore envisioned that this book would be ecumenical in scope, reflecting the contributions of the contemporary liturgical movement, and transcending sectarian lines.

The book was also to provide for daily prayer in a variety of situations. It was to be useful for worship when the church gathers, but also for individuals and families as well. It was to be a resource for daily services in congregations (where such are provided), and for worship in various gatherings of Christians, such as session, committee, and staff meetings, as well as meetings of other groups in the church. It would also provide governing bodies an alternative to worship forms presently used. It was also envisioned that the resource would provide individuals and families with a structure for daily prayer and scripture reading.

Whether used by a group of Christians or by one Christian praying alone, the resource for daily prayer was to be an expression of the church's worship, in accord with the living worship of the ecumenical church of our day and with the church's prayer across the centuries. It was hoped that this resource would help us realize that we are never alone in our praying. In praying the church's prayer, both ancient and contemporary, we discover the unity we have with the "saints" of every time and place and experience the value of common prayer.

In 1981, a task force was appointed to develop the resource for daily prayer. The progress of the task force was charted by the Administrative Committee of the Office of Worship during the years of its development. Those who served on the task force during some portion of the years of its development: Donald W. Stake, chairperson; David Dyer; Howard L. Rice; Robert E. Shelton; Sue Spencer; and Harold M. Daniels, staff. The task force worked in close relationship with another task force developing a psalter, which will provide musical settings for the psalms. The Psalter will be a valuable resource for use in relationship with *Daily Prayer*. Examples of psalms and musical settings projected for inclusion in the Psalter have been published in *A Psalm Sampler* (Philadelphia: The Westminster Press, 1986).

As with all other volumes in the Supplemental Liturgical Resources series, the manuscript for daily prayer was carefully reviewed by the Worship Committee of the Advisory Council on Discipleship and Worship, which made suggestions for its revision. Members of the Worship Committee reviewing *Daily Prayer* were: J. Barrie Shepherd, chairperson; Moffet Swaim Churn; Jay Dee Conrad; Melva W. Costen; Frances M. Gray; Robert S. Moorhead; Irene Overton; Franklin E. Perkins; Donald W. Stake; Helen Wright; Elizabeth J. Villegas, staff; and Harold M. Daniels, adjunct staff.

Evaluations of the manuscript *Daily Prayer* were solicited from pastors and laypersons in a variety of situations. Suggestions were also sought from liturgical scholars both in the Reformed tradition and in other traditions. The evaluations and suggestions contributed greatly to the further refinement of the resource, and we are indebted to many people for their invaluable assistance.

Responding to the field responses and review, the task force prepared the final draft of this resource and presented it to the Administrative Committee of the Office of Worship. The Administrative Committee, which has overseen the work of the task force during the years the resource was being developed, then approved the manuscript for publication. Those who served on the Administrative Committee during the time *Daily Prayer* was being developed were: Melva W. Costen; Arlo D. Duba; Lucile L. Hair (former chairperson); Helen Hamilton; Collier S. Harvey; Robert H. Kempes; James G. Kirk; Wynn McGregor; Ray Meester; Robert D. Miller; Betty Peek; David C. Partington (current chairperson); Dorothea Snyder (former chairperson); Robert Stigall; Darius L. Swann; James Vande Berg; John Weaver; Harold M. Daniels, staff; and Marion L. Liebert, staff.

We invite your evaluation of this resource presented to the church for trial use as it anticipates a new book of services. Send your comments to the Office of Worship, 1044 Alta Vista Road, Louisville, Kentucky 40205.

HAROLD M. DANIELS, Director
*Office of Worship*

# INTRODUCTION

In his First Letter to the Thessalonians (5:17), Paul admonishes his Christian friends to pray constantly. This is the calling of every Christian. But in practical terms, even regular daily prayer seems nearly impossible to many and difficult to most. So it is tempting for many Christians today to consider any full schedule of daily prayer more a luxury than a necessity. Those who would like to pray throughout the day are frustrated by an inability to "find the time" and may envy those whose life is ordered in such a way as to have prayer time "built in," such as those in religious communities.

On the other hand, some Christians are confronted by the great paradox of prayer. Prayer, which is a gift given to us by God, is perceived as work, a religious chore, even a burdensome duty. So they put it off or even try to avoid it, and then wonder why they have so much trouble praying.

This book is a response to this double frustration. For it is possible to experience a profound prayer life even in the busiest of schedules. It is, perhaps, the busyness of schedules that makes us see more clearly our need for prayer in our lives. For when we experience prayer as a joyous gift from God, we can begin to grasp for ourselves the life-giving power of daily communion with God. Only by venturing forth in prayer can we discover new vistas of life lived in the presence of God.

There is within each one of us the drive to pray. As Calvin said, "Genuine and earnest prayer proceeds first from a sense of our need, and next, from faith in the promises of God."[1] For the Christian, then, prayer is a means of grace as well as a result of it. Prayer is not merely an expression of established faith; it is also the food that nourishes faith, giving it strength and energy. By the moving of the Holy Spirit, prayer brings us to new life in the fullness of Jesus Christ. Praying, then, is not a burden under which we labor, but the release of energy for joyful living.

This book offers, therefore, a pattern of prayer designed for use by Christians in the latter part of the twentieth century. Yet it is a pattern that draws on the experience and tradition of the Christian church in all centuries.

## The Nature of Daily Prayer

There are two aspects of daily prayer that need our attention because they are so easily neglected.

The first is *discipline*. Daily prayer deserves a discipline. Sometimes we associate a "discipline" with rigidity and consider it to be opposed to "freedom" that allows the Spirit to work. Discipline in prayer may seem to some to be an obstacle to relevant prayer, preventing prayer from being timely and responsive to the Spirit of God. But this need not be so. The Holy Spirit is the Spirit of order present at the creation. By the Spirit prompting our prayers, we are delivered from aimlessness and emptiness in our praying. A discipline of prayer, therefore, can work with the Spirit as we relate our prayers to the circumstances of our daily life.

The need for a discipline in prayer is apparent. Without some discipline, human frailty takes over. Being a disciple of Jesus Christ does not just happen without our commitment and effort, and that part of our discipleship called prayer deserves no less. The common root of the two words "disciple" and "discipline" indicates that they are related in meaning. To pray without discipline means too often to pray randomly, superficially, and infrequently, thus falling into the trap of irrelevance. A discipline of prayer can open us to the presence of God in everyday situations and keep us alert to the moving of God's Spirit within, among, and around us.

Furthermore, to be a disciple is to be one who learns. With the first disciples, we are always asking the Lord to teach us to pray. The model prayer Jesus gave in answer to this request is a guide to us in our praying, a reminder that we are always to be learning as disciples of Jesus Christ. A discipline of prayer, then, tutors us in prayer so that we continually grow in faith.

The discipline of prayer proposed here is a modification of the most common of all disciplines of daily prayer used by Christians for centuries, going back to the early church of the Bible and even to the ancient Jews. It is a durable discipline, having lasted for ages, adapted repeatedly in different times and situations.

The other aspect of daily prayer easily neglected is that of *commonality*. Too often, individualism is emphasized with regard to prayer, suggesting that all that really matters is our one-to-one relationship to God. On the contrary, there is inherent in Christian prayer a corporateness that draws us to others in the experience of prayer. Even when we pray separately, there is a sense in which we pray together. For we come before God as a people, not simply as a collection of individuals. The opening words of the prayer Jesus taught his disciples instructs us as well about our commonality before God in prayer. And the promise of Jesus is for us also: "Where two or three are gathered in my name, there am I in the midst of them" (Matt. 18:20). This is the "Christian quorum" and requires us to be aware of the commonality of our prayer.

We do not live our lives in isolation from those around us, our families, our friends in faith, even strangers. Praying together, we discover that Christ is present, binding us in a community of faith. Common prayer is itself an act of faith in the promised presence of Jesus Christ with his people.

When we pray for others, we discover a new dimension of the discipline of prayer. For in order to pray together, we have to make practical commitments to one another, and we find ourselves encouraged and even challenged to greater constancy in prayer. Mutual discipline is expressed in mutual support.

Beyond the immediate circle of family and friends with whom we pray daily, we become conscious of the wholeness of Christ's church, the people of God in prayer everywhere. When we adopt a discipline of prayer having much in common with how other Christians pray, we are conscious of being at prayer "with" them as well. Now our prayers are not just our own, nor are they reserved for our immediate community. They are joined to prayers of the whole people of God around the world. We are not preoccupied with personal or local concerns; rather, we are inspired to a broader perspective of prayer. As we pray for others, we are confident that we are lifted up in their prayers as well, and we glimpse something of the fullness of Christ's church at prayer.

Some of the prayers offered in this book are borrowed from many traditions and times other than our own. This reminds us of the resource of the whole Christian church, as the Spirit working in the prayers of others enables us to pray. The prayers suggested here may be used as they are, or may be accepted as the promptings of the Spirit to help us articulate our own prayers. In any case, they remind us of our oneness in Christ with men and women and children around the world.

## Biblical and Written Prayers

The prayer Jesus taught his disciples, which we call the Lord's Prayer, serves as a model for our prayers. The biblical texts (Matt. 6:9–13; Luke 11:2–4) are the basis for versions of the prayer used repeatedly in Christian worship. Our personal prayers as well are shaped by this model, for it is the standard by which all prayers are measured.

There are many other prayers in scripture that serve as a great resource for Christian prayer. The Bible provides for us the content, context, and norm for our praying. Not only do we adopt and adapt scriptural prayers for our use, but the whole of scripture provides us with the language and imagery of prayer. Narratives and histories give us images of the Lord whom we worship and pictures of the faithful life we seek to follow. Prophetic voices instruct and challenge us to see a hurting world and people in need. Doctrinal passages teach us "orthodoxy," which literally means not only "right opinion" but also "right worship," to guard our prayers from eccentricity and narrowness. The reading of scripture is integral to daily prayer, therefore, so that our prayers may be rooted in biblical soil.

Similarly, prayers from all generations of God's people are passed down to us in written form. Although they do not have the same authority as scripture, they nevertheless are aids and encouragements to our practice of prayer. In our own generation we find resources in the prayers of others.

A prayer book, therefore, offers continuity with our heritage and community with our contemporaries. Those who write prayers risk sharing what is most personal and intimate. In reading the prayers of others, we are encouraged to give voice to our own personal prayers. We may even be moved to risk sharing out loud in prayer, and by the grace of God our words may articulate another person's prayer. A prayer book is supposed to be suggestive to us, the first words we pray, perhaps, but by no means the last.

# History of Daily Prayer

It is important for us today to realize that our daily prayer has a long tradition. The history of daily prayer is a complex one and is the subject of scholarly study. A brief sketch of that history, however, will reveal something of the rich heritage that is our legacy.[2]

It is clear that early in Judaism a pattern of prayer evolved including morning and evening sacrifices in the Jerusalem Temple, along with psalms and prayers at mid-morning and mid-afternoon. Devout Jews also engaged in private prayers in the evening and morning and at noon, possibly in preparation for the times of common prayer. Daily prayer was not casually observed by a few, but was highly important in the worship of the synagogue.

The early Christian church continued this pattern built on morning and evening prayer. The book of Acts tells us that the first converts to the Christian faith "devoted themselves to the apostles' teaching and fellowship, to the breaking of bread and the prayers" (Acts 2:42). The prayers referred to are services of morning and evening prayer, probably held in homes.[3] An example of such a prayer service is mentioned later in Acts as Peter and John and their friends praise God in the words of the Second Psalm (Acts 4:25–26). As it did with much of its Jewish inheritance, the early church adapted the daily prayer experience to a peculiarly Christian understanding. They saw in the Psalms a prophetic witness to Jesus Christ, and even the hours of the day set for prayer reminded them of the story of Christ's suffering and death.

Morning and evening continued to be the normative times for daily prayer. While the goal was continuous prayer, assigned times were recognized as helpful means toward its accomplishment. The fact that Christians gathered for prayer is also important to note; common prayer was also normative, encouraging constancy in prayer.

Following the establishment of Christianity under Constantine, the structure of daily prayer became more formalized. Actually it developed in two separate strands. The "congregational" style of daily prayer included participation by parish people in responses and hymns, and centered on morning and evening as the principal times. "Monastic" prayer developed simultaneously in religious communities and among the clergy, and concentrated on praying the entire Psalter on a regular basis. Additional times were set for prayer appropriate for the concentrated prayer life of the monastic community. Throughout the Middle Ages, the "congregational" and the "monastic" styles of daily prayer were woven together in a variety of configurations. Eventually, however, the discipline of daily prayer was carried by the clergy and those in religious orders, and was no longer followed by the common people. It became highly complicated and cumbersome, totally impractical for all but the most diligent of religious orders.

The Reformers, especially in Germany, attempted to revive a congregational use of morning and evening prayer. They were firmly committed to daily prayer as essential in the life of the church. And they understood it to be corporate worship.[4] Among the reforms instituted were the concentration on morning and evening prayer and the use of the common language rather than Latin. The Reformers were also anxious to continue the use of the psalms in daily prayer, as well as other biblical songs. These, then, would have to be translated and arranged for the singing of the common people. Scripture was read in continuous fashion, straight through the Bible, often accompanied by instruction.

In Protestantism, daily prayer found a focus in the family. By the end of the sixteenth century, it was common for families to gather each morning to begin the day with prayer. At the evening dinner table, following the meal, the family would sing a psalm, listen to scripture, and join in prayer, the essential ingredients in any service of daily prayer.

Another Protestant focus of daily prayer was as a discipline for pastors. The pastor was to be a student of scripture, but was also to be diligent in prayer and devotion. The study was also a chapel; the place of learning was a place of piety as well.

The Free Churches, those who have their origin in the radical wing of the Protestant Reformation, have been intentionally free of prescribed forms or liturgies so as to allow the worshiper to be freely guided by the Holy Spirit. Still, this tradition has given emphasis to daily prayer, including the reading of scripture and its exposition, and extemporaneous prayer. Some of this "free church" tradition is expressed within our Presbyterian experience, especially in the racial and ethnic communities. The affirmation of community before God in praise, and holding up the needs of the existential situation in prayer, are characteristic of this discipline. Singing is extremely important in involving people fully in praising God. While this approach to prayer is "free" in the sense of being free of prescribed forms, it is nevertheless disciplined. It brings prayer to focus on immediate struggles of living, and is thus intensely practical. It also recognizes the need for a strong sense of community in coming before God in prayer.

Presbyterians have incorporated much of this "free" tradition and at the same time have persisted in providing prayer books with resources for family worship in the home on a daily basis. In recent decades, worship books in Presbyterian and Reformed lineage have given explicit encouragement to the practice of daily prayer by providing prayers and liturgies.

The rise of ecumenism in this century has witnessed cooperation by Reformed Christians in developing daily worship liturgies, as in the Taizé Community in France and in the Church of South India. Presbyterians in Scotland and in the United States have given renewed attention to daily prayer in recent publications. Common study and worship have taken place among Protestants, Roman Catholics, and Eastern Orthodox Christians, and virtually all major faith communities have taken a fresh look at daily prayer.

## Hours of Prayer and the Meaning of Time

Praying at designated hours of the day is one way of acknowledging the rhythm of time. As the sun rises and sets, so we are summoned by time itself to pray to God who rules over time. Thus morning and evening have naturally become the primary times for prayer. They seem particularly appropriate times to praise the God of creation who gives us the years of our lives. As finite creatures, we humans are subject to the limits of time, and our lives find their rhythms in the cycles of nature, the seasons of the year, even in the daily round of light and darkness. Daily prayer, morning and evening, puts us in touch with the Ruler of creation and all time.

The rhythm of daily prayer is rooted in the experience of ancient Judaism. The day begins with sundown, evening before morning, just as it is recorded in the biblical account of creation (Gen. 1:1–2:4). The onset of night reminds us that the God of creation begins with nothingness and shapes it into new life, just as our day begins with the "nothingness" of sleep anticipating the "new life" that comes with the dawn. The church has often continued this perspective by seeing every morning as a celebration of the resurrection that can only follow the "death" of sleep, thus beginning daily prayer with evening. Whether daily prayer is understood as beginning with morning or evening, there is an overlapping effect so that at the end of one day we already anticipate the beginning of the next, looking forward to God's future.

God's redemption in Jesus Christ involves the redemption of time. Jesus Christ, who took on human nature, accepted and entered into the limitations of human time, thereby transforming the meaning of time itself. "Eternal life" offered in Christ is not simply eternal in the sense of duration or a quantity of time; it has more to do with the quality of time. Life that has this eternal quality is life lived before God. Daily prayer, morning and evening, structures our day in such a manner as to remind us that all our times are lived in God's presence. Time is transformed from a measuring device that marks off our chronology into a kind of time that is filled with the presence of God and divine promises for the future.

Daily prayer, therefore, challenges us to think differently about time. Ordinarily we think of the times of our day being blocked out in terms of various activities: meals, work, relaxation, sleep. A certain amount of time is allotted for each, and specific times noted, so that those activities provide a structure for the rest of the day. In this framework we may want to find a time for prayer, but we tend to see it as one of a number of activities to be inserted in the daily schedule.

If time is transformed, however, so that we are conscious of being in God's presence all the time, then daily prayer becomes itself the framework for our common activities. Time for meals, work, play, and sleep is set in the context of prayer and praise to God. Those activities are thus filled with new meaning, the new quality of life called eternal. All we do, the business and busyness of living, is done before God, and our daily prayer makes us conscious of that fact. At meals we will recognize Christ as our host in the breaking of bread and the sharing of food. Our work will be offered as a part of our Christian discipleship and service. Our play and relaxation is also transformed into an experience of God's renewal of our whole lives in Christ. Sleep becomes an act of trust and surrendering ourselves to the eternal care of God. Daily prayer, morning and evening, enables time to be transformed from a round of activities into events of worship because of the presence of God in Jesus Christ.

Morning and evening are the principal times for prayer, but certainly not the only ones. Calvin mandated prayer on arising in the morning, before starting work, at meals, and at retiring for the night.[5] In fact, the times of morning and evening prayer will tutor us in praying at other times. To this end, we may also want to have prayer in the middle of the day and at night before going to sleep. Midday Prayer and Night Prayer are sometimes observed along with Morning Prayer and Evening Prayer. However, Midday Prayer is simply an extension of Morning Prayer, and Night Prayer is an auxiliary of Evening Prayer.

## Themes of Daily Prayer

There are various themes of the Christian faith traditionally associated with the time of daily prayer.

One theme celebrated in Morning Prayer is that of *creation*. Each day is a gift fresh from God, unspoiled and pure, filled with possibilities. It is as though we are given a new creation every morning, and in our prayer together we praise God for the gift of this day and this world, the time and space in which we live.

Morning Prayer is also a time to praise God for the *re-creation* that we see in the *resurrection* of Jesus Christ. In a sense, each morning is a reflection of Easter, and we all receive new life daily because Christ is raised from the dead. Our waking from sleep is a daily "resurrection" as we are offered the gift of new life.

*Commitment* is another theme of Morning Prayer. As we begin a new day, we confess our failures in order to claim God's power in living the day before us more faithfully. We anticipate our day's work and recreation, consciously giving ourselves in it to the service of God. Praising God for all Christ has done for humankind, we pledge ourselves to Christlike sacrificial living. Our prayers focus on those around us, our families and friends, and strangers too. We intercede for them in prayer as we commit ourselves to serve them in the name of Christ.

Midday Prayer picks up these same themes. We are conscious of being in God's world and give continual praise for the creation around us, filled with wonders and opportunities. We rejoice throughout the day, celebrating the new life in Christ that enables us to live life fully in his service. And we draw on the power of God's Spirit to fulfill the moral and ethical responsibilities of Christian discipleship.

Evening Prayer comes at the end of the workday. So *commitment* is also an evening theme, but now it is the offering of the day past to God. We reflect on what has happened, offering to God our praise for the gifts of opportunity and love and power we received, and confessing our failures as well. So we commit it all, good and bad, to God, recommitting ourselves at the same time.

The theme of *resurrection* is also celebrated in Evening Prayer, but with a different emphasis. As the daylight fades and darkness comes, we celebrate the light of Jesus Christ that will not be extinguished, even by darkness of death. Evening Prayer is a time of preparation for sleep, and the theme of death and resurrection is even more clearly accented in Night Prayer. Here there is a consciousness that we are surrendering our lives into God's keeping in anticipation of our own death, confident that God will "raise us to new life" in the morning as we look toward our resurrection in Jesus Christ.

Evening Prayer also celebrates the theme of *creation*, yet from a different perspective from that of Morning Prayer. To the ancient Hebrews the day began with sundown, evening and night being times of preparation and rest for the next morning's work. Christians too have recognized that the end of one day is the beginning of the next, and the sleep of night is in preparation for the morning's work.

Other, more specific themes emerge in Morning Prayer and Evening Prayer under these broad themes of the Christian faith. Different days of the week will prompt emphases on one aspect or another. Sunday morning, for example, will more strongly stress the theme of resurrection. Different seasons of the church year will also focus the themes. For instance, mornings in Lent will likely stress our commitment in response to the total commitment of Christ's obedience to God. The daily cycle of prayers is influenced and informed by the weekly and yearly worship themes.

### Psalms in Daily Prayer

The book of Psalms is a collection of songs of prayer and praise. These songs were used by the ancient Jews for both corporate and individual worship. Apparently they were sung rather than spoken, and they find their fullest expression of praise of God in musical settings.

Christians quickly adopted the psalms for their worship. One reason was surely that Jesus himself used and quoted the psalms. Another was that the early Christians were Jews and brought with them the heritage of the Hebrew psalms. Still another reason was that Christians have recognized that the psalms point to the Christ. Not only were the psalms used by Jesus, they seemed in the eyes of Christians to be about him as well. So the psalms were adopted and adapted by the followers of Christ for their prayers.

The Reformers easily adopted the psalms as Christian prayer, recognizing the continuity between the Old Testament and the New.[6] Bucer, Calvin, and others interpreted the psalms from a Christian perspective. The Psalms have always been central in Reformed piety and worship, and prayer books in the Reformed tradition are often referred to simply as psalters. The Reformers were aware, however, that not all psalms were of the same quality in revealing Christ, so they became selective in compiling their psalters. As early as 1523, Luther called on German poets to translate the psalms so they could be sung by the people as hymns. In 1539, assisted by the poetic talents of Clement Marot and Theodore Beza, Calvin introduced nineteen metrical psalms, inspired no doubt by the singing of psalms in German in Strasbourg.[7] The entire Psalter was completed in 1562. It was a significant achievement in its literary and musical qualities. The tunes were to accentuate and carry the words, for it was the lyrics that spoke of Christ.[8] Yet singable tunes were chosen as a way of restoring the psalms to the people.

The psalms provide for us today a basis for our prayers as they have for Christians through the centuries. By singing them we lift our praises to Almighty God. By offering them as our own prayers we are guided in candid prayer. Some of the psalms seem very unchristian in their attitude, yet even these are directive for us as we intercede for those who feel pain and injustice as the psalmist did. Above all they are realistic prayers, and they call us to realism in our daily prayer.

The psalms are an essential part of daily prayer. The persistent praying of the psalms over a period of time gives one a repertoire of prayers learned by heart. The prayer language of the psalms finds a natural use in our own prayers, enabling us to articulate the deepest prayers of our souls.

The psalms also lend themselves to group use. They may be sung in a variety of settings, with refrains or responses, chanted, or in metrical versions. They may be shared in improvised ways, as when a single verse is selected as a refrain to be sung by all to a simple tune. Psalm prayers may be used at the conclusion of a psalm, restating the essence of the psalm in the worshiper's words. Psalm prayers are also a means of "Christianizing" a psalm, recognizing Christ in the psalm and being explicitly Christian in praying it. Psalm prayers appeared in the French Psalter in 1561, and were translated into English for inclusion in the Scottish Metrical Psalter of 1595.[9] Psalm prayers are included in this book as a way of reclaiming that part of our Reformed heritage.

## Flexibility of Daily Prayer

In the use of the psalms and in arranging daily prayer for particular situations, there is a need for considerable flexibility. Obviously no one resource could be prepared that would be equally useful in every situation without some adaptation. The resources in this book are intended to be modified from place to place according to the particular need and circumstance. This flexibility is inherent in the history of daily prayer and should be a major principle for our guidance today.

First of all, daily prayer does not require any special leadership. It is truly the worship of the people, and anyone can lead any prayer service. The sharing of leadership of daily prayer, in fact, gives opportunity for broad participation in designing each prayer service, making it as meaningful as possible for the worshipers. In a family, for instance, the children may assume the leader's role from time to time and have ownership of the worship experience in a fuller way.

Daily prayer is not confined to any physical setting either. It may be scheduled for mealtimes at home around the table, or at the beginning or end of various church meetings in the local congregation. It can be shared by a few people in any number of locations from schools to offices. Daily prayer may offer the basis for worship in governing bodies or church conferences, delivering them from attempting to provide miniature Sunday worship services each day. The flexibility of daily prayer in terms of setting is a witness to the fact that Christian prayer is not escapism, but is born in the circumstances of everyday living.

While daily prayer is intended to be a shared experience for two or three or more gathered in the name of Christ, there are times when an individual cannot be present with others. That individual may pray privately using these same resources, with the assurance that his or her prayers are joined with those of others.

Come Holy Spirit, come.
Shape our prayers
that God's will may be done in our lives.
Guide us along the Way of Christ
in our journey each day,
that we may know peace and power
in the presence of God.
Come, Holy Spirit, come!

# HOW TO USE THIS BOOK

This book is offered as a resource for daily prayer in a variety of circumstances, and it will need to be adapted by those who use it to fulfill the requirements of the occasion.

The services are ordered along traditional lines. This pattern of daily prayer has developed over many centuries and has been useful to people of faith. Nevertheless, there is considerable flexibility in these services, and they may be shaped according to particular needs.[10]

It is important to remember that this book is not to be used as a substitute for our most personal prayers, but to prompt and encourage us in our daily worship of Almighty God. The prayers offered here are intended to help us pray our own prayers, perhaps serving as models for our prayers, or even suggesting language to give voice to our deepest prayers.

Music is important in daily prayer. Song can transform what otherwise might be a rather pedestrian service into a liturgy that effectively leads worship into prayer. At least the psalms and biblical songs, as well as the hymns, should be sung.[11]

## Daily Prayer and the Church Year

The services of daily prayer are coordinated with the seasons of the church year. The first set of services (pp. 51–84) is provided for use during the weeks that follow Epiphany (until Lent) and the weeks that follow Pentecost (until Advent). These are the portions of the year that fall outside any of the seasons, and they are often referred to as "ordinary time" or (as here) "ordinary days." Alternative texts are provided for this period; thus there are liturgical texts for two weeks. It is suggested that the texts be alternated from one week to another.

Responses and prayers appropriate to the seasons of Advent (pp. 85–108), Christmas and Epiphany (pp. 109–124), Lent (pp. 125–154), Easter (pp. 155–181), and Pentecost (pp. 182–186) are provided along with material for a number of special days in the church year such as Ash Wednesday, Good Friday, and the Ascension of the Lord.

The psalms as incorporated into the services and the lectionary (see pp. 397–419) are also coordinated to the seasons of the church year and help us see daily prayer in that broader context.

## Singing the Psalms in Daily Prayer

The core of daily prayer is the Psalter. We follow an ancient tradition of God's people when we pray the psalms.[12] The psalms are sung prayer, and across the centuries a rich variety of ways to sing the psalms has developed. All of these are readily available for use today. A congregation will be richly rewarded if it cultivates the use of each form, incorporating those settings that are in keeping with the spirit of prayer.

### Prose Psalms

Fidelity to the prose text of the psalms, such as one finds in the Bible, requires a melodic system that accommodates lines and stanzas of varying lengths. In both Christian and Jewish traditions the prose text of the psalms has been chanted throughout the centuries. Historically, the most widely used system in Western Christianity for singing the psalms has been the Gregorian psalm tones. These melodies have long been associated with the psalms and give them a musical expression that is conducive to sung prayer. They are essentially "sung recitation," since they are expressive of the inflections of speech.

There have been recent efforts to make the simpler Gregorian psalm tones accessible for use by the congregation. These tones may be used to sing the psalms *responsorially*. That is, a person (called a "cantor") or a choir sings the stanzas of the psalm, and the congregation sings a refrain after each verse or group of verses. This is the earliest form of singing the psalms in Christian worship, taken into the church from Jewish usage.

To enable the psalms to be used responsorially, refrains are provided for use with each psalm incorporated into the services (pp. 207–254). A psalm refrain is ordinarily a verse of the psalm that expresses a key thought of the psalm. Often the text is rephrased to lend itself better for use as a refrain. An example is seen in the second refrain offered in this book for Psalm 23 (p. 213). The first refrain for Psalm 23 shows how some paraphrasing adapts a thought from a psalm for use as a refrain. Refrains may be sung by all even if the psalm is spoken. Suggestions for ways to sing the refrains with psalm tones, or when the psalm is spoken, are provided on pages 377–380.

In most versions of the Bible, psalms are laid out so that there are spaces between some verses, dividing the psalms into sections. It is appropriate to use a congregational refrain at each such division as well as at the beginning and end of the psalm.

Psalm tones may also be used to sing the psalms *antiphonally*. In singing the psalms antiphonally, two segments of the gathered community alternate in singing verses of the psalm. For example, the choir might sing antiphonally with the congregation, or female voices might sing antiphonally with male voices, according to the same divisions or by simply alternating verses.

Singing the psalms antiphonally makes possible the utilization of Hebrew parallelisms. For instance, Psalm 23 might begin as follows:

Cantor (or Group 1):          The Lord is my shepherd;

Congregation (or Group 2):    **I shall not want.**

Cantor (or Group 1):          He makes me to lie down in green pastures;

Congregation (or Group 2):    **He leads me beside the still waters.**

In singing prose texts it is important to select a text that adequately captures the poetic imagery of the psalms and is easily intoned. One could use psalm texts directly from the Bible, but a liturgical psalter is preferable, since the texts of liturgical psalters are arranged for singing.[13]

Some liturgical psalters are pointed (marked to indicate how the syllables of the text are to be allotted to the tone), others are not. Until the intoning of psalms becomes second nature, it will be necessary to point an unpointed text in accordance with the particular tones being used. Pointing a text is relatively easy and can be learned by examining pointed texts. A list of liturgical psalters is included on page 386. Suggestions for pointing psalm texts are provided on pages 377–379.

Eight psalm tones and refrains are included in this book for singing prose texts of the psalms (nos. 84–91). They strive for a contemporary character. A tone is provided for each type of psalm. By learning the refrains accompanying the tones, a congregation will know a sufficient number of refrains for use with the entire Psalter. Care will be needed to use the appropriate tone and refrain for the kind of psalm being sung. Prose psalm texts may be sung to other tones found in the resources listed on pages 385–392.

Psalms sung to psalm tones are most effective when sung without accompaniment. There is great power and beauty in unison unaccompanied singing. Handbells may be used to establish pitch at the beginning and at appropriate places during the singing.[14] Accompaniment is provided in most available resources for circumstances where it is felt that organ accompaniment is needed. The accompaniment provided with most sets of psalm tones illustrates the restrained style of accompaniment that is required.

### Gelineau Psalms

Another way to sing the psalms is Gelineau psalmody. This method depends upon a particular text of the psalms, the Grail translation, and corresponding melodies. Unlike metrical psalms and the psalm tones noted above, Gelineau psalmody is organized on an accentual basis. Each line has a prescribed number of accented syllables, even though the total number of syllables in a line will vary. It is called "sprung rhythm." An example of this rhythmic principle is "Three Blind Mice." The rhythmic structure of each line is the same (three beats), although the number of syllables in each line varies between three and eleven. The text in Gelineau psalmody follows this accentual structure.

The Gelineau psalm tones are based on ancient psalm tones from Gregorian, Ambrosian, and other sources. Since their introduction (1953 in French; 1963 in English), Gelineau psalms have found an established place in psalmody. Sources of Gelineau psalmody are listed on page 389.

## Metrical Psalms

For many people, the most familiar way to sing the psalms is to use metrical psalms. A metrical psalm is a psalm in which the psalm text is paraphrased into poetic meter (usually rhyming) and sung to a hymn tune. Such a psalm is sometimes called a "psalm hymn." Familiar metrical psalms include: Psalm 23, "The Lord's My Shepherd, I'll Not Want"; Psalm 42, "As Pants the Hart for Cooling Streams"; Psalm 95, "O Come and Sing Unto the Lord"; Psalm 100, "All People That on Earth Do Dwell"; and Psalm 121, "I to the Hills Will Lift My Eyes."

Introduced in the sixteenth-century Reformation, metrical psalms put the psalms back on the lips of the people. The result was that metrical psalms implanted the spirit of the psalms deep within Reformed piety.

However, in spite of the important role metrical psalms have played, psalms lose something of their lyrical quality when forced into the restrictions of meter and rhyme. Since by their very nature metrical psalms are paraphrases of psalm texts, they reflect a manipulation of the text not required in prose translations. The result is that they do not fully convey the original poetic text of the psalms. They often suffer from contorted syntax that obscures the sense of the poetry. Often the tune drowns the words of the psalm. Furthermore, most congregations are unaware that a metrical psalm is anything other than a hymn. Nevertheless, metrical psalms have a continuing place of importance in psalmody and should be embraced alongside other ways of singing the psalms. Metrical psalms are readily available in many hymnals. See page 390 for suggested sources for metrical psalms.

While it is desirable to sing the psalms, it may not always be possible. Therefore prose texts of the psalms may be spoken and shared by the worshipers responsorially or antiphonally.

## Psalms Used Daily

Certain psalms have long been associated with Morning and Evening Prayer. Those included in this resource (nos. 92–95) are Psalms 95; 100; 63; and 51. One of these is suggested for use each morning. Psalms 67 and 24 have also been long used in Morning Prayer. They provide further alternatives.

The use of Psalm 141 in Evening Prayer is rooted in a long tradition. This psalm leads us to reflection and repentance. It is suggested for use on each Saturday and Sunday evening. A metrical setting (no. 96) and a responsorial version (no. 112) are provided.

Since Psalm 141 speaks of our prayers rising like incense before God, it is appropriate that incense be used as the psalm is sung. The Christian use of incense is rooted in Jewish Temple worship. In the Bible, as is clear in Psalm 141, incense symbolizes our prayer ascending before God. Heaven and earth are thus joined in a visible and sensuous way.

An unthreatening way to introduce the use of incense is to place one or two pieces of self-starting charcoal in a metal bowl filled with sand. The bowl is placed on a small stand. The charcoal is lighted in advance of the service so that it is red hot by the time the service begins. As the words from Rev. 8:3–4 and Psalm 141 are sung or said, grains of incense resin are sprinkled on the charcoal. Such use of incense is unobtrusive, yet the fragrance of the incense fills the space. Epiphany is a particularly fitting occasion to use incense, since on that day we recall the visit of the magi, who brought frankincense as a gift for the infant Jesus.[15]

### Psalm Prayers

Psalm prayers are provided for each of the psalms incorporated into the services (pp. 207–254) and are suggested for use with all psalms except the opening psalms in Morning Prayer. Each psalm prayer captures some theme or image from the psalm and usually adds Christian implications drawn from the psalm. The prayer helps us to pray the psalm ourselves and also helps us see Christ in the psalm as we pray. Psalm prayers may be composed in this way to focus on emphases of immediate need to the worshipers. The psalm prayer is spoken by the leader following a period of silent reflection after the psalm is sung or read. The psalm prayers in this resource are from various traditions; many are based upon psalm prayers from the Scottish Psalter (1595).[16]

### Biblical Songs

In addition to psalms, daily prayer incorporates the singing of other biblical texts. Three songs from the Gospel of Luke are traditionally used in daily prayer in Western Christianity: the Song of

Zechariah or *Benedictus* (Luke 1:68–79), the Song of Mary or *Magnificat* (Luke 1:46–55), and the Song of Simeon or *Nunc Dimittis* (Luke 2:29–32). They are called Gospel Canticles, not only because they come from a Gospel, but because they witness to the message of the gospel. Since these are used most often, musical settings are provided in this book (see nos. 96–99, 112). Other available settings are suggested on page 390.

The Song of Zechariah is traditionally sung in Morning Prayer. It is particularly appropriate for use in the morning because of the words, "The dawn from on high shall break upon us." In this song, Zechariah, the father of John the Baptist, sings, assured of the fulfillment of God's ancient promise. He addresses his son, "You, my child, shall be called the prophet of the Most High." This song looks toward the future, to the dawn of the day when God's purpose for humanity will be fulfilled, when we shall dwell in the full light of the kingdom of God.

The Song of Mary is traditionally sung in Evening Prayer. As the darkness deepens and the lamps are lit, Mary's song becomes the church's song. Like Mary bearing the fulfillment of the promise of the ages in her womb, so we wait for the fulfillment of God's promises in the kingdom of God.

The Song of Simeon is traditionally sung in Night Prayer. The aged Simeon had long awaited and watched for the coming of Christ. At last, he held the Savior in his arms. Knowing that the ancient promises were now fulfilled, he was content to die.

A variety of other biblical songs are suggested in the orders of the services, appropriate for the changing liturgical seasons. When the traditional song is not used, it is suggested that a biblical song from the Old Testament be used in the morning and one from the New Testament be used in the evening. Texts of biblical songs are provided (nos. 7–25). They may be sung or said in the same manner as suggested for the psalms. An Index of Biblical Songs and Ancient Hymns is provided at the end of this book.

## Hymns

The traditional hymn sung at the lighting of the candles at Evening Prayer is the ancient Greek hymn *Phos Hilaron*, referred to in this resource as the Hymn of Light. Its use dates from very early in Christian history. Basil the Great in the fourth century spoke of the singing of this ancient hymn as a cherished tradition. One setting is included in this book (no. 100); sources for additional settings may be found in the resources listed on page 390.

Other hymns may be sung as noted, some familiar hymns being particularly suited for Morning Prayer and others for Evening Prayer (see pp. 381–384). The Song of Simeon (without refrain) is an appropriate alternative to the optional hymn or spiritual at the end of Evening Prayer when there is to be no Night Prayer.

### Singing Other Texts

There may be occasions when it is desirable to sing more of the liturgy than the psalms, hymns, and biblical songs. Certain litanies are effective when sung. The opening sentences and the dismissal might be sung. Such occasions for singing the full service might include vespers on an occasional Sunday evening, or on the eve or evening of major festivals. The singing of Night Prayer is an effective way to end the day and is usable after an evening committee meeting, or by a group in a retreat setting. Consequently, a musical setting is provided for alternate use. This book includes some music for singing many of the texts in the services (nos. 83–113). A tone is provided (no. 83) that may be used with most of the opening sentences and dismissals. Other music may be found in the resources listed on pages 385–392. (Note that in the rubrics of the services, an asterisk [*] after a number indicates a musical setting.)

In building a service, careful attention should be given to each detail. Care should also be taken to select musical settings that are in keeping with the mood of the liturgical season. For example, musical settings during Lent will be more restrained than those used during the season of Easter.

### Lectionary

A daily lectionary is also included in this resource (pp. 397–419). Three readings are provided for each day. The readings may be incorporated into Morning and Evening Prayer as suggested in the introduction to the lectionary (p. 395), or in other ways that may be useful.

Many of the readings in this lectionary are a series of consecutive readings from a book of the Bible. This lectionary therefore has its greatest value when used daily, since the reading for a particular day is read in relation to the readings that have immediately preceded.

For this reason, when Morning and Evening Prayer are not held daily (as may be the case in a congregation, meetings of committees or governing bodies, or retreats), it may be preferable to select the readings by some other method than this lectionary. One such method is to use the Sunday lectionary, choosing readings appointed for the nearest Sunday in the table of readings for the years not in current use. For example, on a day following the Fourth Sunday of Easter during a year when Cycle B is being used, readings may be chosen from Cycles A and C for the Fourth Sunday of Easter.

The scripture reading may be briefly interpreted, or discussed. While a sermon is not ordinarily a part of daily prayer, there may be occasions when the proclamation of the Word may be desirable. Or other devotional readings from Christian literature may be shared.[17] In any event, the reading of scripture should be followed by a period of silence, time for personal reflection and meditation on the Word, and listening for that Word spoken personally.

## Other Use of Scripture in Daily Prayer

It is fitting that a resource for daily prayer in the Reformed tradition be firmly rooted in scripture. Not only do the services include psalms, biblical songs, and scripture readings, but much of the liturgical text is also in words of scripture. The versicles, the verses that begin the service and introduce the prayers, are taken from scripture. Morning Prayer begins with words from Psalm 51:15, "O Lord, open my lips. . . ." Evening Prayer and Night Prayer begin with Psalm 70:1: "O God, come to our assistance. . . ." Midday Prayer begins with Psalm 124:8. The opening sentences that follow are ordinarily verses from scripture. The references are displayed in the text.

Biblical verses also introduce the prayers of thanksgiving and intercession. The verse used in Morning Prayer, "Satisfy us with your love in the morning . . . ," is based on Psalm 90:14. The verse used in Evening Prayer on Sundays and Saturdays, "Receive my prayer as incense . . . ," is Psalm 141:2. The verse used in Evening Prayer on Mondays through Fridays, "Let us walk in love . . . ," is Ephesians 5:2. Psalm 31:5 and Psalm 17:8 comprise the major part of the versicles introducing the prayers in Night Prayer.

The dismissals are also in words of scripture. The references for these are included in the text of the services.

## Prayers of Thanksgiving and Intercession

This resource includes a series of prayers (nos. 26–72) for use in daily prayer. These prayers can prompt us in thanksgiving and intercession over a broader range of concern than we might otherwise pray. Most of the prayers are structured to include free prayer by providing an opportunity for the leader or worshipers to offer those concerns that are currently paramount. Prayers are provided for use throughout the week, both for "ordinary days" and for the seasons and festivals. The litanies will be particularly useful in groups.

The Litany (no. 40) is an ancient prayer and comes from the Eastern Orthodox tradition. It is most effective when sung. The Great Litany (no. 41) is very old, having roots in a variety of sources in Western Christianity. It was revised and incorporated in both Anglican and Lutheran service books of the sixteenth century. A version of it appeared in *The Book of Common Worship* (1946). There is a long tradition of singing the Great Litany in procession on Sundays of Advent and Lent, and at penitential times "as a dramatization of our passage through this world toward that which is to come."[18] The *Lutheran Book of Worship*, as noted on page 391, includes musical settings for both of these litanies.

The prayers of thanksgiving and intercession may be used as they are, or may serve as models for free prayer. In any event, the prayers of thanksgiving and intercession should be offered in a manner that is appropriate for the particular group.[19]

## Silence in the Service of Daily Prayer

Silence is particularly important in these services, for they are services of prayer. Silence helps us to be more deliberate than rushed in our worship, and encourages a contemplative attitude.

The services might begin with silence as a way of "centering" and beginning to focus one's whole person on God in prayer. This is particularly desirable in Morning Prayer, when silence is broken with the first words of the service, "O Lord, open my lips."

In addition to a period of meditation and reflection following the hearing of scripture, there are other places in the service where silence is incorporated.

There should be a time of silence following the singing or speaking of each psalm. This is not only for reflecting on the meaning of the psalm but more especially for absorbing the psalm as a personal prayer. In this way the words of the psalmist give guidance to the words of our own prayers, and we learn to listen to the promptings of the Spirit within us.

Similarly, there is silence incorporated into the prayers of thanksgiving and intercession. Again, this allows the prayers of the people to be personalized.

During these periods of silence a comfortable posture of prayer should be adopted as one's breathing is allowed to deepen and one fulfills the command, "Be still, and know that I am God" (Ps. 46:10).

### The Service of Light

Since the beginning of civilization, people have lit lamps as darkness approached. It has always been more than a utilitarian act, for associated with it have been the ancient symbols of darkness—light and fire. In Jewish worship the Sabbath begins with the blessing of the evening light. In Christian worship the lighting of lights as worship begins has continued.

In early centuries, Christians marked the eve of Sundays and major festivals in cathedrals and parish churches in a special way in the service of light *(lucernarium)*.

This ancient service of light is incorporated into the services of this book on all Saturday and Sunday evenings and on the eve of major festivals. The services include the lighting of a candle and carrying it in procession into the midst of the assembly. The Hymn of Light *(Phos Hilaron)*, the thanksgiving for light, and the singing of Psalm 141 follow. A musical setting for the service of light is provided (nos. 102–109).

The service of light is a dramatic portrayal of creation and resurrection. The candle symbolizes Christ the Light of the world, who shines in the midst of this world's night. The God who in the darkness of the first creation said, "Let there be light," in the new creation called forth Christ from the darkness of death. We are reminded that the darkness of chaos, fear, and defeat, though always threatening, is driven back by the coming of the light of Christ.

The church should be very dimly lighted before the service, the people waiting in silence. The service beginning with a procession in which a large candle is carried into the darkened church gives drama to the emphasis of Christ as the light of the world. A large unadorned candle is used. Although the candle should be the size of the paschal candle, the paschal candle should not be used, to avoid confusing the symbolism. The one carrying the candle leads the procession, since the candle as the representation of Christ is the principal focus of attention. The one carrying the candle sings the verses responsorially with the congregation, during the procession, or after the candle is placed in its stand. The stand for the candle should be placed in the center of the chancel or in the center of the assembly.

On Epiphany the people may be given candles as they enter. These may be lit from the large candle during the singing of the Hymn of Light, *Phos Hilaron*, thereby filling the space with light.

Other lights may be turned up after the candles are lighted. Nevertheless, the light should not be too bright, in order to ensure an environment conducive to a meditative spirit.

Following the singing of the hymn, the thanksgiving for light is offered. Sources for music to sing the thanksgivings are noted in the list of resources on page 391. When the thanksgiving for light is sung, the versicle introducing the prayer is also sung. Musical settings for the thanksgivings also include music for the versicle.

The thanksgiving for light concludes the portion of Evening Prayer called the service of light. The service continues with Psalm 141 and the remainder of the order for Evening Prayer.

## The Environment for Daily Prayer

Effective services of prayer require a sensitivity to environmental aspects of the actions. The space and all of the visual aspects should contribute to the spirit of prayer.

Worship leaders ought not to dominate in services of prayer. Since the services center on praise and prayer, and unordained as well as ordained persons may lead them, a simple white alb without stole is a fitting vestment for leaders.

Since services of daily prayer are not centered on the Eucharist, and normally do not include preaching, a different kind of worship space is desirable. Neither the holy table nor the pulpit is the focus. A different seating configuration is preferable to one designed to gather the people around the holy table or to hear a sermon. Furthermore, a configuration in which everyone faces forward militates against this form of prayer.

If the seating is movable, an effective configuration is to arrange the seats in rows facing each other across a broad center aisle, with a reading desk closing one end of the aisle. For Evening Prayer, candles may be placed beside the reading desk. If the service of light is used, the large candle is placed in front of the reading desk between the rows. In this configuration, leaders of worship do not dominate, since they are in the midst of the worshipers (see Diagram A).

**Diagram A. Arrangements for Daily Prayer**

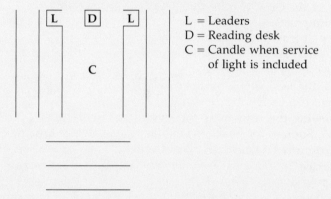

L = Leaders
D = Reading desk
C = Candle when service
    of light is included

In buildings having a divided chancel in which the choir is divided into two sections facing each other, small groups might gather in the choir stalls for daily prayer. The reading desk is placed at the open end opposite the holy table (see Diagram B).

**Diagram B. Daily Prayer in Chancel**

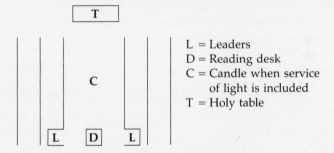

L = Leaders
D = Reading desk
C = Candle when service
    of light is included
T = Holy table

## Adapting the Prayer Services

While the suggested format is a traditional one, it is not necessary that it be rigidly followed. However, it is suggested that initially these services be used essentially as presented here so that the worshipers may become familiar with the rhythm and flow of the services.

The following outlines of the services for Morning and Evening Prayer may be useful in adapting the material for particular occasions or circumstances. The basic order set forth in this resource is displayed in the center. The abbreviated order is suggested for situations requiring an abbreviated service. In this order some elements are deleted without destroying the integrity of the service. In situations where some form of interpretation of the Word is desired, the expanded order is suggested.

| *Abbreviated Order* | *Basic Order* | *Expanded Order* |
|---|---|---|
| Opening Sentences | Opening Sentences | Opening Sentences |
| | Morning Psalm | Morning Psalm |
| | or Morning Hymn | or Morning Hymn |
| Psalm | Psalmody | Psalmody |
| Psalm Prayer | Psalm and Prayer | Psalm and Prayer |
| | Psalm and Prayer | Psalm and Prayer |
| Scripture Reading | Scripture Reading | Scripture Reading |
| | | Interpretation |
| Silence | Silence | Silence |
| | Biblical Song | Biblical Song |
| Prayers | Prayers | Prayers |
| of Thanksgiving | of Thanksgiving | of Thanksgiving |
| and Intercession | and Intercession | and Intercession |
| Lord's Prayer | Lord's Prayer | Lord's Prayer |
| | | Hymn or Spiritual |
| Dismissal | Dismissal | Dismissal |

Adaptations of the order for Saturday and Sunday evening may be similarly made as follows:

| *Abbreviated Order* | *Basic Order* | *Expanded Order* |
|---|---|---|
| | Entrance of Light and | Entrance of Light and |
| Opening Sentences | Opening Sentences | Opening Sentences |
| second set beginning: | first set | first set |
| "O God, come . . ." | | |
| | Hymn of Light | Hymn of Light |
| | or Evening Hymn | or Evening Hymn |
| | Thanksgiving | Thanksgiving |
| | for Light | for Light |
| | | Incense |
| | Psalm 141 | Psalm 141 |
| | Psalm Prayer | Psalm Prayer |

| Psalter | Psalter | Psalter |
|---|---|---|
| Psalm Prayer | Psalm and Prayer | Psalm and Prayer |
|  | Psalm and Prayer | Psalm and Prayer |
| Scripture Reading | Scripture Reading | Scripture Reading |
|  |  | Interpretation |
| Silence | Silence | Silence |
|  | Biblical Song | Biblical Song |
| Prayers | Prayers | Prayers |
| of Thanksgiving | of Thanksgiving | of Thanksgiving |
| and Intercession | and Intercession | and Intercession |
| Lord's Prayer | Lord's Prayer | Lord's Prayer |
|  |  | Hymn or Spiritual |
| Dismissal | Dismissal | Dismissal |

When worshiping *alone* one may wish to abbreviate the services even more than is suggested here. The basic elements of psalm, scripture, prayer, and silence may be sufficient for individual use. However, even individuals may find it helpful if the opening sentences and dismissal are spoken aloud, and the hymns sung. An individual may want to change the language of prayer from plural to singular, or the plural may be retained as a reminder that though we may be alone when worshiping, we are still part of the fellowship of Christ's church.

In a *family* the services may be used at meals or other convenient times of the day. Children should be encouraged to take part in the leadership of the services. Younger children may help with lighting the candle, and older children may read scripture. Leadership of the services may be rotated among family members. Special decorations may be made by family members for particular days or seasons of the year. Familiar hymns or songs may be sung from memory, or from songbooks or hymnals kept handy. The service may be streamlined as desired.

In a *small church group,* the services may also be useful. Morning Prayer may be adapted for the beginning of church staff meetings or other group meetings at church. Evening Prayer may begin the meetings of boards or committees. Or a time may be set aside in advance of regular church group meetings for daily prayer. Meetings may incorporate Midday Prayer or end with Night Prayer as appropriate.

*Larger church groups* may also find use for daily prayer services in this format. Annual church meetings or dinner meetings may incorporate Evening Prayer. Longer meetings, such as those of presbyteries or retreats, may make use of several times of worship according to the outline of daily prayer. Particular scripture readings appropriate to the theme or emphasis of such meetings, or related to the Sunday Lectionary, may be used. Sermons may be preached as the "interpretation" of scripture.

It is difficult to suggest the possibilities because there are so many, and various circumstances call forth different and creative adaptations. Worshipers are encouraged to develop their own style and particular expressions. It is important to remember that a prayer book is a resource to encourage our prayer life and is not to be used slavishly.

Finally, while these services may be adapted to very brief time constraints, it is helpful if they are not rushed. The Orthodox tradition is very explicit in this. Guidance for Morning Prayer states: "If the time at disposal is short, and the need to begin work is pressing, it is preferable to say only a few of the suggested prayers, with attention and zeal, rather than to recite them all in haste and without due concentration."[20] Daily prayer should not be driven, but should be relaxed in order that the Spirit of God might be given opportunity to prompt our prayers and surprise us.

### Preparing to Lead a Service

There are certain things that should be done in advance of a service of daily prayer.

1. The leader should be selected or determined. Usually it is helpful for one person to be in charge of a particular service, although many may have different leadership roles.

2. The structure of the service should be determined. The leader will want to decide which optional parts will be included and the specific order. For instance, if it is Evening Prayer, the leader will have to decide whether or not the service of light is to be included. If so, a suitable candle will need to be secured. If not, will a candle be lighted anyway, and will a hymn be sung? Other choices will be similarly made. Which opening psalm or hymn, which psalms selected from those listed, and which biblical song will be used, these are among other choices to be made.

3. Responsibilities should be assigned to other participants. For example, who will lead the opening sentences and the psalter; who will read the scripture, lead the prayer?

4. Participants should prepare their individual parts. For instance, the person leading a psalm should decide how it will be shared—re-

sponsorially, or antiphonally, or sung in a metrical version, or in some other way. The person reading scripture should consult the lectionary and determine which passages should be read, or decide on other appropriate texts. The person leading in the prayer may want to solicit concerns to include in prayer, or decide how to invite the participation of others at that time of the service.

5. The room or place should be prepared so that the setting is conducive for worship. Where seating is movable, a decision needs to be made relative to the arrangement of the seats, the location of a reading desk, and the placement of candles if it is Evening Prayer. In the home, the family dinner table may be arranged with an open Bible and candles. Or another place in the home may be similarly set aside for such prayer services. Other arrangements may be made according to the season. Bibles and songbooks or hymnals or other worship resources should be made available.

6. A time should be set. For individuals this may be a regular time each day; for families it may be at meals or other times in the day; for church groups the times of prayer may be determined in relation to meeting times. In all cases, it is desirable to have a regular time clearly set aside for daily prayer. The time should be announced to all concerned in advance.

# ORDER
# FOR
# DAILY
# PRAYER

# ORDER FOR
# MORNING PRAYER

*Opening Sentences*
   The opening petition and response are followed by other biblical
   sentences appropriate for the day.

*Morning Psalm or Morning Hymn*
   One of the morning psalms (95; 100; 63; or 51), a doxology, or a
   morning hymn is sung (see pp. 381–382).

*Psalter*
   One or more of the psalms appointed for the day may be sung or
   said. A refrain may be sung or said before and after the psalm, or
   at the end of each division of the psalm. Silence for meditation
   follows each psalm. A psalm prayer appropriate to each psalm
   follows the silence. Suggested refrains and psalm prayers may be
   found on pages 207–254.

*Scripture Reading*
   A reading of scripture from the lectionary (pp. 397–419) is followed
   by:
      This is the Word of the Lord.

      **Thanks be to God.**

   The scripture may be interpreted, discussed, or augmented by
   nonbiblical readings. A time of silence may be included for reflection on the meaning of the scripture.

*Biblical Song*
   The Song of Zechariah (nos. 1, 97\*) or an Old Testament song (nos.
   7–14) may be sung or said.

*Prayers of Thanksgiving and Intercession*
   Following the introductory sentences, free prayer may be offered,
   giving thanks for God's blessings and expressing concerns for the

---

\*Asterisk indicates a musical setting.

needs of others; or an appropriate prayer may be selected from prayers numbered 26–72. There may be a time of silent prayer before the concluding prayer and the Lord's Prayer.

*Hymn or Spiritual*
If desired, a song of affirmation may be sung.

*Dismissal*
Following the dismissal, a sign of peace may be exchanged.

# ORDER FOR
# EVENING PRAYER

## Sunday and Saturday
## (including Service of Light)

## Monday Through Friday

*Entrance of the Light
and Opening Sentences*
When this service of light begins
Evening Prayer, the room is dimly
lit. A large candle is lighted and
brought in procession to a promi-
nent place as the opening sentences are sung or said.

*Opening Sentences*
The opening petition and
response are followed by
other biblical sentences
appropriate for the day.

*Hymn of Light*
The Hymn of Light (*Phos Hilaron;*
4, 100\*) or another hymn of the
same theme may be sung. Other
candles may be lighted from the
flame of the large candle as other
lights are turned up.

*Hymn of Light and
Lighting of the Candle*
The traditional Hymn of
Light (*Phos Hilaron;* 4,
100\*) or an evening
hymn may be sung as a
candle is lighted.

*Thanksgiving for Light*
Following the introductory sentences, the thanksgiving for light
is offered.

*Incense*
As a symbol of our prayers pleas-
ingly offered to God, incense may
be burned as the verses from Rev.
8:3–4 are sung or said, introducing
Psalm 141.

*Evening Psalm—Psalm 141*
This prayer for forgiveness begins
the Psalter. It should include the
refrain and conclude with the
psalm prayer.

*Psalter*
One or more of the psalms appointed for the day may be sung or
said. A refrain may be sung or said before and after the psalm, or
at the end of each division of the psalm. Silence for meditation
follows each psalm. A psalm prayer appropriate to each psalm
follows the silence. Suggested refrains and psalm prayers may be
found on pages (207–254).

*Scripture Reading*
A reading of scripture from the lectionary (pp. 397–419) is followed
by:
This is the Word of the Lord.

**Thanks be to God.**

The scripture may be interpreted, discussed, or augmented by
nonbiblical readings. A time of silence may be included for reflection on the meaning of the scripture.

*Biblical Song*
The Song of Mary (2, 98*) or a New Testament song (nos. 15–25)
may be sung or said.

*Prayers of Thanksgiving and Intercession*
Following the introductory sentences, free prayer may be offered,
giving thanks for God's blessings and expressing concerns for the
needs of others; or an appropriate prayer may be selected from
those numbered 26–72. There may be a time of silent prayer before
the concluding prayer and the Lord's Prayer.

*Hymn or Spiritual*
If desired, a song of affirmation may be sung.

*Dismissal*
Following the dismissal, a sign of peace may be exchanged.

# MORNING
# AND
# EVENING
# PRAYER

# ORDINARY DAYS

## SUNDAY
### MORNING PRAYER

**OPENING SENTENCES**

O Lord, open my lips.

**And my mouth shall proclaim your praise.**

*And*

Thanks be to God,

**who gives us the victory through our Lord Jesus Christ.**

*1 Cor. 15:56*

By our baptism we were buried with Christ and shared his death,

**so that as Christ was raised from the dead,
we too might live a new life.**

*Rom. 6:4*

*Or*

If God be for us, who can be against us?

**There is nothing in all creation**

that can separate us from the love of God,

**which is ours in Christ Jesus our Lord.**

*Rom. 8:31, 39*

**MORNING PSALM** (95; 100; 63; or 51) *or* **MORNING HYMN**

**PSALTER** *One or more of the following:*
(A) Psalms 103; 150    (C) Psalms 67; 150
(B) Psalms 19; 150      (D) Psalms 108; 150

**SCRIPTURE READING** *followed by silent reflection*

**BIBLICAL SONG** *Song of Zechariah (1, 97\*) or Old Testament song (7–14)*

## PRAYERS OF THANKSGIVING AND INTERCESSION

Satisfy us with your love in the morning,

**and we will live this day in joy and praise.**

*Free prayer (or prayer 26)*

*Silent prayer*

*And*

Eternal and almighty God,
we praise you that you cause the sun to rise
to bring us the light of this new day,
and that you raised Christ from the dead
to bring us the new life.
May our lives always face his brightness
so we may go wherever he leads,
serving in gladness and peace. **Amen.**

*Or*

You have brought us again to new life, Almighty God,
and gathered us in the community of faith
to be your people
as we work and witness in this world.
Feed us today with the presence of our risen Lord Jesus Christ,
and breathe into us your Spirit,
that we may be bold witnesses in all we say and do
to the glory of your holy name. **Amen.**

*The Lord's Prayer*

**HYMN** *or* **SPIRITUAL**

**DISMISSAL**

To God be honor and glory forever and ever!          *1 Tim. 1:17*

**Amen.**

Bless the Lord.

**The Lord's name be praised.**

## EVENING PRAYER

## OPENING SENTENCES AT ENTRANCE OF THE LIGHT

Jesus Christ is the light of the world,

**the light no darkness can overcome.**

Stay with us, Lord, for it is evening,

**and the day is almost over.**

Let your light scatter the darkness

**and illumine your church.**

*Based on John 1:5; 8:12; Luke 24:29*

*Or*

O God, come to our assistance.

**O Lord, hasten to help us.**

*And*

In the beginning was the Word:

**The Word was with God and the Word was God.**

The Word was with God in the beginning.

**Through the Word all things came to be.**          *John 1:1–3*

**HYMN OF LIGHT** *(4, 100\*) or other evening hymn*

**THANKSGIVING FOR LIGHT**

The Lord be with you.

**And also with you.**

Let us give thanks to the Lord our God.

**It is right to give our thanks and praise.**

We praise and thank you, O God,
for you are without beginning and without end.
Through Christ you are the creator and preserver of the whole
   world;
but, above all, you are his God and Father,
the Giver of the Spirit,
and the Ruler of all that is, seen and unseen.
You made the day for the works of light,
and the night for the refreshment of our minds and our bodies.
O loving Lord and source of all that is good,
graciously accept our evening sacrifice of praise.
As you have led us through the day
and brought us to night's beginning,
keep us now in Christ;
grant us a peaceful evening
and a night free from sin,
and bring us at last to eternal life.
Through Christ and in the Holy Spirit,
we offer you all glory, honor, and worship
now and forever and ever. **Amen.**

*Apostolic Constitutions (c. A.D. 380)*

*Or*

We praise you, O Lord our God, Ruler of the universe,
by whose word the shadows of evening fall.
Your wisdom opens the gates of morning;
your understanding orders the changes of time and seasons;
your will controls the stars as they travel through the skies.
You are the Creator of both night and day,

making light recede before darkness,
and darkness before light.
You cause day to pass,
and bring on the night,
setting day and night apart.
You are the Lord of Hosts.

Living and eternal God, rule over us always,
to the end of time.
Blessed are you, O Lord,
whose word makes evening fall. **Amen.**

*Jewish Berakah of the Evening*

## INCENSE

An angel, holding a golden censer full of incense,
stood before the altar.
The smoke of the incense went up before God,
mingled with the prayers of the people.          *Rev. 8:3–4*

## EVENING PSALM Psalm 141

**PSALTER** *One or more of the following:*
  (A) Psalms 117; 139   (C) Psalms 46; 93
  (B) Psalms 81; 113    (D) Psalms 66; 23

## SCRIPTURE READING *followed by silent reflection*

## BIBLICAL SONG *Song of Mary (2, 98\*) or New Testament song (15–25)*

## PRAYERS OF THANKSGIVING AND INTERCESSION

Let us walk in love, as Christ loved us and gave himself up for us,

**a fragrant offering and sacrifice to God.**

*Free prayer (or prayer 27 or 40)*

*Silent prayer*

*And*

Eternal God,
in Jesus Christ you poured out your love for us
and claimed us as your own.
Keep us secure in your gracious embrace
this day and in every tomorrow,
by the power of your Spirit,
in the name of Christ our risen Lord. **Amen.**

*Or*

Mighty and loving God,
in Jesus Christ you have brought us all to new life.
Mend what is broken in us,
and restore us to communion with you
by the power of the Holy Spirit,
that we may be glad and gracious followers
of our risen Lord and Savior, Jesus Christ. **Amen.**

*The Lord's Prayer*

## HYMN *or* SPIRITUAL

## DISMISSAL

To God be honor and glory forever and ever!    *1 Tim. 1:17*

**Amen.**

Bless the Lord.

**The Lord's name be praised.**


## MONDAY
### MORNING PRAYER

## OPENING SENTENCES

O Lord, open my lips.

**And my mouth shall proclaim your praise.**

*And*

The Lord's unfailing love and mercy still continue,

**fresh as the morning and sure as the sunrise.**

The Lord is all I have,

**in the Lord I put my hope.**                    *Lam. 3:22–24*

*Or*

Since we have died with Christ,

**we believe that we will also live with him.**

For we know that Christ has been raised from death
and will never die again.

**Death will no longer rule over him.**          *Rom. 6:8–9*

**MORNING PSALM** (95; 100; 63; or 51) *or* **MORNING HYMN**

**PSALTER** *One or more of the following:*
(A)  Psalms 5; 145      (C)  Psalms 57; 145
(B)  Psalms 135; 145    (D)  Psalms 62; 145

**SCRIPTURE READING** *followed by silent reflection*

**BIBLICAL SONG** *Song of Zechariah (1, 97\*) or Old Testament song
(7–14)*

**PRAYERS OF THANKSGIVING AND INTERCESSION**

Satisfy us with your love in the morning,

**and we will live this day in joy and praise.**

*Free prayer (or prayer 28)*

*Silent prayer*

*And*

Eternal God,
our beginning and our end,
be our starting point and our haven,
and accompany us in this day's journey.
Use our hands
to do the work of your creation,
and use our lives
to bring to others the new life you give this world
in Jesus Christ, Redeemer of all. **Amen.**

*Or*

Before we know what to ask, O God,
you are fashioning out of your love everything we can need.
Today give us courage
to witness to your wondrous love
and to share in your work
which you have given us as disciples of Jesus Christ,
our Servant Lord. **Amen.**

*The Lord's Prayer*

**HYMN** *or* **SPIRITUAL**

**DISMISSAL**

May we continue to grow in the grace and knowledge
of Jesus Christ, our Lord and Savior.                    *2 Peter 3:18*

**Amen.**

Bless the Lord.

**The Lord's name be praised.**

## OPENING SENTENCES

O God, come to our assistance.

**O Lord, hasten to help us.**

*And*

You created the day, O God, and the night;

**you set the sun and the moon in their places;**

you made summer and winter;

**you set the limits of the earth.**                          *Ps. 74:16–17*

*Or*

Let us give thanks to the God of our Lord Jesus Christ.

**God has blessed us in Christ with every spiritual blessing.**

Before the world was made, God chose us in Christ,

**that we might be holy and blameless before God.**     *Eph. 1:3–4*

**HYMN OF LIGHT** *(4, 100\*) or other evening hymn, and*
**LIGHTING OF THE CANDLE**

**PSALTER** *One or more of the following:*
  (A)  Psalms 82; 29    (C)  Psalms 85; 47
  (B)  Psalms 97; 112    (D)  Psalms 73; 9

**SCRIPTURE READING** *followed by silent reflection*

**BIBLICAL SONG** *Song of Mary (2, 98\*) or New Testament song (15–25)*

## PRAYERS OF THANKSGIVING AND INTERCESSION

Receive my prayer as incense, O God,

**my uplifted hands as an evening sacrifice.**

*Free prayer (or prayer 29)*

*Silent prayer*

*And*

Great God, you are one God,
and you bring together what is scattered
and mend what is broken.
Unite us with the scattered peoples of the earth
that we may be one family of your children.
Bind up all our wounds,
and heal us in spirit,
that we may be renewed as disciples
of Jesus Christ, our Master and Savior. **Amen.**

*Or*

God of wonders,
you work your will
and claim us to serve your purposes
as you have revealed them in Jesus Christ.
Take us and all we are and all we do;
forgive what is imperfect and flawed
and show us how to make amends,
so that our lives may be better witnesses
to the presence of our risen Lord and Savior,
Jesus Christ. **Amen.**

*The Lord's Prayer*

**HYMN** *or* **SPIRITUAL**

**DISMISSAL**

May we continue to grow in the grace and knowledge
of Jesus Christ, our Lord and Savior.           *2 Peter 3:18*

**Amen.**

Bless the Lord.

**The Lord's name be praised.**

### TUESDAY
#### MORNING PRAYER

**OPENING SENTENCES**

O Lord, open my lips.

**And my mouth shall proclaim your praise.**

*And*

I pray to you, O Lord;

**you hear my voice in the morning;**

at sunrise I offer my prayer

**and wait for your answer.**           *Ps. 5:2–3*

*Or*

God helps us in all our troubles,

**so we are able to help others
using what we have received from God.**

Just as we have a share in the suffering of Christ,

**so also through Christ we share in God's great help.**     *2 Cor. 1:4–5*

**MORNING PSALM** (95; 100; 63; or 51) *or* **MORNING HYMN**

**PSALTER** *One or more of the following:*
(A) Psalms 42; 146   (C) Psalms 54; 146
(B) Psalms 123; 146  (D) Psalms 12; 146

**SCRIPTURE READING** *followed by silent reflection*

**BIBLICAL SONG** *Song of Zechariah (1, 97\*) or Old Testament song
(7–14)*

**PRAYERS OF THANKSGIVING AND INTERCESSION**

Satisfy us with your love in the morning,

**and we will live this day in joy and praise.**

*Free prayer (or prayer 30)*

*Silent prayer*

*And*

As you cause the sun to rise, O God,
bring the light of Christ to dawn in our souls
and dispel all darkness.
Give us grace to reflect Christ's glory;
and let his love show in our deeds,
his peace shine in our words,
and his healing in our touch,
that all may give him praise. **Amen.**

*Or*

Eternal God,
open our eyes to see your hand at work
in the splendor of creation,
in the beauty of human life.
Your touch makes this world holy.
Help us to cherish the gifts that surround us,
to share your blessings with our brothers and sisters,

and to experience the joy of life in your presence.
We ask this through Christ our Lord. **Amen.**

*The Lord's Prayer*

## HYMN *or* SPIRITUAL

## DISMISSAL

The grace of God be with us all, now and always.     *1 Tim. 6:21*

**Amen.**

Bless the Lord.

**The Lord's name be praised.**

EVENING PRAYER

## OPENING SENTENCES

O God, come to our assistance.

**O Lord, hasten to help us.**

*And*

God is light.

**In God there is no darkness.**

If we live in the light,

**as God is in the light,**

we have fellowship with one another,

**and the blood of Jesus, God's Son,
purifies us from every sin.**     *1 John 1:5, 7*

*Or*

Let us give praise for God's glorious grace,

**for the free gift we received in God's dear Son.**

By the death of Christ, our sins are forgiven.

**How great is the grace of God,
given to us in such large measure!**                    *Eph. 1:6–8*

**HYMN OF LIGHT** *(4, 100\*) or other evening hymn, and*
**LIGHTING OF THE CANDLE**

**PSALTER** *One or more of the following:*
(A) Psalms 102; 133   (C) Psalms 28; 99
(B) Psalms 30; 86      (D) Psalms 36; 7

**SCRIPTURE READING** *followed by silent reflection*

**BIBLICAL SONG** *Song of Mary (2, 98\*) or New Testament song (15–25)*

**PRAYERS OF THANKSGIVING AND INTERCESSION**

Receive my prayer as incense, O God,

**my uplifted hands as an evening sacrifice.**

*Free prayer (or prayer 31)*

*Silent prayer*

*And*

God of glory,
no darkness of despair nor gloom of sin
can eclipse the light of your love
revealed in Jesus Christ.
May we shine brightly in serving him,
and reflect something of your overwhelming love
for the whole world
in Jesus Christ our Lord. **Amen.**

*Or*

God of all who fear you,
make us one with all your saints
and with any who are in need.
Teach us to befriend the weak,
and honor the outcast,
that we may serve the Lord Jesus Christ
and live to give him glory.
In his holy name we pray. **Amen.**

*The Lord's Prayer*

## HYMN *or* SPIRITUAL

## DISMISSAL

The grace of God be with us all, now and always.     *1 Tim. 6:21*

**Amen.**

Bless the Lord.

**The Lord's name be praised.**

**WEDNESDAY**
**MORNING PRAYER**

## OPENING SENTENCES

O Lord, open my lips.

**And my mouth shall proclaim your praise.**

*And*

Lord, have mercy on us.

**We have put our hope in you.**

Uphold us every morning,

**and save us in times of trouble.**                *Isa. 33:2*

*Or*

Let us keep our eyes fixed on Jesus,

**on whom our faith depends from beginning to end.**

He freely died on the cross for us

**and is now seated at the right hand of God.** *Heb. 12:2*

**MORNING PSALM** (95; 100; 63; or 51) *or* **MORNING HYMN**

**PSALTER** *One or more of the following:*
 (A) Psalms 89:1–18; 147:1–11   (C) Psalms 65; 147:1–11
 (B) Psalms 15; 147:1–11        (D) Psalms 96; 147:1–11

**SCRIPTURE READING** *followed by silent reflection*

**BIBLICAL SONG** *Song of Zechariah (1, 97\*) or Old Testament song (7–14)*

**PRAYERS OF THANKSGIVING AND INTERCESSION**

Satisfy us with your love in the morning,

**and we will live this day in joy and praise.**

 *Free prayer (or prayer 32)*

 *Silent prayer*

 *And*

Eternal God,
you never fail to give us each day all that we ever need,
and even more.
Give us such joy in living
and such peace in serving Christ,
that we may gratefully make use of all your blessings,
and joyfully seek our risen Lord
in everyone we meet.
In Jesus Christ we pray. **Amen.**

*Or*

God of grace,
we praise you for the richness of your love,
for you rescue those in peril
and ransom the captives.
Give us grace
to proclaim your mighty acts of redemption in Jesus Christ,
in our lives,
in our community,
in our nation,
and throughout the world.
Then all will turn again
to give you glory and honor. **Amen.**

*The Lord's Prayer*

## HYMN *or* SPIRITUAL

## DISMISSAL

May the Lord, who is our peace,
give us peace at all times and in every way.          *2 Thess. 3:16*

**Amen.**

Bless the Lord.

**The Lord's name be praised.**

### EVENING PRAYER

## OPENING SENTENCES

O God, come to our assistance.

**O Lord, hasten to help us.**

*And*

In the city of God, night shall be no more;

**they need no light of lamp or sun,**

for the Lord God will be their light,

**And they will reign forever and ever.**               *Rev. 22:5*

*Or*

Now that we have been put right with God through faith,

**we have peace with God through our Lord Jesus Christ.**

He has brought us by faith into the grace of God.

**We rejoice in the hope of sharing God's glory!**        *Rom. 5:1–2*

**HYMN OF LIGHT** *(4, 100\*) or other evening hymn, and*
**LIGHTING OF THE CANDLE**

**PSALTER** *One or more of the following:*
   (A) Psalms 1; 33   (C) Psalms 125; 91
   (B) Psalms 48; 4   (D) Psalms 132; 134

**SCRIPTURE READING** *followed by silent reflection*

**BIBLICAL SONG** *Song of Mary (2, 98\*) or New Testament song (15–25)*

**PRAYERS OF THANKSGIVING AND INTERCESSION**

Receive my prayer as incense, O God,

**my uplifted hands as an evening sacrifice.**

*Free prayer (or prayer 33)*

*Silent prayer*

*And*

O God, our God,
you are one,
complete and sufficient in yourself.
We praise you
that you offer us yourself in Jesus Christ our Savior,
and so invite us to be reconciled,
healed, whole, and holy,
bound with you and one another
in Christ's powerful peace. **Amen.**

*Or*

O God,
you have brought us through this day
to a time of reflection and rest.
Calm our souls within us,
and give us a sense of your peace that will refresh us.
Keep us close to Christ
that we may be closer to one another
because of his wondrous love.
In his name we pray. **Amen.**

*The Lord's Prayer*

## HYMN *or* SPIRITUAL

## DISMISSAL

May the Lord, who is our peace,
give us peace at all times in every way.    *2 Thess. 3:16*

**Amen.**

Bless the Lord.

**The Lord's name be praised.**

## OPENING SENTENCES

O Lord, open my lips.

**And my mouth shall proclaim your praise.**

*And*

Sing psalms, hymns, and sacred songs;

**let us sing to God with thanksgiving in our hearts.**

Let everything you do or say be done in the name of the Lord Jesus,

**giving thanks to God through Jesus Christ.**      *Col. 3:16–17*

*Or*

O depth of wealth, wisdom, and knowledge of God!

**How unsearchable are God's judgments,
how untraceable are God's ways!**

Source, Guide, and Goal of all that is,

**to God be glory forever! Amen.**      *Rom. 11:33, 36*

**MORNING PSALM** (95; 100; 63; or 51) *or* **MORNING HYMN**

**PSALTER** *One or more of the following:*
(A) Psalms 97; 147:12–20      (C) Psalms 143; 147:12–20
(B) Psalms 36; 147:12–20      (D) Psalms 116; 147:12–20

**SCRIPTURE READING** *followed by silent reflection*

**BIBLICAL SONG** *Song of Zechariah (1, 97\*) or Old Testament song (7–14)*

## PRAYERS OF THANKSGIVING AND INTERCESSION

Satisfy us with your love in the morning,

**and we will live this day in joy and praise.**

*Free prayer (or prayer 34)*

*Silent prayer*

*And*

Great God,
you sent Jesus Christ
that we might trust in him
and live as his faithful followers.
Uplift us when we stumble,
steady us when we falter,
that we may walk in righteousness
and work for reconciliation
in the way of Jesus Christ.
Give us grace
to be a blessing to all we meet today
in the name of the One who is Savior of all. **Amen.**

*Or*

Mighty God,
you have given us life and all goodness,
and you bring us daily to new life in Jesus Christ.
Re-create us in Christ's image,
and fill us anew with your Spirit,
that we may be your new creation
and bring about your purpose in this world you love,
through Jesus Christ. **Amen.**

*The Lord's Prayer*

**HYMN** *or* **SPIRITUAL**

**DISMISSAL**

May the God of hope fill us with all joy and peace
through the power of the Holy Spirit. *Rom. 15:13*

**Amen.**

Bless the Lord.

**The Lord's name be praised.**

## EVENING PRAYER

**OPENING SENTENCES**

O God, come to our assistance.

**O Lord, hasten to help us.**

*And*

God reveals deep and mysterious things,

**and knows what is hidden in darkness.**

God is surrounded by light.

**To you, O God, we give thanks and praise.** *Dan. 2:22–23*

*Or*

All that came to be had life in the Word

**and that life was the light of the world,**

a light that shines in the dark,

**a light that darkness could not overpower.** *John 1:4–5*

**HYMN OF LIGHT** *(4, 100\*) or other evening hymn, and*
**LIGHTING OF THE CANDLE**

**PSALTER** *One or more of the following:*
  (A) Psalms 16; 62   (C) Psalms 81; 116
  (B) Psalms 80; 27   (D) Psalms 26; 130

**SCRIPTURE READING** *followed by silent reflection*

**BIBLICAL SONG** *Song of Mary (2, 98\*) or New Testament song (15–25)*

**PRAYERS OF THANKSGIVING AND INTERCESSION**

Receive my prayer as incense, O God,

**my uplifted hands as an evening sacrifice.**

*Free prayer (or prayer 35)*

*Silent prayer*

*And*

To you, O God,
we give up the burdens of this day,
trusting your love and mercy.
To you, O God,
we surrender ourselves,
trusting our risen Lord to lead us always
in the way of peace,
today, tomorrow, and forever. **Amen.**

*Or*

God,
you are everything to us,
giving us life,
filling it with love,
and setting us free from sin
that we might live in love.
Take the work of our hands this day,
and let good come of it;
take our lives this night,
and let good come to us.

May our rest refresh our souls,
and renew us in the service of Jesus Christ. **Amen.**

*The Lord's Prayer*

**HYMN** *or* **SPIRITUAL**

**DISMISSAL**

May the God of hope fill us with all joy and peace
through the power of the Holy Spirit.                    *Rom. 15:13*

**Amen.**

Bless the Lord.

**The Lord's name be praised.**

## FRIDAY
### Morning Prayer

**OPENING SENTENCES**

O Lord, open my lips.

**And my mouth shall proclaim your praise.**

*And*

When we were still helpless

**Christ died for the ungodly.**

The proof of God's amazing love is this:

**While we were still sinners, Christ died for us.**        *Rom. 5:6, 8*

*Or*

God, who began a good work in us,

**will bring it to completion
at the day of Christ Jesus.**

May our love grow in wisdom
that we may choose what is best.

**Then, on the day of Christ,
we will be pure and without blame.**              *Phil. 1:6, 9–10*

## MORNING PSALM (95; 100; 63; or 51) *or* MORNING HYMN

**PSALTER** *One or more of the following:*
(A) Psalms 51; 148   (C) Psalms 88; 148
(B) Psalms 130; 148   (D) Psalms 84; 148

**SCRIPTURE READING** *followed by silent reflection*

**BIBLICAL SONG** *Song of Zechariah (1, 97\*) or Old Testament song (7–14)*

## PRAYERS OF THANKSGIVING AND INTERCESSION

Satisfy us with your love in the morning,

**and we will live this day in joy and praise.**

*Free prayer (or prayer 36)*

*Silent prayer*

*And*

Eternal God,
remind us always
that you have gone before us
through every dark valley,
and that Christ walks with us still.
Free us from fear
that we may be firm in our discipleship.
Lead us to stand with all who suffer
and to champion the cause of justice and truth
in Christ's name. **Amen.**

*Or*

Eternal God,
you gave supremely of your love for us
in the death of Christ on the cross.
Give us grace
that we may reflect something of that sacrifice
in the words and deeds of our daily living.
Mighty God,
in the resurrection of Christ from the dead
you conquered death out of love for us.
Give us grace
that we may reflect his life
in all we say and do
and be faithful followers of Christ the Lord. **Amen.**

*The Lord's Prayer*

## HYMN *or* SPIRITUAL

## DISMISSAL

May God's peace, which is far beyond our understanding,
keep us safe in union with Christ Jesus.                    *Phil. 4:7*

**Amen.**

Bless the Lord.

**The Lord's name be praised.**

### EVENING PRAYER

## OPENING SENTENCES

O God, come to our assistance.

**O Lord, hasten to help us.**

*And*

The Lord made the stars, the Pleiades and Orion.

**The Lord turns darkness into daylight,
and day into night.**

The Lord calls for the waters of the sea
and pours them out upon the earth.

**The one who does this is the Lord.**                    *Amos 5:8*

*Or*

The city of God has no need of sun or moon,

**for the glory of God is its light,
and its lamp is the Lamb.**

By its light shall the nations walk,

**and the rulers of earth shall bring their treasures into it.**
*Rev. 21:23–24*

**HYMN OF LIGHT** *(4, 100\*) or other evening hymn, and*
**LIGHTING OF THE CANDLE**

**PSALTER** *One or more of the following:*
  (A) Psalms 142; 65  (C) Psalms 6; 20
  (B) Psalms 32; 139  (D) Psalms 25; 40

**SCRIPTURE READING** *followed by silent reflection*

**BIBLICAL SONG** *Song of Mary (2, 98\*) or New Testament song (15–25)*

**PRAYERS OF THANKSGIVING AND INTERCESSION**

Receive my prayer as incense, O God,

**my uplifted hands as an evening sacrifice.**

*Free prayer (or prayer 37)*

*Silent prayer*

*And*

God of mercy and might,
all creation exists and is sustained
by your righteous rule.
Govern our lives
by your powerful and gracious Spirit,
that we may reflect the glory of your righteousness
which we have seen in Jesus Christ,
Savior of the world. **Amen.**

*Or*

As you have made this day, O God,
you also make the night.
Give light for our comfort.
Come upon us with quietness and still our souls
that we may listen for the whisper of your Spirit
and be attentive to your nearness in our dreams.
Empower us to rise again in new life
to proclaim your praise,
and show Christ to the world. **Amen.**

*The Lord's Prayer*

**HYMN** *or* **SPIRITUAL**

**DISMISSAL**

May God's peace, which is far beyond our understanding,
keep us safe in union with Christ Jesus.                    *Phil. 4:7*

**Amen.**

Bless the Lord.

**The Lord's name be praised.**

## OPENING SENTENCES

O Lord, open my lips.

**And my mouth shall proclaim your praise.**

*And*

Lord, we are clay,

**and you are the potter.**

We are all the work of your hand.

**Be merciful to us.**                               *Isa. 64:8, 9c*

*Or*

Jesus says: Listen! I am coming soon!

**I will bring my rewards with me.**

I am the first and the last,

**the beginning and the end.**                      *Rev. 22:12–13*

## MORNING PSALM (95; 100; 63; or 51) *or* MORNING HYMN

**PSALTER** *One or more of the following:*
(A) Psalms 104; 149    (C) Psalms 122; 149
(B) Psalms 56; 149     (D) Psalms 63; 149

## SCRIPTURE READING *followed by silent reflection*

## BIBLICAL SONG *Song of Zechariah (1, 97\*) or Old Testament song (7–14)*

## PRAYERS OF THANKSGIVING AND INTERCESSION

Satisfy us with your love in the morning,

**and we will live this day in joy and praise.**

*Free prayer (or prayer 38)*

*Silent prayer*

*And*

Take our lives, great God,
and mold us into the image of Jesus Christ our Lord.
Forgive all waywardness in us,
and move us beyond our sin
to set out afresh with Christ,
who is the only way.
Give peace to us,
to all your children,
and to the whole world
for which Christ died. **Amen.**

*Or*

Re-create us, O God,
that in our work and play
we may know the new life
which you give us and all people
in Jesus Christ.
Keep us alert to your presence,
and stir a deep longing in us
for the coming of your rule,
that we may sit at table
to celebrate your love and truth,
rejoicing with all the saints
in communion with Christ,
our Lord and Savior. **Amen.**

*The Lord's Prayer*

**HYMN** *or* **SPIRITUAL**

**DISMISSAL**

May the grace of the Lord Jesus Christ be with us all.    *Phil. 4:23*

**Amen.**

Bless the Lord.

**The Lord's name be praised.**

### EVENING PRAYER

## OPENING SENTENCES AT ENTRANCE OF THE LIGHT

Jesus Christ is the light of the world,

**the light no darkness can overcome.**

Stay with us, Lord, for it is evening,

**and the day is almost over.**

Let your light scatter the darkness

**and illumine your church.**

*Based on John 1:5; 8:12; Luke 24:29*

*Or*

O God, come to our assistance.

**O Lord, hasten to help us.**

*And*

I could ask the darkness to hide me

**or the light around me to become night,**

but even darkness is not dark for you,
and the night is as bright as the day;

**for darkness is as light with you.**              *Ps. 139:11–12*

**HYMN OF LIGHT** *(4, 100\*) or other evening hymn*

## THANKSGIVING FOR LIGHT

The Lord be with you.

**And also with you.**

Let us give thanks to the Lord our God.

**It is right to give our thanks and praise.**

*And*

Blessed are you, O Lord our God, Ruler of the universe.
You led your people Israel by a pillar of cloud by day
and a pillar of fire by night.

Enlighten our darkness by the light of your Christ.
May his Word be a lamp to our feet
and a light to our path;
for you are full of loving-kindness for your whole creation,
and we, your creatures, glorify you,
Father, Son, and Holy Spirit. **Amen.**

*Or*

We praise and thank you, O God,
through your Son, Jesus Christ our Lord,
through whom you have enlightened us
by revealing the light that never fades.
Having ended the course of this day
and reached the edge of night,
having been filled by the light of day
which you created for our joy,
we now possess, through your kindness,
the evening light.
Therefore, we praise and glorify you
through your Son, Jesus Christ our Lord.

Through him be glory, honor, and power to you
in the Holy Spirit,
now and forever and ever. **Amen.**

Apostolic Tradition (c. A.D. 215)

## INCENSE

An angel, holding a golden censer full of incense,
stood before the altar.
The smoke of the incense went up before God,
mingled with the prayers of the people.          *Rev. 8:3–4*

## EVENING PSALM Psalm 141

## PSALTER *One or more of the following:*
(A) Psalms 138; 98    (C) Psalms 100; 63
(B) Psalms 118; 111    (D) Psalms 125; 90

## SCRIPTURE READING *followed by silent reflection*

## BIBLICAL SONG *Song of Mary (2, 98*) or New Testament song (15–25)*

## PRAYERS OF THANKSGIVING AND INTERCESSION

Let us walk in love, as Christ loved us and gave himself up for us,

**a fragrant offering and sacrifice to God.**

*Free prayer (or prayer 39 or 40)*

*Silent prayer*

*And*

Inspire us, great God,
that we may wait expectantly for all you promise,
and look forward to new life in Jesus Christ.
Keep us moving on life's journey,
traveling with our companion Christ,
through every darkness
toward the dawn of the Lord's Day. **Amen.**

*Or*

God, you alone are to be trusted,
for only you can redeem us
and set us free from sin.
Deliver us from false hopes,
from counterfeit claims on us,
from wistful allegiances.
Gather us again to yourself
and bring us to your presence,
that we may be renewed and refreshed
in body and in soul,
through Jesus Christ our Lord. **Amen.**

*The Lord's Prayer*

**HYMN** *or* **SPIRITUAL**

**DISMISSAL**

May the grace of the Lord Jesus Christ be with us all.    *Phil. 4:23*

**Amen.**

Bless the Lord.

**The Lord's name be praised.**

# ADVENT

**OPENING SENTENCES**

O Lord, open my lips.

**And my mouth shall proclaim your praise.**

The mountains and the hills shall break forth into singing,

**and all the trees of the forest shall clap their hands.**     *Isa. 55:12*

For behold, our Lord and Ruler is coming to reign forever.

**Alleluia!**

**MORNING PSALM** (95; 100; 63; or 51) *or* **MORNING HYMN** *or* **ADVENT HYMN**

**PSALTER** *One or both of the following:* Psalms 24; 150

**SCRIPTURE READING** *followed by silent reflection*

**BIBLICAL SONG** *Song of Zechariah (1, 97\*) or The New Jerusalem (10) or other Old Testament song (7–14)*

**PRAYERS OF THANKSGIVING AND INTERCESSION**

Satisfy us with your love in the morning,

**and we will live this day in joy and praise.**

*Free prayer (or prayer 42 or 43)*

*Silent prayer*

*And*

God of all wisdom,
our hearts yearn for the warmth of your love,
and our minds search for the light of your Word.
Increase our longing for Christ our Savior,
and strengthen us to grow in love,
that at the dawn of his coming
we may rejoice in his presence
and welcome the light of his truth.
This we ask in the name of Jesus Christ. **Amen.**

*The Lord's Prayer*

## HYMN *or* SPIRITUAL

## DISMISSAL

To God be honor and glory forever and ever!          *1 Tim. 1:17*

**Amen.**

Bless the Lord.

**The Lord's name be praised.**

### EVENING PRAYER

## OPENING SENTENCES AT ENTRANCE OF THE LIGHT

The Spirit and the church cry out:

**Come, Lord Jesus.**

All those who await his appearance pray:

**Come, Lord Jesus.**

The whole creation pleads:

**Come, Lord Jesus.**                    *Based on Rev. 22:20*

*Or*

O God, come to our assistance.

**O Lord, hasten to help us.**

*And*

Rejoice greatly, O daughter of Zion!

**Shout aloud, O daughter of Jerusalem!**

The Lord your God will come, with all the holy ones.

**On that day, at evening time there shall be light.**   *Zech. 9:9; 14:5–7*

**HYMN OF LIGHT** *(4, 100\*) or other evening hymn or Advent hymn*

**THANKSGIVING FOR LIGHT**

The Lord be with you.

**And also with you.**

Let us give thanks to the Lord our God.

**It is right to give our thanks and praise.**

Blessed are you, O Lord our God, Ruler of the universe,
creator of light and darkness.
In this holy season,
when the sun's light is swallowed up
by the growing darkness of the night,
you renew your promise to reveal among us
the splendor of your glory,
made flesh and visible to us in Jesus Christ, your Son.
Through the prophets
you teach us to hope for his reign of peace.

----

Through the outpouring of your Spirit
you give sight to our souls,
that we may see your glory
in the presence of Christ.
Strengthen us where we are weak,
support us in our efforts to do your will,
and free our tongues to sing your praise,
for to you all honor and blessing are due,
now and forever. **Amen.**

## INCENSE

An angel, holding a golden censer full of incense,
stood before the altar.
The smoke of the incense went up before God,
mingled with the prayers of the people.                    *Rev. 8:3–4*

## EVENING PSALM Psalm 141

**PSALTER** *One or both of the following:* Psalms 25; 110

**SCRIPTURE READING** *followed by silent reflection*

**BIBLICAL SONG** *Song of Mary (2, 98\*) or Song of the Redeemed (16) or other New Testament song (15–25)*

## PRAYERS OF THANKSGIVING AND INTERCESSION

Let us walk in love, as Christ loved us and gave himself up for us,

**a fragrant offering and sacrifice to God.**

*Free prayer (or prayer 44, 45, or 40)*

*Silent prayer*

*And*

Faithful God,
give us the joy of your love
to prepare the way for Christ our Lord.

Help us to serve you and one another,
in Jesus Christ,
who lives and reigns with you and the Holy Spirit,
one God, forever and ever. **Amen.**

*The Lord's Prayer*

## HYMN *or* SPIRITUAL

## DISMISSAL

To God be honor and glory forever and ever!          *1 Tim. 1:17*

**Amen.**

Bless the Lord.

**The Lord's name be praised.**

## MONDAY
### MORNING PRAYER

## OPENING SENTENCES

O Lord, open my lips.

**And my mouth shall proclaim your praise.**

The time has come for you to wake from sleep.

**The night is nearly over, day is almost here.**

Let us stop doing the things that belong to the night.

**Let us conduct ourselves properly,
as people who live in the light of day.**          *Rom. 13:11–13*

**MORNING PSALM** (95; 100; 63; or 51) *or* **MORNING HYMN** *or*
**ADVENT HYMN**

**PSALTER** *One or both of the following:* Psalms 122; 145

**SCRIPTURE READING** *followed by silent reflection*

**BIBLICAL SONG** *Song of Zechariah (1, 97\*) or The New Jerusalem (10) or other Old Testament song (7–14)*

## PRAYERS OF THANKSGIVING AND INTERCESSION

Satisfy us with your love in the morning,

**and we will live this day in joy and praise.**

*Free prayer (or prayer 42 or 43)*

*Silent prayer*

*And*

Eternal God,
drive away the night of our sin
by the gracious dawn of the coming of your Son,
that we may be awake in faith
to welcome him who lives and reigns
with you and the Holy Spirit,
one God, forever and ever. **Amen.**

*The Lord's Prayer*

## HYMN *or* SPIRITUAL

## DISMISSAL

May we continue to grow in the grace and knowledge
of Jesus Christ, our Lord and Savior.                    *2 Peter 3:18*

**Amen.**

Bless the Lord.

**The Lord's name be praised.**

## Evening Prayer

**OPENING SENTENCES**

O God, come to our assistance.

**O Lord, hasten to help us.**

A voice cries out:
Prepare a road for the Lord through the wilderness,

**clear a highway across the desert for our God.**          *Isa. 40:3*

**HYMN OF LIGHT** *(4, 100\*) or other evening hymn or Advent hymn, and*
**LIGHTING OF THE CANDLE**

**PSALTER** *One or both of the following:* Psalms 40; 67

**SCRIPTURE READING** *followed by silent reflection*

**BIBLICAL SONG** *Song of Mary (2, 98\*) or Song of the Redeemed (16) or other New Testament song (15–25)*

**PRAYERS OF THANKSGIVING AND INTERCESSION**

Receive my prayer as incense, O God,

**my uplifted hands as an evening sacrifice.**

*Free prayer (or prayer 44 or 45)*

*Silent prayer*

*And*

God of the prophets,
you sent your messenger into the wilderness of Jordan
to prepare human hearts for the coming of your Son.
Help us to prepare for Christ's coming,
to hear the good news and repent,
that we may be ready to welcome the Lord,
our Savior, Jesus Christ. **Amen.**

*The Lord's Prayer*

**HYMN** *or* **SPIRITUAL**

**DISMISSAL**

May we continue to grow in the grace and knowledge
of Jesus Christ, our Lord and Savior.                    *2 Peter 3:18*

**Amen.**

Bless the Lord.

**The Lord's name be praised.**

## TUESDAY
### MORNING PRAYER

**OPENING SENTENCES**

O Lord, open my lips.

**And my mouth shall proclaim your praise.**

Love and faithfulness will meet;

**justice and peace will embrace.**

Faithfulness will spring from the earth

**and justice will look down from heaven.**            *Ps. 85:10–11*

**MORNING PSALM** (95; 100; 63; or 51) *or* **MORNING HYMN** *or*
**ADVENT HYMN**

**PSALTER** *One or both of the following:* Psalms 33; 146

**SCRIPTURE READING** *followed by silent reflection*

**BIBLICAL SONG** *Song of Zechariah (1, 97\*) or The New Jerusalem (10)
or other Old Testament song (7–14)*

# PRAYERS OF THANKSGIVING AND INTERCESSION

Satisfy us with your love in the morning,

**and we will live this day in joy and praise.**

*Free prayer (or prayer 42 or 43)*

*Silent prayer*

*And*

Lord our God,
let your glory dawn to take away our darkness,
that at the coming of your Son
we may be revealed as children of light,
through Jesus Christ our Lord. **Amen.**

*The Lord's Prayer*

# HYMN *or* SPIRITUAL

# DISMISSAL

The grace of God be with us all, now and always.　　　*1 Tim. 6:21*

**Amen.**

Bless the Lord.

**The Lord's name be praised.**

## EVENING PRAYER

# OPENING SENTENCES

O God, come to our assistance.

**O Lord, hasten to help us.**

Drop down the dew from above, O heavens,

**and let the clouds rain justice.**

Let the earth's womb be opened,

**and bring forth a Savior.** *Based on Isa. 45:8*

**HYMN OF LIGHT** *(4, 100\*) or other evening hymn or Advent hymn, and*
**LIGHTING OF THE CANDLE**

**PSALTER** *One or both of the following:* Psalms 85; 94

**SCRIPTURE READING** *followed by silent reflection*

**BIBLICAL SONG** *Song of Mary (2, 98\*) or Song of the Redeemed (16) or other New Testament song (15–25)*

**PRAYERS OF THANKSGIVING AND INTERCESSION**

Receive my prayer as incense, O God,

**my uplifted hands as an evening sacrifice.**

*Free prayer (or prayer 44 or 45)*

*Silent prayer*

*And*

God of hope and joy,
the day draws near when the glory of your Son
will brighten the night of the waiting world.
Let no vanity hinder the joy
of those who seek him.
Let no sin obscure the vision of wisdom
seen by those who find him.
We ask this through Christ our Lord. **Amen.**

*The Lord's Prayer*

**HYMN** *or* **SPIRITUAL**

## DISMISSAL

The grace of God be with us all, now and always.　　*1 Tim. 6:21*

**Amen.**

Bless the Lord.

**The Lord's name be praised.**

## WEDNESDAY
### MORNING PRAYER

## OPENING SENTENCES

O Lord, open my lips.

**And my mouth shall proclaim your praise.**

The Lord shall come when morning dawns,

**and earth's dark night is past.**

As the sentry waits for daybreak,

**so my soul hopes for the Lord.**

**MORNING PSALM** (95; 100; 63; or 51) *or* **MORNING HYMN** *or* **ADVENT HYMN**

**PSALTER** *One or both of the following:* Psalms 50; 147:1–11

**SCRIPTURE READING** *followed by silent reflection*

**BIBLICAL SONG** *Song of Zechariah (1, 97\*) or The New Jerusalem (10) or other Old Testament song (7–14)*

## PRAYERS OF THANKSGIVING AND INTERCESSION

Satisfy us with your love in the morning,

**and we will live this day in joy and praise.**

*Free prayer (or prayer 42 or 43)*

*Silent prayer*

*And*

O Lord our God,
by your wisdom you created us,
and by your providence you lead us.
Let the dawn of your goodness shine in our hearts,
that we may always live for you,
through Jesus Christ our Lord. **Amen.**

*The Lord's Prayer*

## HYMN *or* SPIRITUAL

## DISMISSAL

May the Lord, who is our peace,
give us peace at all times and in every way.     *2 Thess. 3:16*

**Amen.**

Bless the Lord.

**The Lord's name be praised.**

### EVENING PRAYER

## OPENING SENTENCES

O God, come to our assistance.

**O Lord, hasten to help us.**

My soul yearns for you in the night.

**My spirit eagerly seeks you when dawn is breaking.**

Those who sleep in the dust will awake and shout for joy;

**for your dew shines forth with sparkling light,**

and the earth will bring those long dead to birth again.    *Isa. 26:9, 19*

**HYMN OF LIGHT** *(4, 100\*) or other evening hymn or Advent hymn, and*
**LIGHTING OF THE CANDLE**

**PSALTER** *One or both of the following:* Psalms 53; 17

**SCRIPTURE READING** *followed by silent reflection*

**BIBLICAL SONG** *Song of Mary (2, 98\*) or Song of the Redeemed (16) or
other New Testament song (15–25)*

## PRAYERS OF THANKSGIVING AND INTERCESSION

Receive my prayer as incense, O God,

**my uplifted hands as an evening sacrifice.**

*Free prayer (or prayer 44 or 45)*

*Silent prayer*

*And*

God of grace,
ever faithful to your promises,
the earth rejoices in hope of the Savior's coming
and looks forward with longing
to his return at the end of time.
Prepare our hearts to receive him when he comes,
for he is Lord forever and ever. **Amen.**

*The Lord's Prayer*

## HYMN *or* SPIRITUAL

## DISMISSAL

May the Lord, who is our peace,
give us peace at all times and in every way.          2 Thess. 3:16

**Amen.**

Bless the Lord.

**The Lord's name be praised.**

## THURSDAY
### MORNING PRAYER

**OPENING SENTENCES**

O Lord, open my lips.

**And my mouth shall proclaim your praise.**

Your light will come, O Jerusalem.

**The Lord will dawn on you in radiant beauty.**

**MORNING PSALM** (95; 100; 63; or 51) *or* **MORNING HYMN** *or* **ADVENT HYMN**

**PSALTER** *One or both of the following:* Psalms 18:1–20; 147:12–20

**SCRIPTURE READING** *followed by silent reflection*

**BIBLICAL SONG** *Song of Zechariah (1, 97\*) or The New Jerusalem (10) or other Old Testament song (7–14)*

**PRAYERS OF THANKSGIVING AND INTERCESSION**

Satisfy us with your love in the morning,

**and we will live this day in joy and praise.**

*Free prayer (or prayer 42 or 43)*

*Silent prayer*

*And*

O Christ, splendor of the glory of God,
and perfect image of the Father who begot you:
we praise you for the infinite love which sent you among us;
we confess you as the light and life of the world;

and we adore you as our Lord and our God,
now and forever. **Amen.**

*The Lord's Prayer*

## HYMN *or* SPIRITUAL

## DISMISSAL

May the God of hope fill us with all joy and peace
through the power of the Holy Spirit.                    *Rom. 15:13*

**Amen.**

Bless the Lord.

**The Lord's name be praised.**

### EVENING PRAYER

## OPENING SENTENCES

O God, come to our assistance.

**O Lord, hasten to help us.**

From the root of Jesse a flower will blossom,
and the glory of the Lord will fill the earth.

**All creation shall see the saving power of God.**
                                             *Based on Isa. 11:11; 52:10*

**HYMN OF LIGHT** *(4, 100\*) or other evening hymn or Advent hymn, and*
**LIGHTING OF THE CANDLE**

**PSALTER** *One or both of the following:* Psalms 126; 62

**SCRIPTURE READING** *followed by silent reflection*

**BIBLICAL SONG** *Song of Mary (2, 98\*) or Song of the Redeemed (16) or
other New Testament song (15–25)*

## PRAYERS OF THANKSGIVING AND INTERCESSION

Receive my prayer as incense, O God,

**my uplifted hands as an evening sacrifice.**

*Free prayer (or prayer 44 or 45)*

*Silent prayer*

*And*

God of power and mercy,
open our hearts in welcome.
Remove all that hinders us from receiving Christ with joy,
that we may share his wisdom
and become one with him when he comes in glory,
for he lives and reigns with you and the Holy Spirit,
one God, forever and ever. **Amen.**

*The Lord's Prayer*

## HYMN *or* SPIRITUAL

## DISMISSAL

May the God of hope fill us with all joy and peace
through the power of the Holy Spirit.              *Rom. 15:13*

**Amen.**

Bless the Lord.

**The Lord's name be praised.**

### FRIDAY
#### MORNING PRAYER

## OPENING SENTENCES

O Lord, open my lips.

**And my mouth shall proclaim your praise.**

Like the sun in the morning sky,
the Savior of the world will come.

**Like rain on the meadow,
he will descend.**

**MORNING PSALM** (95; 100; 63; or 51) *or* **MORNING HYMN** *or*
**ADVENT HYMN**

**PSALTER** *One or both of the following:* Psalms 102; 148

**SCRIPTURE READING** *followed by silent reflection*

**BIBLICAL SONG** *Song of Zechariah (1, 97\*) or The New Jerusalem (10)
or other Old Testament song (7–14)*

**PRAYERS OF THANKSGIVING AND INTERCESSION**

Satisfy us with your love in the morning,

**and we will live this day in joy and praise.**

*Free prayer (or prayer 42 or 43)*

*Silent prayer*

*And*

All-powerful God,
help us to look forward in hope
to the coming of our Savior.
May we live by his teachings,
ready to welcome him with burning love and faith.
We ask this through the same Christ our Lord. **Amen.**

*The Lord's Prayer*

**HYMN** *or* **SPIRITUAL**

## DISMISSAL

May God's peace, which is far beyond our understanding,
keep us safe in union with Christ Jesus.                    *Phil. 4:7*

**Amen.**

Bless the Lord.

**The Lord's name be praised.**

### EVENING PRAYER

## OPENING SENTENCES

O God, come to our assistance.

**O Lord, hasten to help us.**

The angel said to Mary:
Hail, O favored one, the Lord is with you!

**Do not be afraid, Mary, for you have found favor with God.**

You will conceive and bear a son,

**and you shall call his name Jesus.**

The Holy Spirit will come upon you,

**and the power of the Most High will overshadow you.**
                                        *Luke 1:28, 30–31, 35*

**HYMN OF LIGHT** *(4, 100\*) or other evening hymn or Advent hymn, and*
**LIGHTING OF THE CANDLE**

**PSALTER** *One or both of the following:* Psalms 130; 16

**SCRIPTURE READING** *followed by silent reflection*

**BIBLICAL SONG** *Song of Mary (2, 98\*) or Song of the Redeemed (16) or
other New Testament song (15–25)*

## PRAYERS OF THANKSGIVING AND INTERCESSION

Receive my prayer as incense, O God,
**my uplifted hands as an evening sacrifice.**

*Free prayer (or prayer 44 or 45)*

*Silent prayer*

*And*

Holy God,
you show the world the splendor of your glory
in the coming of Christ,
born of the Virgin Mary.
Give us true faith and love
to celebrate the mystery of God made flesh
in Jesus Christ our Lord. **Amen.**

*The Lord's Prayer*

## HYMN *or* SPIRITUAL

## DISMISSAL

May God's peace, which is far beyond our understanding,
keep us safe in union with Christ Jesus.                    *Phil. 4:7*

**Amen.**

Bless the Lord.

**The Lord's name be praised.**

## SATURDAY
### MORNING PRAYER

## OPENING SENTENCES

O Lord, open my lips.

**And my mouth shall proclaim your praise.**

Behold, a young woman shall conceive and bear a son,

**and shall call his name Immanuel, God-with-us.**

And his name will be called Wonderful Counselor,

**Mighty God, Everlasting Father, Prince of Peace.**     *Isa. 7:14; 9:6*

**MORNING PSALM** (95; 100; 63; or 51) *or* **MORNING HYMN** *or* **ADVENT HYMN**

**PSALTER** *One or both of the following:* Psalms 90; 149

**SCRIPTURE READING** *followed by silent reflection*

**BIBLICAL SONG** *Song of Zechariah (1, 97\*) or The New Jerusalem (10) or other Old Testament song (7–14)*

**PRAYERS OF THANKSGIVING AND INTERCESSION**

Satisfy us with your love in the morning,

**and we will live this day in joy and praise.**

*Free prayer (or prayer 42 or 43)*

*Silent prayer*

*And*

Holy God,
the mystery of your eternal Word
took flesh among us in Jesus Christ.
At the message of an angel,
the Virgin Mary placed her life
at the service of your will.
Filled with the light of your Spirit,
she became the temple of your Word.
Strengthen us by the example of her humility,
that we may always be ready to do your will
and welcome Christ into our lives. **Amen.**

*The Lord's Prayer*

**HYMN** *or* **SPIRITUAL**

**DISMISSAL**

May the grace of the Lord Jesus Christ be with us all.    *Phil. 4:23*
**Amen.**

Bless the Lord.
**The Lord's name be praised.**

## EVENING PRAYER

## OPENING SENTENCES AT ENTRANCE OF THE LIGHT

The Spirit and the church cry out:
**Come, Lord Jesus.**

All those who await his appearance pray:
**Come, Lord Jesus.**

The whole creation pleads:
**Come, Lord Jesus.**                               *Based on Rev. 22:20*

*Or*

O God, come to our assistance.
**O Lord, hasten to help us.**

*And*

Let the heavens be glad and let the earth rejoice,
**for the Lord comes to judge the earth,**
to judge the world with justice
**and the nations with truth.**                          *Ps. 96:11, 13*

Blessed are those servants

**whom the master finds awake when he comes.** *Luke 12:37*

**HYMN OF LIGHT** *(4, 100\*) or other evening hymn or Advent hymn, and* **LIGHTING OF THE CANDLE**

**THANKSGIVING FOR LIGHT**

The Lord be with you.

**And also with you.**

Let us give thanks to the Lord our God.

**It is right to give our thanks and praise.**

Blessed are you, O Lord our God, Ruler of the universe,
creator of light and darkness.
In this holy season,
when the sun's light is swallowed up
by the growing darkness of the night,
you renew your promise to reveal among us
the splendor of your glory,
made flesh and visible to us in Jesus Christ, your Son.
Through the prophets
you teach us to hope for his reign of peace.
Through the outpouring of your Spirit,
you give sight to our souls
that we may see your glory
in the presence of Christ.

Strengthen us where we are weak,
support us in our efforts to do your will,
and free our tongues to sing your praise,
for to you all honor and blessing are due,
now and forever. **Amen.**

---

Text beginning "Blessed are you, O Lord our God, Ruler" is by John Allyn Melloh, S.M., and is copyright © 1979 G.I.A. Publications, Inc., Chicago, Illinois. Altered with permission. All rights reserved.

## INCENSE

An angel, holding a golden censer full of incense,
stood before the altar.
The smoke of the incense went up before God,
mingled with the prayers of the people.                    *Rev. 8:3–4*

**EVENING PSALM** Psalm 141

**PSALTER** *One or both of the following:* Psalms 80; 72

**SCRIPTURE READING** *followed by silent reflection*

**BIBLICAL SONG** *Song of Mary (2, 98\*) or Song of the Redeemed (16) or other New Testament song (15–25)*

## PRAYERS OF THANKSGIVING AND INTERCESSION

Let us walk in love, as Christ loved us and gave himself up for us,

**a fragrant offering and sacrifice to God.**

*Free prayer (or prayer 44, 45, or 40)*

*Silent prayer*

*And*

Lord God,
may we live simply, justly, and devoutly
as we await the coming of our God and Savior Jesus Christ,
who gave himself for us,
and set us apart as his own people,
for he lives and reigns forever. **Amen.**

*The Lord's Prayer*

## HYMN *or* SPIRITUAL

## DISMISSAL

May the grace of the Lord Jesus Christ be with us all.    *Phil. 4:23*

**Amen.**

Bless the Lord.

**The Lord's name be praised.**

# CHRISTMAS

*For use December 25 to January 5*

## OPENING SENTENCES

O Lord, open my lips.

**And my mouth shall proclaim your praise.**

*And*

Glory to God in the highest,

**and peace to God's people on earth. Alleluia!**          *Luke 2:14*

*Or*

The Word became flesh and dwelt among us,

**and we beheld his glory. Alleluia!**          *John 1:14*

*Or, for Holy Innocents (December 28)*

Those who had been slain for the word of God cried out:

**O sovereign Lord, holy and true,
how long before you will avenge us?**          *Rev. 6:9–10*

*Or, for January 1*

Proclaim with me the greatness of the Lord;

**let us exalt the name of the Lord together.**          *Ps. 34:3*

**PSALM** (95; 100; 63; or 51) *or* **MORNING HYMN** *or*
**CHRISTMAS HYMN**

**PSALTER** *One of the following may be read; and one of the Laudate psalms.**

| | | | |
|---|---|---|---|
| Dec. 25 | Psalm 2 | Dec. 31 | Psalm 98 |
| Dec. 26 | Psalm 116 | Jan. 1 | Psalm 98 |
| Dec. 27 | Psalm 34 | Jan. 2 | Psalm 48 |
| Dec. 28 | Psalm 2 | Jan. 3 | Psalm 111 |
| Dec. 29 | Psalm 96 | Jan. 4 | Psalm 20 |
| Dec. 30 | Psalm 93 | Jan. 5 | Psalm 99 |

*Laudate psalms:*

Sunday—Psalm 150
Monday—Psalm 145
Tuesday—Psalm 146
Wednesday—Psalm 147:1–11

Thursday—Psalm 147:12–20
Friday—Psalm 148
Saturday—Psalm 149

**SCRIPTURE READING** *followed by silent reflection*

**BIBLICAL SONG** *Song of Zechariah (1, 97*) or Te Deum (5) or Old Testament song (7–14)*

**PRAYERS OF THANKSGIVING AND INTERCESSION**

Satisfy us with your love in the morning,

**and we will live this day in joy and praise.**

*Free prayer (or prayer 46 or 47)*

*Silent prayer*

*And*

All-powerful and unseen God,
the coming of your light into our world
has made the darkness vanish.
Teach us to proclaim the birth of your Son Jesus Christ,
who lives and reigns with you and the Holy Spirit,
one God, forever and ever. **Amen.**

*The Lord's Prayer*

**HYMN** *or* **SPIRITUAL**

## DISMISSAL

May the Lord bless us,
protect us from all evil,
and bring us to eternal life.

**Amen.**

Bless the Lord.

**The Lord's name be praised.**

### EVENING PRAYER

*For use December 24 and 25; also Saturday and Sunday*

## OPENING SENTENCES AT ENTRANCE OF THE LIGHT

The people who walked in darkness
have seen a great light.

**The light shines in the darkness,
and the darkness has not overcome it.**

Those who dwell in the land of deep darkness,
on them has the light shined.

**We have beheld Christ's glory,
glory as of the only Son of the Father.**

For to us a child is born, to us a Son is given.

**In him was life,
and the life was the light of all people.**

*Based on Isa. 9:2, 6; John 1:4–5, 14*

*Or*

O God, come to our assistance.

**O Lord, hasten to help us.**

*And*

Today Christ is born;

**today salvation has appeared;**

today angels are singing and archangels rejoicing;

**today the just exult and say:**
**Glory to God in the highest. Alleluia!**

**HYMN OF LIGHT** *(4, 100\*) or other evening hymn or Christmas hymn*

**THANKSGIVING FOR LIGHT**

The Lord be with you.

**And also with you.**

Let us give thanks to the Lord our God.

**It is right to give our thanks and praise.**

Blessed are you, O Lord our God,
our eternal Father and David's Ruler.
You have made our gladness greater and increased our joy
by sending to dwell among us
the Wonderful Counselor, the Prince of Peace.
Born of Mary,
proclaimed to the shepherds
and acknowledged to the ends of the earth,
your unconquered Sun of righteousness
destroys our darkness and establishes us in freedom.

All glory in the highest be to you,
through Christ, the Son of your favor,
in the anointing love of your Spirit,
this night and forever and ever. **Amen.**

---

## INCENSE

An angel, holding a golden censer full of incense,
stood before the altar.
The smoke of the incense went up before God,
mingled with the prayers of the people.                    *Rev. 8:3–4*

## EVENING PSALM Psalm 141

**PSALTER** *One or both of the following:*

| Dec. 24 | Psalms 132; 114 | Dec. 31 | Psalms 45; 96 |
|---------|-----------------|---------|---------------|
| Dec. 25 | Psalms 98; 96 | Jan. 1 | Psalms 99; 8 |
| Dec. 26 | Psalms 119:1–24; 27 | Jan. 2 | Psalms 9, 29 |
| Dec. 27 | Psalms 19; 121 | Jan. 3 | Psalms 107; 15 |
| Dec. 28 | Psalms 110; 111 | Jan. 4 | Psalms 93; 97 |
| Dec. 29 | Psalms 132; 97 | Jan. 5 | Psalms 96; 110 |
| Dec. 30 | Psalms 89:1–18; 89:19–52 | Jan. 6 | Psalms 100; 67 |

## SCRIPTURE READING *followed by silent reflection*

**BIBLICAL SONG** *Song of Mary (2, 98\*), Jesus Christ Is Lord (20),
Christ, the Head of All Creation (19), or other New Testament song (15–25)*

## PRAYERS OF THANKSGIVING AND INTERCESSION

Let us walk in love, as Christ loved us and gave himself up for us,

**a fragrant offering and sacrifice to God.**

*Free prayer (or prayer 48, 49, or 40)*

*Silent prayer*

Eternal God,
in Jesus Christ your light shines in our darkness,
giving joy in our sorrow
and presence in loneliness.
Fill us with the mystery of your Word made flesh,
until our hearts overflow with praise and joy,
for he is the beginning and the end of all that exists,
living forevermore. **Amen.**

*The Lord's Prayer*

**HYMN** *or* **SPIRITUAL**

**DISMISSAL**

May the Lord, who is our peace,
give us peace at all times and in every way.　　　　*2 Thess. 3:16*

**Amen.**

Bless the Lord.

**The Lord's name be praised.**

## EVENING PRAYER

*For use December 26 to January 4 (except Saturday and Sunday)*

**OPENING SENTENCES**

O God, come to our assistance.

**O Lord, hasten to help us.**

*And*

Today Christ is born;

**today salvation has appeared;**

today angels are singing and archangels rejoicing;

**today the just exult and say:
Glory to God in the highest. Alleluia!**

*Or*

Jesus Christ is the true light

**that enlightens all who come into the world.**　　　　*John 1:9*

*Or*

Christ, the light of the world, is born to us.

**Come, let us adore him. Alleluia!**

*Or, for Holy Innocents (December 28)*

A sound of moaning is heard in Ramah,
the sound of bitter weeping.

**Rachel is crying for her children;
she refuses to be comforted,**

because her children are no more.                              *Jer. 31:15*

*For January 1*

To us a child is born, to us a Son is given,

**and he shall be called the Prince of Peace. Alleluia!**     *Isa. 9:6*

**HYMN OF LIGHT** *(4, 100\*) or other evening hymn or Christmas hymn,
and* **LIGHTING OF THE CANDLE**

**PSALTER** *One or both of the following:*

| | | | | |
|---|---|---|---|---|
| *Dec. 24* | Psalms 132; 114 | | *Dec. 30* | Psalms 89:1–18; 89:19–52 |
| *Dec. 25* | Psalms 98; 96 | | *Dec. 31* | Psalms 45; 96 |
| *Dec. 26* | Psalms 119:1–24; 27 | | *Jan. 1* | Psalms 99; 8 |
| *Dec. 27* | Psalms 19; 121 | | *Jan. 2* | Psalms 9; 29 |
| *Dec. 28* | Psalms 110; 111 | | *Jan. 3* | Psalms 107; 15 |
| *Dec. 29* | Psalms 132; 97 | | *Jan. 4* | Psalms 93; 97 |

**SCRIPTURE READING** *followed by silent reflection*

**BIBLICAL SONG** *Song of Mary (2, 98\*), Jesus Christ Is Lord (20),
Christ, the Head of All Creation (19), or other New Testament song (15–25)*

## PRAYERS OF THANKSGIVING AND INTERCESSION

Receive my prayer as incense, O God,

**my uplifted hands as an evening sacrifice.**

*Free prayer (or prayer 48 or 49)*

*Silent prayer*

*And*

O God,
you loved the world so much
that you gave your only Son for us.
Increase and strengthen our faith
and fix it firmly on the mystery of your Word made flesh,
that we may triumph over all evil
through Christ who reigns now and forever. **Amen.**

*The Lord's Prayer*

## HYMN *or* SPIRITUAL

## DISMISSAL

May the Lord, who is our peace,
give us peace at all times and in every way.        *2 Thess. 3:16*

**Amen.**

Bless the Lord.

**The Lord's name be praised.**

# EPIPHANY

## THE EPIPHANY OF THE LORD
### MORNING PRAYER

*For use January 6 through the following Sunday (Baptism of the Lord)*

**OPENING SENTENCES**

O Lord, open my lips.

**And my mouth shall proclaim your praise.**

*And*

Today the church is joined to her heavenly bridegroom;

**the magi hasten with their gifts to the royal wedding,**

where the guests rejoice with water made wine.

**Alleluia!**

*Or*

The Lord has shown forth his glory;

**come, let us adore him. Alleluia!**

*Or*

Arise, shine, for your light is come!

**The glory of the Lord is risen upon you!**

Nations shall come to your light,

**and rulers to the brightness of your rising.**

They shall come from Sheba, bearing gold and incense,

**singing the praise of God.**                    *Isa. 60:1, 3, 6*

*Or, for Baptism of the Lord*

Sealed with the sign of the Spirit,

**Jesus rises from the waters.**

The Baptizer knows him and foretells:

**This is the Lamb of God
who takes away the sin of the world.**

**PSALM** (95; 100; 63; or 51) *or* **MORNING HYMN** *or*
**EPIPHANY HYMN**

**PSALTER** *One of the following may be read: Psalms 72 (Jan. 6); 46; 97; or
104 (Baptism of the Lord); and one of the Laudate psalms:*
| | |
|---|---|
| *Sunday*—Psalm 150 | *Thursday*—Psalm 147:12–20 |
| *Monday*—Psalm 145 | *Friday*—Psalm 148 |
| *Tuesday*—Psalm 146 | *Saturday*—Psalm 149 |
| *Wednesday*—Psalm 147:1–11 | |

**SCRIPTURE READING** *followed by silent reflection*

**BIBLICAL SONG** *Song of Zechariah (1, 97\*) or an Old Testament song
such as The New Jerusalem (10, Epiphany) or Isaiah 42:1–8 (Baptism of the
Lord)*

**PRAYERS OF THANKSGIVING AND INTERCESSION**

Satisfy us with your love in the morning,

**and we will live this day in joy and praise.**

*Free prayer (or prayer 50 or 51)*

*Silent prayer*

*And*

O Christ, light made manifest as the true light of God;
gladden our hearts on the joyful morning of your glory,
call us by our name on the great Day of your coming,

and give us grace to offer,
with all the hosts of heaven,
unending praise to God
in whom all things find their ending,
now and ever. **Amen.**

*The Lord's Prayer*

**HYMN** *or* **SPIRITUAL**

**DISMISSAL**

The grace of God be with us all, now and always.     *1 Tim. 6:21*

**Amen.**

Bless the Lord.

**The Lord's name be praised.**

*From Monday morning after Baptism of the Lord through Shrove Tuesday (the day before Ash Wednesday), the liturgy for Ordinary Days is used (pp. 51–84).*

## EVENING PRAYER

*For use on January 5; Epiphany (January 6); also Saturday and the Sunday after Epiphany (Baptism of the Lord)*

**OPENING SENTENCES AT ENTRANCE OF THE LIGHT**

The people who walked in darkness
have seen a great light.

**The light shines in the darkness,
and the darkness has not overcome it.**

Those who dwell in the land of deep darkness,
on them has the light shined.

**We have beheld Christ's glory,
glory as of the only Son of the Father.**

For to us a child is born, to us a Son is given.

**In him was life,
and the life was the light of all people.**

*Based on Isa. 9:2, 6; John 1:4–5, 14*

*Or*

O God, come to our assistance,

**O Lord, hasten to help us.**

*And*

This is a holy day adorned with three mysteries:

**Today a star leads the magi to the manger;**

today water is made wine at the wedding;

**today Christ is baptized by John in the Jordan to save us.
Alleluia!**

**HYMN OF LIGHT** *(4, 100\*) or other evening hymn or Christmas hymn*

**THANKSGIVING FOR LIGHT**

The Lord be with you.

**And also with you.**

Let us give thanks to the Lord our God.

**It is right to give our thanks and praise.**

Blessed are you, O Lord our God,
our eternal Father and David's Ruler.
You have made our gladness greater and increased our joy
by sending to dwell among us
the Wonderful Counselor, the Prince of Peace.
Born of Mary,

---

proclaimed to the shepherds
and acknowledged to the ends of the earth,
your unconquered Sun of righteousness
destroys our darkness and establishes us in freedom.

All glory in the highest be to you,
through Christ, the Son of your favor,
in the anointing love of your Spirit,
this night and forever and ever. **Amen.**

## INCENSE

An angel, holding a golden censer full of incense,
stood before the altar.
The smoke of the incense went up before God,
mingled with the prayers of the people.               *Rev. 8:3–4*

## EVENING PSALM Psalm 141

**PSALTER** *One or more of the following:*
        *Jan. 5*—Psalms 96; 110
        *Jan. 6*—Psalms 100; 67
        *Baptism of the Lord*—Psalm 29

## SCRIPTURE READING *followed by silent reflection*

**BIBLICAL SONG** *Song of Mary (2, 98\*), Jesus Christ Is Lord (20), Christ, the Head of All Creation (19), or other New Testament song (15–25)*

## PRAYERS OF THANKSGIVING AND INTERCESSION

Let us walk in love, as Christ loved us and gave himself up for us,

**a fragrant offering and sacrifice to God.**

*Free prayer (or prayer 52, 53, or 40)*

*Silent prayer*

*And*

Almighty God,
who anointed Jesus at his baptism with the Holy Spirit,
and revealed him as your beloved Son,
keep us, your children born of water and the Spirit,
faithful in your service,
that we may rejoice to be called children of God,
through the same Jesus Christ our Lord. **Amen.**

*The Lord's Prayer*

## HYMN *or* SPIRITUAL

## DISMISSAL

May the Lord, who is our peace,
give us peace at all times and in every way.     *2 Thess. 3:16*

**Amen.**

Bless the Lord.

**The Lord's name be praised.**

*From Monday morning after Baptism of the Lord through Shrove Tues-
day (the day before Ash Wednesday), the liturgy for Ordinary Days is
used (pp. 51–84).*

### EVENING PRAYER

*For use January 7 through Friday before Baptism of the Lord*

## OPENING SENTENCES

O God, come to our assistance.

**O Lord, hasten to help us.**

*And*

We have seen his star in the East

**and have come to worship him. Alleluia!**     *Matt. 2:2*

*Or*

Declare the glory of God among the nations,

**God's marvelous works among all people! Alleluia!**     *Ps. 96:3*

*Or*

This is a holy day adorned with three mysteries:

**Today a star leads the magi to the manger;**

today water is made wine at the wedding;

**today Christ is baptized by John in the Jordan to save us. Alleluia!**

**HYMN OF LIGHT** *(4,100\*) or other evening hymn or Epiphany hymn*

**PSALTER** *One or more of the following:* Psalms 27; 93; 114

**SCRIPTURE READING** *followed by silent reflection*

**BIBLICAL SONG** *Song of Mary (2, 98\*), Jesus Christ Is Lord (20), Christ, the Head of All Creation (19), or other New Testament song (15–25)*

**PRAYERS OF THANKSGIVING AND INTERCESSION**

Receive my prayer as incense, O God,

**my uplifted hands as an evening sacrifice.**

*Free prayer (or prayer 52 or 53)*

*Silent prayer*

*And*

Eternal Light,
you have shown us your glory in Christ,
the Word made flesh.

Your light is strong,
your love is near.
Draw us beyond the limits which this world imposes,
to the life where the Spirit makes all life complete,
through Jesus Christ our Lord. **Amen.**

*The Lord's Prayer*

**HYMN** *or* **SPIRITUAL**

**DISMISSAL**

The grace of God be with us all, now and always.     *1 Tim. 6:21*

**Amen.**

Bless the Lord.

**The Lord's name be praised.**

*From Monday morning after Baptism of the Lord through Shrove Tues-*
*day (the day before Ash Wednesday), the liturgy for Ordinary Days is*
*used (pp. 51–84).*

# LENT

## SUNDAY
### MORNING PRAYER

**OPENING SENTENCES**

O Lord, open my lips.

**And my mouth shall proclaim your praise.**

*And*

O Lord, you are kind and forgiving,

**full of love to all who call on you.**

Listen to my prayer, O Lord;

**hear the cries of my pleading.** *Ps. 86:5–6*

*Or, for Passion/Palm Sunday*

Tell the daughter of Zion: Behold, your king is coming to you!

**He is humble and rides on a donkey.**

Hosanna to the Son of David!

**Blessed is he who comes in the name of the Lord!**
**Hosanna in the highest!** *Matt. 21:5, 9*

**MORNING PSALM** (95; 100; 63; or 51) *or* **MORNING HYMN** *or*
**LENTEN HYMN**

**PSALTER** *One or both of the following:* Psalms 84; 150

**SCRIPTURE READING** *followed by silent reflection*

**BIBLICAL SONG** *Song of Zechariah (1, 97\*), Seek the Lord (9), Song of
Penitence (13), or Old Testament song (7–14)*

## PRAYERS OF THANKSGIVING AND INTERCESSION

Satisfy us with your love in the morning,

**and we will live this day in joy and praise.**

*Free prayer (or prayer 56 or 57)*

*Silent prayer*

*And*

God of all joy,
fill our souls to overflowing
with the fullness of your grace.
In this season, remind us
of your triumph over the tragedy of the cross,
and your victory for us over the powers of sin and death,
so that we may reflect your glory
as disciples of Jesus Christ,
our risen Lord. **Amen.**

*The Lord's Prayer*

## HYMN *or* SPIRITUAL

## DISMISSAL

To God be honor and glory forever and ever!           *1 Tim. 1:17*

**Amen.**

Bless the Lord.

**The Lord's name be praised.**

### EVENING PRAYER

## OPENING SENTENCES AT THE ENTRANCE OF THE LIGHT

Behold, now is the acceptable time;

**now is the day of salvation.**

Turn us again, O God of our salvation,

**that the light of your face may shine on us.**

May your justice shine like the sun;

**and may the poor be lifted up.**

*Based on 2 Cor. 6:2; Pss. 85:4; 80:3*

*Or*

O God, come to our assistance.

**O Lord, hasten to help us.**

*And*

All the nations shall come, O Lord.

**They will bow down before you and praise your name.**

For you are great, your works are wonderful;

**you alone are God.** *Ps. 86:9–10*

**HYMN OF LIGHT** *(4, 100\*) or other evening hymn or Lenten hymn*

**THANKSGIVING FOR LIGHT**

The Lord be with you.

**And also with you.**

Let us give thanks to the Lord our God.

**It is right to give our thanks and praise.**

Blessed are you, O Lord our God,
the Shepherd of Israel,
their pillar of cloud by day,
their pillar of fire by night.

------

In these forty days
you lead us into the desert of repentance
that in this pilgrimage of prayer
we might learn to be your people once more.
In fasting and service
you bring us back to your heart.
You open our eyes to your presence in the world
and you free our hands
to lead others to the radiant splendor of your mercy.

Be with us in these journey days,
for without you we are lost and will perish.
To you alone be dominion and glory,
forever and ever. **Amen.**

## INCENSE

An angel, holding a golden censer full of incense,
stood before the altar.
The smoke of the incense went up before God,
mingled with the prayers of the people.                    *Rev. 8:3–4*

**EVENING PSALM** Psalm 141

**PSALTER** *One or both of the following:* Psalms 42; 32

**SCRIPTURE READING** *followed by silent reflection*

**BIBLICAL SONG** *Song of Mary (2, 98\*), The Beatitudes (21), Jesus Christ
Is Lord (20), Song of the Redeemed (16), Christ the Servant (22), or other
New Testament song (15–25)*

## PRAYERS OF THANKSGIVING AND INTERCESSION

Let us walk in love, as Christ loved us and gave himself up for us,

**a fragrant offering and sacrifice to God.**

*Free prayer (or prayer 58, 59, or 40)*

*Silent prayer*

*And*

God of creation,
you formed us out of the dust of the earth
and breathed life into us.
By your Spirit breathe your new life into us.
Lead us to life eternal
by the mighty love of Jesus Christ,
who suffered on the cross
and was raised from the dead.
You lifted him to glory,
where with outstretched arms
he welcomes the world in his strong embrace of salvation.
In his holy name we pray. **Amen.**

*The Lord's Prayer*

## HYMN *or* SPIRITUAL

## DISMISSAL

To God be honor and glory forever and ever!     *1 Tim. 1:17*
**Amen.**

Bless the Lord.

**The Lord's name be praised.**

## MONDAY
### MORNING PRAYER

## OPENING SENTENCES

O Lord, open my lips.

**And my mouth shall proclaim your praise.**

*And*

Show me your way, O Lord,

**that I may walk in your truth.**

Teach me to fear your name,

**and my whole heart will praise you.** *Ps. 86:11–12*

*For Monday in Holy Week*

When Jesus saw Jerusalem, he wept over it:

**If only you had known the way to peace!** *Luke 19:41*

**MORNING PSALM** (95; 100; 63; or 51) *or* **MORNING HYMN** *or* **LENTEN HYMN**

**PSALTER** *One or both of the following:* Psalms 119:73–80; 145

**SCRIPTURE READING** *followed by silent reflection*

**BIBLICAL SONG** *Song of Zechariah (1, 97\*), Seek the Lord (9), Song of Penitence (13), or Old Testament song (7–14)*

**PRAYERS OF THANKSGIVING AND INTERCESSION**

Satisfy us with your love in the morning,

**and we will live this day in joy and praise.**

*Free prayer (or prayer 56 or 57)*

*Silent prayer*

*And*

Eternal God,
give us such grace and generosity
that this day we may bring your love and peace and joy
to the lonely, the troubled, the grieving.
Help us by your Spirit
to recognize your presence with us throughout the day,
that we may do what is good
in the name of Jesus Christ, our Redeemer. **Amen.**

*The Lord's Prayer*

**HYMN** *or* **SPIRITUAL**

**DISMISSAL**

May we continue to grow in the grace and knowledge
of Jesus Christ, our Lord and Savior. *2 Peter 3:18*

**Amen.**

Bless the Lord.

**The Lord's name be praised.**

## EVENING PRAYER

**OPENING SENTENCES**

O God, come to our assistance.

**O Lord, hasten to help us.**

*And*

With all my heart I will praise you, O Lord my God!

**I will glorify your name forever.**

For great is your constant love for me!

**You have rescued my soul from the depths of the grave.**

*Ps. 86:12–13*

*For Monday in Holy Week*

Jesus drove the sellers out of the temple:

**It is written in the scriptures that God said:**

My temple will be called a house of prayer.

**But you are making it a den of thieves.** *Matt. 21:12–13*

**HYMN OF LIGHT** *(4, 100\*) or other evening hymn or Lenten hymn, and*
**LIGHTING OF THE CANDLE**

**PSALTER** *One or both of the following:* Psalms 121; 6

**SCRIPTURE READING** *followed by silent reflection*

**BIBLICAL SONG** *Song of Mary (2, 98\*), The Beatitudes (21), Jesus Christ Is Lord (20), Song of the Redeemed (16), Christ the Servant (22), or other New Testament song (15–25)*

## PRAYERS OF THANKSGIVING AND INTERCESSION

Receive my prayer as incense, O God,

**my uplifted hands as an evening sacrifice.**

*Free prayer (or prayer 58 or 59)*

*Silent prayer*

*And*

Loving God,
fill us with a full measure of grace,
that we may be agents of your love in this world.
By the power of your Holy Spirit,
sustain us in the struggle for peace and justice.
Keep us constant in the service of Jesus Christ
the Savior of the world. **Amen.**

*The Lord's Prayer*

## HYMN *or* SPIRITUAL

## DISMISSAL

May we continue to grow in the grace and knowledge
of Jesus Christ, our Lord and Savior.                    *2 Peter 3:18*

**Amen.**

Bless the Lord.

**The Lord's name be praised.**

# TUESDAY
## MORNING PRAYER

**OPENING SENTENCES**

O Lord, open my lips.

**And my mouth shall proclaim your praise.**

*And*

Happy are those whose sins are forgiven,

**whose wrongs are pardoned.**

Happy are those to whom the Lord imputes no guilt,

**in whose spirit there is no guile.**                    *Ps. 32:1–2*

*For Tuesday in Holy Week*

The children were shouting in the temple:

**Hosanna to the Son of David!**

And Jesus justified them with scripture:

**Out of the mouths of children and infants
you have brought perfect praise.**          *Matt. 21:15–16*

**MORNING PSALM** (95; 100; 63; or 51) *or* **MORNING HYMN** *or*
**LENTEN HYMN**

**PSALTER** *One or both of the following:* Psalms 34; 146

**SCRIPTURE READING** *followed by silent reflection*

**BIBLICAL SONG** *Song of Zechariah (1, 97\*), Seek the Lord (9), Song of
Penitence (13), or Old Testament song (7–14)*

**PRAYERS OF THANKSGIVING AND INTERCESSION**

Satisfy us with your love in the morning,

**and we will live this day in joy and praise.**

*Free prayer (or prayer 56 or 57)*

*Silent prayer*

*And*

God of love,
as you have given your life to us,
so may we live according to your holy will
revealed in Jesus Christ.
Make us bold to share your life,
and show your love,
in the power of your Holy Spirit. **Amen.**

*The Lord's Prayer*

## HYMN *or* SPIRITUAL

## DISMISSAL

The grace of God be with us all, now and always.     *1 Tim. 6:21*

**Amen.**

Bless the Lord.

**The Lord's name be praised.**

## EVENING PRAYER

## OPENING SENTENCES

O God, come to our assistance.

**O Lord, hasten to help us.**

*And*

In the time of trouble,
the faithful will pray to you.

**The great waters may overflow,
but they shall not reach me.**

O Lord, you are my hiding place.
You are my refuge from distress;

**you guard me and enfold me in salvation,
beyond all reach of harm.**                    *Ps. 32:6–7*

*For Tuesday in Holy Week*

Jesus cursed the fruitless fig tree and it died; so he said:

**When you pray, believe, and you will receive.**    *Matt. 21:19, 22*

When you pray, forgive,

**so God will forgive the wrongs you have done.**    *Mark 11:25*

**HYMN OF LIGHT** *(4, 100\*) or other evening hymn or Lenten hymn, and*
**LIGHTING OF THE CANDLE**

**PSALTER** *One or both of the following:* Psalms 25; 91

**SCRIPTURE READING** *followed by silent reflection*

**BIBLICAL SONG** *Song of Mary (2, 98\*), The Beatitudes (21), Jesus Christ
Is Lord (20), Song of the Redeemed (16), Christ the Servant (22), or other
New Testament song (15–25)*

**PRAYERS OF THANKSGIVING AND INTERCESSION**

Receive my prayer as incense, O God,

**my uplifted hands as an evening sacrifice.**

*Free prayer (or prayer 58 or 59)*

*Silent prayer*

*And*

Great God,
keep our feet firmly in the Way
where Christ leads us;

sound from our mouths the Truth
which Christ teaches us;
and fill our bodies with the Life
that is Christ within us,
by the power of your Holy Spirit. **Amen.**

*The Lord's Prayer*

## HYMN *or* SPIRITUAL

## DISMISSAL

The grace of God be with us all, now and always.     *1 Tim. 6:21*

**Amen.**

Bless the Lord.

**The Lord's name be praised.**

## WEDNESDAY
### MORNING PRAYER

## OPENING SENTENCES

O Lord, open my lips.

**And my mouth shall proclaim your praise.**

*And*

*For Ash Wednesday*

Create in me a clean heart, O God,

**and renew a right spirit within me.**

Cast me not away from your presence,

**and take not your Holy Spirit from me.**     *Ps. 51:10–11*

*For other days in Lent*

You look for truth deep within me,

**and teach me wisdom in my heart.**

Purify me, and I shall be clean;

**wash me, and I shall be whiter than snow.**  *Ps. 51:6–7*

*For Wednesday in Holy Week*

Jesus said: Soon it will be the Passover,

**and the Son of man will be handed over to be crucified.**

*Matt. 26:1–2*

**MORNING PSALM** (95; 100; 63; or 51) *or* **MORNING HYMN** *or* **LENTEN HYMN**

**PSALTER** *One or both of the following:* Psalms 5; 147:1–11

**SCRIPTURE READING** *followed by silent reflection*

**BIBLICAL SONG** *Song of Zechariah (1, 97\*), Seek the Lord (9), Song of Penitence (13), or Old Testament song (7–14)*

**PRAYERS OF THANKSGIVING AND INTERCESSION**

Satisfy us with your love in the morning,

**and we will live this day in joy and praise.**

*Free prayer (or prayer 54 Ash Wednesday, 56, 57, or 41)*

*Silent prayer*

*And*

*For Ash Wednesday*

Relying on your grace, O God,
we ask mercy and strength

for ourselves and for all who take up disciplines today,
that we may know the peace of humility,
the joy of service,
and the power of your Holy Spirit.
In the name of Jesus Christ we pray. **Amen.**

*Or*

Almighty and everlasting God,
you hate nothing you have made
and forgive the sins of all who are penitent.
Create in us new and contrite hearts,
that, lamenting our sins and acknowledging our wretchedness,
we may receive from you, the God of all mercy,
perfect forgiveness and peace;
through Jesus Christ our Lord. **Amen.**

*For other days in Lent*

Lord,
as daylight fills the sky,
fill us with your holy light.
May our lives mirror your great love.
Your wisdom has brought us into being,
and your care guides us
on the way of Jesus Christ our Lord. **Amen.**

*Or*

Send us forth this day, great God,
to be your people,
ready to do your will,
eager to speak your Word.
Lift us up by your Spirit
that we may be followers of Jesus Christ,
our Lord and Savior. **Amen.**

*The Lord's Prayer*

**HYMN** *or* **SPIRITUAL**

## DISMISSAL

May the Lord, who is our peace,
give us peace at all times and in every way.     *2 Thess. 3:16*

**Amen.**

Bless the Lord.

**The Lord's name be praised.**

### EVENING PRAYER

## OPENING SENTENCES

O God, come to our assistance.

**O Lord, hasten to help us.**

*And*

*For Ash Wednesday*

Have mercy on me, O God, according to your loving-kindness;

**in your great compassion blot out my offenses.**

Wash me thoroughly from my wickedness,

**and cleanse me from my sin!**     *Ps. 51:1–2*

*For other days in Lent*

Hide your face, O God, from my sins,

**and blot out all my iniquities.**

Give me the joy of your saving help,

**and sustain me with your bountiful spirit.**     *Ps. 51:9, 12*

*For Wednesday in Holy Week*

Mary washed Jesus' feet with expensive perfume, and they said:

**This should have been sold, and the money given to the poor.**

But Jesus said: Leave her alone! She has done a beautiful thing.

**She has poured the perfume on me to prepare me for burial.**

*Mark 14:3–6, 8*

**HYMN OF LIGHT** *(4, 100\*) or other evening hymn or Lenten hymn, and* **LIGHTING OF THE CANDLE**

**PSALTER** *One or both of the following:* Psalms 27; 51

**SCRIPTURE READING** *followed by silent reflection*

**BIBLICAL SONG** *Song of Mary (2, 98\*), The Beatitudes (21), Jesus Christ Is Lord (20), Song of the Redeemed (16), Christ the Servant (22), or other New Testament song (15–25)*

**PRAYERS OF THANKSGIVING AND INTERCESSION**

Receive my prayer as incense, O God,

**my uplifted hands as an evening sacrifice.**

*Free prayer (or prayer 55 Ash Wednesday, 58, 59, or 41)*

*Silent prayer*

*And*

*For Ash Wednesday*

Without your breath in us, O God,
we wither and are gone.
Calm us by your Spirit,
and renew your life within us,
that we may journey with Christ
and come at last to the home he has prepared for us,
welcomed in your eternal embrace.
In Jesus Christ we pray. **Amen.**

*For other days in Lent*

Eternal God,
we pray that you will change the grief of our guilt
into the joy of forgiveness,
that we may be delivered from sin
and set free to serve Jesus Christ,
our crucified and risen Lord. **Amen.**

*The Lord's Prayer*

**HYMN** *or* **SPIRITUAL**

**DISMISSAL**

May the Lord, who is our peace,
give us peace at all times and in every way.      *2 Thess. 3:16*

**Amen.**

Bless the Lord.

**The Lord's name be praised.**

## THURSDAY
### MORNING PRAYER

**OPENING SENTENCES**

O Lord, open my lips.

**And my mouth shall proclaim your praise.**

*And*

Deliver me from death, O God,

**and my tongue shall sing of your righteousness,
O God of my salvation.**      *Ps. 51:14*

Save your people, O Lord,

**by the cross of our Lord Jesus Christ.**

*For Maundy Thursday*

Jesus said: I give you a new commandment.
Love one another as I have loved you.

**By this the world will know
that we are his disciples,
if we love one another.**                    *John 13:34–35*

**MORNING PSALM** (95; 100; 63; or 51) *or* **MORNING HYMN** *or*
**LENTEN HYMN**

**PSALTER** *One or both of the following:* Psalms 27; 147:12—20

**SCRIPTURE READING** *followed by silent reflection*

**BIBLICAL SONG** *Song of Zechariah (1, 97\*), Seek the Lord (9), Song of
Penitence (13), or Old Testament song (7–14)*

**PRAYERS OF THANKSGIVING AND INTERCESSION**

Satisfy us with your love in the morning,

**and we will live this day in joy and praise.**

*Free prayer (or prayer 56, 57, or 60 Maundy Thursday)*

*Silent prayer*

*And*

Remember us, O God,
so we may not forget you this day.
Direct our steps in discipleship,
and protect our souls in faith,
that we may be steadfast in your service,
because we are secure in your love
which we know in Jesus Christ,
Savior of all. **Amen.**

*For Maundy Thursday*

Loving God,
as you have shared life and love with us,
lead us to share ourselves,
that in the giving of our lives
others may recognize your love.
In the name of Jesus Christ,
who commanded us to love
by his righteous example. **Amen.**

*The Lord's Prayer*

**HYMN** *or* **SPIRITUAL**

**DISMISSAL**

May the God of hope fill us with all joy and peace
through the power of the Holy Spirit.                     *Rom. 15:13*

**Amen.**

Bless the Lord.

**The Lord's name be praised.**

## EVENING PRAYER

**OPENING SENTENCES**

O God, come to our assistance.

**O Lord, hasten to help us.**

*And*

You, O Lord, are gracious and full of compassion,
slow to anger, and full of kindness and truth.          *Ps. 103:8*

**Turn to me in your abundant mercy.**                  *Ps. 69:16*

*For Maundy Thursday*

When it was evening, they sat down to eat, and Jesus said:

**I tell you, one of you will betray me.**

The disciples were very upset, and began to ask him:

**Is it I, Lord?**                                    *Matt. 26:21–22*

**HYMN OF LIGHT** *(4, 100\*) or other evening hymn or Lenten hymn, and* **LIGHTING OF THE CANDLE**

**PSALTER** *One or both of the following:* Psalms 126; 102

**SCRIPTURE READING** *followed by silent reflection*

**BIBLICAL SONG** *Song of Mary (2, 98\*), The Beatitudes (21), Jesus Christ Is Lord (20), Song of the Redeemed (16), Christ the Servant (22), or other New Testament song (15–25)*

**PRAYERS OF THANKSGIVING AND INTERCESSION**

Receive my prayer as incense, O God,

**my uplifted hands as an evening sacrifice.**

*Free prayer (or prayer 58, 59, or 61 Maundy Thursday)*

*Silent prayer*

*And*

Gracious God,
you know our frailty
and understand our failures.
Cleanse us by your forgiveness,
purge the stain of sin,
and make pure our hearts within us.
Mend what is broken in our lives,
that we may be made whole with the peace of Jesus Christ,
your Son, our Savior. **Amen.**

*For Maundy Thursday*

Holy God,
keep us in communion with you
and in community with one another,
that we may always be ready to eat at table with Christ.
Protect and preserve us from all evil,
and deliver us from the pitfalls of sin,
that, ransomed and restored,
we may be loyal followers of Jesus Christ,
our Lord and Savior. **Amen.**

*The Lord's Prayer*

## HYMN *or* SPIRITUAL

## DISMISSAL

May the God of hope fill us with all joy and peace
through the power of the Holy Spirit.                    *Rom. 15:13*

**Amen.**

Bless the Lord.

**The Lord's name be praised.**

## FRIDAY
### Morning Prayer

## OPENING SENTENCES

O Lord, open my lips.

**And my mouth shall proclaim your praise.**

*And*

Out of the depths I cry to you, O Lord!

**Lord, hear my voice!**
**Let your ears attend to my pleading.**

If you, O Lord, should keep an account of our sins, who will survive?

**But you always forgive us, and for this we revere you.**   *Ps. 130:1–4*

*For Good Friday*

Keep watch and pray that you will not fall into temptation.

**The spirit is willing, but the flesh is weak.**

The hour has come for the Son of man to be handed over.

**Lord, lead us not into temptation.**   *Matt. 26:41, 45; 6:13*

**MORNING PSALM** (95; 100; 63; or 51) *or* **MORNING HYMN** *or* **LENTEN HYMN**

**PSALTER** *One or both of the following:* Psalms 22; 148

**SCRIPTURE READING** *followed by silent reflection*

**BIBLICAL SONG** *Song of Zechariah (1, 97\*), Seek the Lord (9), Song of Penitence (13), or Old Testament song (7–14)*

**PRAYERS OF THANKSGIVING AND INTERCESSION**

Satisfy us with your love in the morning,

**and we will live this day in joy and praise.**

*Free prayer (or prayer 56, 57, 41, or 62 Good Friday)*

*Silent prayer*

*And*

Stay with us, great God,
in the joys and difficulties of this day.
Remember us
when we are in trouble for Christ's sake.
Remember us also
when we forget you in the easy times.

In every time
defend us from evil.
In the name of Jesus Christ we pray. **Amen.**

*For Good Friday*

Holy God,
your Word, Jesus Christ, spoke peace to a sinful world
and brought humanity the gift of reconciliation
by the suffering and death he endured.
Teach those who bear his name
to follow the example he gave us.
May our faith, hope, and charity
turn hatred to love, conflict to peace, and death to eternal life,
through Christ our Lord. **Amen.**

*The Lord's Prayer*

## HYMN *or* SPIRITUAL

## DISMISSAL

May God's peace, which is far beyond our understanding,
keep us safe in union with Christ Jesus.              *Phil. 4:7*

**Amen.**

Bless the Lord.

**The Lord's name be praised.**

### EVENING PRAYER

## OPENING SENTENCES

O God, come to our assistance.

**O Lord, hasten to help us.**

*And*

He was wounded for our transgressions,

**he was bruised for our iniquities;**

upon him was the chastisement that made us whole,

**and with his stripes we are healed.** *Isa. 53:5*

*For Good Friday*

They took Jesus out to the place called The Skull,

**and they crucified Jesus there.**

Jesus said: Father, forgive them!

**They do not know what they are doing.** *Luke 23:33–34*

**HYMN OF LIGHT** *(4, 100\*) or other evening hymn or Lenten hymn, and* **LIGHTING OF THE CANDLE**

**PSALTER** *One or both of the following:* Psalms 105; 130

**SCRIPTURE READING** *followed by silent reflection*

**BIBLICAL SONG** *Song of Mary (2, 98\*), The Beatitudes (21), Jesus Christ Is Lord (20), Song of the Redeemed (16), Christ the Servant (22), or other New Testament song (15–25)*

**PRAYERS OF THANKSGIVING AND INTERCESSION**

Receive my prayer as incense, O God,

**my uplifted hands as an evening sacrifice.**

*Free prayer (or prayer 58, 59, 41, or 63 Good Friday)*

*Silent prayer*

*And*

Loving God,
do not forsake us with the coming of night.
Though we may walk in darkness,
lead us by the hand
and calm our fears.
Then at last
bring us to the dawning of your eternal day,
in Jesus Christ our Lord. **Amen.**

*For Good Friday*

Eternal God,
as we are baptized into the death of Jesus Christ,
so give us the grace of repentance
that we may pass through the grave with him
and be born again to eternal life.
For he is the One
who was crucified, dead, and buried,
and rose again for us,
Jesus our Savior. **Amen.**

*The Lord's Prayer*

**HYMN** *or* **SPIRITUAL**

**DISMISSAL**

May God's peace, which is far beyond our understanding,
keep us safe in union with Christ Jesus.　　　　　　　*Phil. 4:7*

**Amen.**

Bless the Lord.

**The Lord's name be praised.**

# SATURDAY
## MORNING PRAYER

**OPENING SENTENCES**

O Lord, open my lips.

**And my mouth shall proclaim your praise.**

*And*

O God, you are my God, for you I long;
for you my soul is thirsting.

**My whole being desires you,**
**like a dry and barren land without water.**

Because your love is better than life itself,
my lips will give you praise.

**I will raise my hands to you in prayer,**
**and praise you with joy.**                     *Ps. 63:1, 3–4*

*For Holy Saturday*

Joseph had taken down his body, wrapped it in linen,

**and placed it in a new tomb cut from solid rock.**

The women had gone home to prepare spices for the body.

**It was the Sabbath, so they rested as the Law commanded.**
                                          *Luke 23:53, 56*

**MORNING PSALM** (95; 100; 63; or 51) *or* **MORNING HYMN** *or* **LENTEN HYMN**

**PSALTER** *One or both of the following:* Psalms 43; 149

**SCRIPTURE READING** *followed by silent reflection*

**BIBLICAL SONG** *Song of Zechariah (1, 97\*), Seek the Lord (9), Song of Penitence (13), or Old Testament song (7–14)*

## PRAYERS OF THANKSGIVING AND INTERCESSION

Satisfy us with your love in the morning,

**and we will live this day in joy and praise.**

*Free prayer (or prayer 56, 57, or 62 Holy Saturday)*

*Silent prayer*

*And*

Take all doubts and uncertainties, O God,
and fill us with such faith
that we may be confident of your love
and loyal in the service of him
who died and yet lives for us,
Jesus Christ the Lord. **Amen.**

*The Lord's Prayer*

## HYMN *or* SPIRITUAL

## DISMISSAL

May the grace of the Lord Jesus Christ be with us all.     *Phil. 4:23*

**Amen.**

Bless the Lord.

**The Lord's name be praised.**

### EVENING PRAYER

## OPENING SENTENCES AT ENTRANCE OF THE LIGHT

Behold, now is the acceptable time;

**now is the day of salvation.**

Turn us again, O God of our salvation,

**that the light of your face may shine on us.**

May your justice shine like the sun;

**and may the poor be lifted up.**

*Based on 2 Cor. 6:2; Pss. 85:4; 80:3*

*Or*

O God, come to our assistance.

**O Lord, hasten to help us.**

*And*

Teach me to do your will,

**for you are my God.**

For your name's sake,

**let your gracious Spirit lead me on a safe path.**          *Ps. 143:10*

**HYMN OF LIGHT** *(4, 100\*) or other evening hymn or Lenten hymn*

**THANKSGIVING FOR LIGHT**

The Lord be with you.

**And also with you.**

Let us give thanks to the Lord our God.

**It is right to give our thanks and praise.**

Blessed are you, O Lord our God,
the Shepherd of Israel,
their pillar of cloud by day,
their pillar of fire by night.
In these forty days
you lead us into the desert of repentance
that in this pilgrimage of prayer

---

we might learn to be your people once more.
In fasting and service
you bring us back to your heart.
You open our eyes to your presence in the world
and you free our hands
to lead others to the radiant splendor of your mercy.

Be with us in these journey days,
for without you we are lost and will perish.
To you alone be dominion and glory,
forever and ever. **Amen.**

## INCENSE

An angel, holding a golden censer full of incense,
stood before the altar.
The smoke of the incense went up before God,
mingled with the prayers of the people.                    *Rev. 8:3–4*

**EVENING PSALM** Psalm 141

**PSALTER** *One or both of the following:* Psalms 31; 143

**SCRIPTURE READING** *followed by silent reflection*

**BIBLICAL SONG** *Song of Mary (2, 98\*), The Beatitudes (21), Jesus Christ
Is Lord (20), Song of the Redeemed (16), Christ the Servant (22), or other
New Testament song (15–25)*

## PRAYERS OF THANKSGIVING AND INTERCESSION

Let us walk in love, as Christ loved us and gave himself up for us,

**a fragrant offering and sacrifice to God.**

*Free prayer (or prayer 58, 59, 64 Holy Saturday, or 40)*

*Silent prayer*

*And*

God our Redeemer,
keep us firm in faith
and safe from all evil.
Open our eyes,
that we may awaken
and watch for the coming of your dawn,
and the establishment of your rule,
when there is no more pain or sorrow,
in your eternal life
with Jesus Christ our risen Lord. **Amen.**

*The Lord's Prayer*

**HYMN** *or* **SPIRITUAL**

**DISMISSAL**

May the grace of the Lord Jesus Christ be with us all.    *Phil. 4:23*

**Amen.**

Bless the Lord.

**The Lord's name be praised.**

# EASTER

## OPENING SENTENCES

O Lord, open my lips.

**And my mouth shall proclaim your praise.**

*And*

Alleluia! Christ is risen!

**Christ is risen indeed, Alleluia!**

Do not seek the living among the dead.

**The living Lord is risen. Alleluia!**

**MORNING PSALM** (95; 100; 63; or 51) *or* **MORNING HYMN** *or* **EASTER HYMN**

**PSALTER** *One or both of the following:* Psalms 93; 150

**SCRIPTURE READING** *followed by silent reflection*

**BIBLICAL SONG** *Song of Zechariah (1, 97\*), Te Deum (5), Glory to God (6), Song of Miriam and Moses (7), Song of Thanksgiving (8), or Old Testament song (7–14)*

## PRAYERS OF THANKSGIVING AND INTERCESSION

Satisfy us with your love in the morning,

**and we will live this day in joy and praise.**

*Free prayer (or prayer 65 or 66)*

*Silent prayer*

*And*

God of mercy,
we no longer look for Jesus among the dead,
for he is alive and has become the Lord of life.
From the waters of death you raise us with him
and renew your gift of life within us.
Increase in our minds and hearts
the risen life we share with Christ,
and help us to grow as your people
toward the fullness of eternal life with you,
through Christ our Lord. **Amen.**

*The Lord's Prayer*

## HYMN *or* SPIRITUAL

## DISMISSAL

To God be honor and glory forever and ever!          *1 Tim. 1:17*

**Amen.**

Bless the Lord.

**The Lord's name be praised.**

### EVENING PRAYER

## OPENING SENTENCES AT ENTRANCE OF THE LIGHT

Jesus Christ is risen from the dead.

**Alleluia, Alleluia, Alleluia!**

We are illumined by the brightness of his rising.

**Alleluia, Alleluia, Alleluia!**

Death has no more dominion over us.

**Alleluia, Alleluia, Alleluia!**

*Or*

O God, come to our assistance.

**O Lord, hasten to help us.**

*And*

Alleluia! Christ is risen!

**Christ is risen indeed! Alleluia!**

The risen Christ says: Peace be with you.

**We have seen the Lord! Alleluia!**

The risen Christ says: Receive the Holy Spirit.

**We are filled with joy because he lives! Alleluia!**

*Based on Luke 24:34; John 20:18–20, 22*

**HYMN OF LIGHT** *(4, 100\*) or other evening hymn or Easter hymn*

**THANKSGIVING FOR LIGHT**

The Lord be with you.

**And also with you.**

Let us give thanks to the Lord our God.

**It is right to give our thanks and praise.**

We praise and thank you, O God,
through your Son, Jesus Christ our Lord.
You have enlightened us
by revealing the light that never fades.
Dark death has been destroyed
and radiant life is everywhere restored.
What was promised is fulfilled:
we have been joined to God,
through renewed life in the Spirit of the risen Lord.

---

Glory and praise to you, our Father,
through Jesus your Son,
who lives and reigns with you and the Spirit,
in the kingdom of light eternal,
forever and ever. **Amen.**

## INCENSE

An angel, holding a golden censer full of incense,
stood before the altar.
The smoke of the incense went up before God,
mingled with the prayers of the people. *Rev. 8:3–4*

## EVENING PSALM Psalm 141

## PSALTER *One or both of the following:* Psalms 136; 117

## SCRIPTURE READING *followed by silent reflection*

## BIBLICAL SONG *Song of Mary (2, 98\*), Christ Our Passover (23), Jesus Christ Is Lord (20), Christ, the Head of All Creation (19), Worthy Is the Lamb (25), Song of the Redeemed (16), or other New Testament song (15–25)*

## PRAYERS OF THANKSGIVING AND INTERCESSION

Let us walk in love, as Christ loved us and gave himself up for us,

**a fragrant offering and sacrifice to God.**

*Free prayer (or prayer 67, 68, or 40)*

*Silent prayer*

*And*

Stay with us, Lord Jesus,
for evening draws near.
Be our companion on our way
to set our hearts on fire with new hope.

Help us to recognize your presence among us
in the scriptures we read
and in the breaking of bread.
You live and reign with the Father and the Holy Spirit,
one God, forever and ever. **Amen.**

*The Lord's Prayer*

**HYMN** *or* **SPIRITUAL**

**DISMISSAL**

To God be honor and glory forever and ever!        *1 Tim. 1:17*

**Amen.**

Bless the Lord.

**The Lord's name be praised.**

## MONDAY
### MORNING PRAYER

**OPENING SENTENCES**

O Lord, open my lips.

**And my mouth shall proclaim your praise.**

*And*

I know that my Redeemer lives!

**Christ is risen to be our Savior. Alleluia!**

We shall see Christ with our own eyes!

**In our flesh we shall see God! Alleluia!**        *Based on Job 19:25–26*

**MORNING PSALM** (95; 100; 63; or 51) *or* **MORNING HYMN** *or*
**EASTER HYMN**

**PSALTER** *One or both of the following:* Psalms 97; 145

**SCRIPTURE READING** *followed by silent reflection*

**BIBLICAL SONG** *Song of Zechariah (1, 97\*), Te Deum (5), Glory to God (6), Song of Miriam and Moses (7), Song of Thanksgiving (8), or Old Testament song (7–14)*

## PRAYERS OF THANKSGIVING AND INTERCESSION

Satisfy us with your love in the morning,

**and we will live this day in joy and praise.**

*Free prayer (or prayer 65 or 66)*

*Silent prayer*

*And*

Mighty God,
as you invite all to share in your new creation
and work with you in the world,
we pray that you will take our labors
and make them useful in Christ's service.
May we always recognize him
in those whom we would serve,
and may our work be as ministry
in his holy name. **Amen.**

*The Lord's Prayer*

## HYMN *or* SPIRITUAL

## DISMISSAL

May we continue to grow in the grace and knowledge
of Jesus Christ, our Lord and Savior.         *2 Peter 3:18*

**Amen.**

Bless the Lord.

**The Lord's name be praised.**

## OPENING SENTENCES

O God, come to our assistance.

**O Lord, hasten to help us.**

*And*

The risen Christ says: Peace be with you.

**We are filled with joy because he lives! Alleluia!**

The risen Christ says: Reach out, touch, and believe!

**Our Lord and our God! Alleluia!** *Based on John 20:26–28*

**HYMN OF LIGHT** *(4, 100\*) or other evening hymn or Easter hymn, and* **LIGHTING OF THE CANDLE**

**PSALTER** *One or both of the following:* Psalms 124; 115

**SCRIPTURE READING** *followed by silent reflection*

**BIBLICAL SONG** *Song of Mary (2, 98\*), Christ Our Passover (23), Jesus Christ Is Lord (20), Christ, the Head of All Creation (19), Worthy Is the Lamb (25), Song of the Redeemed (16), or other New Testament song (15–25)*

## PRAYERS OF THANKSGIVING AND INTERCESSION

Receive my prayer as incense, O God,

**my uplifted hands as an evening sacrifice.**

*Free prayer (or prayer 67 or 68)*

*Silent prayer*

*And*

Good and mighty God,
we ask your blessing anew on us
and your whole church here and in every place.

Calm and steady us in the peace of Jesus Christ.
Lift us up when we fall,
and guide us when we fail,
that we may always be joyful disciples of Jesus Christ,
our risen Lord. **Amen.**

*The Lord's Prayer*

## HYMN *or* SPIRITUAL

## DISMISSAL

May we continue to grow in the grace and knowledge
of Jesus Christ, our Lord and Savior.                    *2 Peter 3:18*

**Amen.**

Bless the Lord.

**The Lord's name be praised.**

## TUESDAY
### MORNING PRAYER

## OPENING SENTENCES

O Lord, open my lips.

**And my mouth shall proclaim your praise.**

*And*

The tomb is empty—do not be afraid!

**We are looking for Jesus, who was crucified!**

He is not here; he is risen as he said! Alleluia!

**He has been raised from death! Alleluia!**
                    *Based on Matt. 28:5–6; 1 Cor. 15:20*

**MORNING PSALM** (95; 100; 63; or 51) *or* **MORNING HYMN** *or* **EASTER HYMN**

**PSALTER** *One or both of the following:* Psalms 98; 146

**SCRIPTURE READING** *followed by silent reflection*

**BIBLICAL SONG** *Song of Zechariah (1, 97\*), Te Deum (5), Glory to God (6), Song of Miriam and Moses (7), Song of Thanksgiving (8), or Old Testament song (7–14)*

**PRAYERS OF THANKSGIVING AND INTERCESSION**

Satisfy us with your love in the morning,

**and we will live this day in joy and praise.**

*Free prayer (or prayer 65 or 66)*

*Silent prayer*

*And*

God of grace,
you have caused the sun to rise
and chase away the shadows of death.
Each day you promise resurrection,
that we may be born again to new life
and overcome with you all that would hurt or destroy.
Fill us with the Holy Spirit,
that we may be alive again
with the power and the peace of Jesus Christ,
our risen Lord. **Amen.**

*The Lord's Prayer*

**HYMN** *or* **SPIRITUAL**

## DISMISSAL

The grace of God be with us all, now and always.    *1 Tim. 6:21*

**Amen.**

Bless the Lord.

**The Lord's name be praised.**

### EVENING PRAYER

## OPENING SENTENCES

O God, come to our assistance.

**O Lord, hasten to help us.**

*And*

The Lord our God gives us salvation and victory! Alleluia!

**The Lord our God brings us light and life! Alleluia!**

God's right hand has done wonders! Alleluia!

**So let us proclaim the works of our God! Alleluia!**

**HYMN OF LIGHT** *(4, 100\*) or other evening hymn or Easter hymn, and*
**LIGHTING OF THE CANDLE**

**PSALTER** *One or both of the following:* Psalms 66; 116

**SCRIPTURE READING** *followed by silent reflection*

**BIBLICAL SONG** *Song of Mary (2, 98\*), Christ Our Passover (23), Jesus Christ Is Lord (20), Christ, the Head of All Creation (19), Worthy Is the Lamb (25), Song of the Redeemed (16), or other New Testament song (15–25)*

## PRAYERS OF THANKSGIVING AND INTERCESSION

Receive my prayer as incense, O God,

**my uplifted hands as an evening sacrifice.**

*Free prayer (or prayer 67 or 68)*

*Silent prayer*

*And*

God of comfort and strength,
revive us when we are weary,
console us when we are full of woe,
and set our feet anew in the way Christ leads us.
Protect us from sin
so we may always be glad disciples,
diligent in service
and bold in witness for our risen Lord,
Jesus Christ, Savior of the world. **Amen.**

*The Lord's Prayer*

## HYMN *or* SPIRITUAL

## DISMISSAL

The grace of God be with us all, now and always.      *1 Tim. 6:21*

**Amen.**

Bless the Lord.

**The Lord's name be praised.**

## WEDNESDAY
### MORNING PRAYER

## OPENING SENTENCES

O Lord, open my lips.

**And my mouth shall proclaim your praise.**

*And*

The God of our ancestors raised Jesus from death!

**He is at God's right side, our Lord and Savior! Alleluia!**

We are witnesses to these things!

**So is the Holy Spirit, God's gift to those who obey! Alleluia!**

*Acts 5:30–32*

**MORNING PSALM** (95; 100; 63; or 51) *or* **MORNING HYMN** *or* **EASTER HYMN**

**PSALTER** *One or both of the following:* Psalms 99; 147:1–11

**SCRIPTURE READING** *followed by silent reflection*

**BIBLICAL SONG** *Song of Zechariah (1, 97\*), Te Deum (5), Glory to God (6), Song of Miriam and Moses (7), Song of Thanksgiving (8), or Old Testament song (7–14)*

**PRAYERS OF THANKSGIVING AND INTERCESSION**

Satisfy us with your love in the morning,

**and we will live this day in joy and praise.**

*Free prayer (or prayer 65 or 66)*

*Silent prayer*

*And*

We have seen your glory, O God,
and we have witnessed your mighty acts.
By your Holy Spirit
put your voice in our mouths,
fill our arms with your strength,
and warm our hearts with your love.
Then we will be worthy disciples of Jesus Christ,
the living Lord. **Amen.**

*The Lord's Prayer*

**HYMN** *or* **SPIRITUAL**

## DISMISSAL

May the Lord, who is our peace,
give us peace at all times and in every way.          *2 Thess. 3:16*

**Amen.**

Bless the Lord.

**The Lord's name be praised.**

### EVENING PRAYER

## OPENING SENTENCES

O God, come to our assistance.

**O Lord, hasten to help us.**

*And*

Stay with us, Lord, for it is evening,

**and the day is almost over.**

Break bread, and give it to us, Lord.

**Open our eyes, Lord, that we may recognize you.**
*Based on Luke 24:29–31*

**HYMN OF LIGHT** *(4, 100\*) or other evening hymn or Easter hymn, and*
**LIGHTING OF THE CANDLE**

**PSALTER** *One or both of the following:* Psalms 9; 118

**SCRIPTURE READING** *followed by silent reflection*

**BIBLICAL SONG** *Song of Mary (2, 98\*), Christ Our Passover (23), Jesus Christ Is Lord (20), Christ, the Head of All Creation (19), Worthy Is the Lamb (25), Song of the Redeemed (16), or other New Testament song (15–25)*

## PRAYERS OF THANKSGIVING AND INTERCESSION

Receive my prayer as incense, O God,

**my uplifted hands as an evening sacrifice.**

*Free prayer (or prayer 67 or 68)*

*Silent prayer*

*And*

Generous God,
feed us by the Bread of Jesus Christ,
that we may be strong
and grow into his stature.
Nourish us by your Holy Spirit,
that we may receive strength
in every difficulty of life
and every demand of discipleship.
Guide us to our eternal home,
where we may rest in your peace
which we know in Jesus Christ,
our Lord and Savior. **Amen.**

*The Lord's Prayer*

## HYMN *or* SPIRITUAL

## DISMISSAL

May the Lord, who is our peace,
give us peace at all times and in every way.          *2 Thess. 3:16*

**Amen.**

Bless the Lord.

**The Lord's name be praised.**

# THURSDAY
## MORNING PRAYER

**OPENING SENTENCES**

O Lord, open my lips.

**And my mouth shall proclaim your praise.**

*And*

Christ died for our sins, as written in the scriptures. Alleluia!

**He was buried and raised to life three days later. Alleluia!**

He appeared to Peter, the apostles, and many others. Alleluia!

**By God's grace, Christ is risen for us. Alleluia!**

*Based on 1 Cor. 15:3–6*

*For Ascension Day*

Jesus lifted up his hands.

**While blessing his disciples,
he parted from them. Alleluia!**                    *Luke 24:50–51*

Christ went up, above and beyond the heavens,

**to fill the whole universe with his presence. Alleluia!**   *Eph. 4:10*

**MORNING PSALM** (95; 100; 63; or 51) *or* **MORNING HYMN** *or*
**EASTER HYMN**

**PSALTER** *One or both of the following:* Psalms 47; 147:12–20

**SCRIPTURE READING** *followed by silent reflection*

**BIBLICAL SONG** *Song of Zechariah (1, 97\*), Te Deum (5), Glory to God (6), Song of Miriam and Moses (7), Song of Thanksgiving (8), or Old Testament song (7–14)*

## PRAYERS OF THANKSGIVING AND INTERCESSION

Satisfy us with your love in the morning,

**and we will live this day in joy and praise.**

*Free prayer (or prayer 65, 66, or 69 Ascension Day)*

*Silent prayer*

*And*

Mighty God,
you have raised Christ Jesus from death
that we might be brought to new life.
Wake us from the sleep of sin,
that we may live in the light,
and by the power of the Holy Spirit
do wonderful works
in ministry with Jesus Christ,
your Son, Savior of us all. **Amen.**

*For Ascension*

O King of glory and Lord of hosts,
who ascended triumphantly above all the heavens,
do not abandon us,
but send us the Promised One,
the Spirit of truth.
Blessed be the holy and undivided Trinity now and forever. **Amen.**

*The Lord's Prayer*

## HYMN *or* SPIRITUAL

## DISMISSAL

May the God of hope fill us with all joy and peace
through the power of the Holy Spirit.                    *Rom. 15:13*

**Amen.**

Bless the Lord.

**The Lord's name be praised.**

## OPENING SENTENCES

O God, come to our assistance.

**O Lord, hasten to help us.**

*And*

You have died with Christ.

**So we are set free from the dominion of this world. Alleluia!**

You are raised to life with Christ.

**So we set our hearts on heaven. Alleluia!**

*For Ascension*

We see Jesus,
who for a little while was made lower than the angels.

**He is crowned with glory and honor.**         *Heb. 2:9*
**Alleluia!**

We have a great high priest who has passed into the heavens,
Jesus, the Son of God.

**Let us with confidence draw near to the throne of grace.**
**Alleluia!**
        *Heb. 4:14, 16*

**HYMN OF LIGHT** *(4, 100\*) or other evening hymn or Easter hymn, and*
**LIGHTING OF THE CANDLE**

**PSALTER** *One or both of the following:* Psalms 68; 113

**SCRIPTURE READING** *followed by silent reflection*

*Easter—Thursday* 171

**BIBLICAL SONG** *Song of Mary (2, 98\*), Christ Our Passover (23), Jesus Christ Is Lord (20), Christ, the Head of All Creation (19), Worthy Is the Lamb (25), Song of the Redeemed (16), or other New Testament song (15–25)*

## PRAYERS OF THANKSGIVING AND INTERCESSION

Receive my prayer as incense, O God,

**my uplifted hands as an evening sacrifice.**

*Free prayer (or prayer 67, 68, or 69 Ascension Day)*

*Silent prayer*

*And*

Sovereign God,
the whole universe is within your reach,
and all things are ordered by your hand.
You have claimed us to be your people
and set us to be disciples of Jesus Christ, our risen Lord.
As you have protected our lives,
so preserve our souls
and keep before us always
the vision of our Redeemer,
that we may see and follow. **Amen.**

*For Ascension*

Holy God, creator of all,
the risen Christ taught from scripture
of his death, resurrection,
and ascension into your glorious presence.
May the living Lord
breathe on us his peace,
that our eyes may be opened to recognize him in breaking bread,
and to follow wherever he leads. **Amen.**

*The Lord's Prayer*

## HYMN *or* SPIRITUAL

## DISMISSAL

May the God of hope fill us with all joy and peace
through the power of the Holy Spirit.                    *Rom. 15:13*

**Amen.**

Bless the Lord.

**The Lord's name be praised.**

### FRIDAY
### MORNING PRAYER

## OPENING SENTENCES

O Lord, open my lips.

**And my mouth shall proclaim your praise.**

*And*

In baptism, you were buried with Christ.

**In baptism we were also raised with Christ. Alleluia!**

You were at one time spiritually dead.

**God has now brought us life with Christ. Alleluia!**

*Based on Rom. 6:4–11*

**MORNING PSALM** (95; 100; 63; or 51) *or* **MORNING HYMN** *or*
**EASTER HYMN**

**PSALTER** *One or both of the following:* Psalms 96; 148

**SCRIPTURE READING** *followed by silent reflection*

**BIBLICAL SONG** *Song of Zechariah (1, 97\*), Te Deum (5), Glory to God
(6), Song of Miriam and Moses (7), Song of Thanksgiving (8), or Old
Testament song (7–14)*

## PRAYERS OF THANKSGIVING AND INTERCESSION

Satisfy us with your love in the morning,

**and we will live this day in joy and praise.**

*Free prayer (or prayer 65 or 66)*

*Silent prayer*

*And*

You sent your Son to us, O God,
to show your wondrous love
and to bring us again to you.
He emptied himself
and went to the depths of suffering,
crucified, and abandoned.
Yet you have lifted him up
and filled him with glory,
that we and all people
might worship him with our lives
and witness for him with our love.
Give us your Holy Spirit,
that we may go into this world
and follow our risen Lord, Jesus Christ. **Amen.**

*The Lord's Prayer*

## HYMN *or* SPIRITUAL

## DISMISSAL

May God's peace, which is far beyond our understanding,
keep us safe in union with Christ Jesus.                    *Phil. 4:7*

**Amen.**

Bless the Lord.

**The Lord's name be praised.**

# EVENING PRAYER

## OPENING SENTENCES

O God, come to our assistance.

**O Lord, hasten to help us.**

*And*

Keep working out your salvation
with fear and trembling.

**God is always at work in us
to make us willing and able to obey. Alleluia!**

Be innocent and pure as God's perfect children.

**May we shine like stars lighting up the sky. Alleluia!**

*Phil. 2:12–15*

*Or*

Christ is risen from the dead,

**trampling down death by death,
and giving life to those in the grave.**

**HYMN OF LIGHT** *(4, 100*) or other evening hymn or Easter hymn, and*
**LIGHTING OF THE CANDLE**

**PSALTER** *One or both of the following:* Psalms 49; 138

**SCRIPTURE READING** *followed by silent reflection*

**BIBLICAL SONG** *Song of Mary (2, 98*), Christ Our Passover (23), Jesus
Christ Is Lord (20), Christ, the Head of All Creation (19), Worthy Is the
Lamb (25), Song of the Redeemed (16), or other New Testament song (15–25)*

## PRAYERS OF THANKSGIVING AND INTERCESSION

Receive my prayer as incense, O God,

**my uplifted hands as an evening sacrifice.**

*Free prayer (or prayer 67 or 68)*

*Silent prayer*

*And*

We have seen your glory, O God, in Jesus Christ,
who lived among us in grace and truth.
May we welcome him to dwell among us anew
by the power of the Holy Spirit.
Then we shall know his peace
and be strong in the service of the One you glorified
in death and resurrection,
who lives and reigns eternally with you,
Jesus Christ, our Lord and Savior. **Amen.**

*The Lord's Prayer*

## HYMN *or* SPIRITUAL

## DISMISSAL

May God's peace, which is far beyond our understanding,
keep us safe in union with Christ Jesus.                    *Phil. 4:7*

**Amen.**

Bless the Lord.

**The Lord's name be praised.**

## SATURDAY
### MORNING PRAYER

## OPENING SENTENCES

O Lord, open my lips.

**And my mouth shall proclaim your praise.**

*And*

Listen to the truth: we shall not all die. Alleluia!

**When the last trumpet sounds,
we shall be changed in an instant. Alleluia!**

Death is destroyed; victory is complete. Alleluia!

**Thanks be to God who gives us the victory. Alleluia!**

*1 Cor. 15:51–52, 54, 57*

**MORNING PSALM** (95; 100; 63; or 51) *or* **MORNING HYMN** *or*
**EASTER HYMN**

**PSALTER** *One or both of the following:* Psalms 92; 149

**SCRIPTURE READING** *followed by silent reflection*

**BIBLICAL SONG** *Song of Zechariah (1, 97\*), Te Deum (5), Glory to God
(6), Song of Miriam and Moses (7), Song of Thanksgiving (8), or Old
Testament song (7–14)*

**PRAYERS OF THANKSGIVING AND INTERCESSION**

Satisfy us with your love in the morning,

**and we will live this day in joy and praise.**

*Free prayer (or prayer 65 or 66)*

*Silent prayer*

*And*

Holy God,
yours is the morning
and yours is the evening.
Let the sun of justice, Jesus Christ,
shine for ever in our hearts
and draw us to that light
where you live in radiant glory.
We ask this through our Lord Jesus Christ, your Son,

who lives and reigns with you and the Holy Spirit,
one God, forever and ever. **Amen.**

*Or*

Awaken your people, O God,
that we may rise with Christ
and go into the world with him.
Give us grace to be a blessing
among the peoples of every land,
to speak his truth in love
and do justice and mercy
in the strong name of Jesus Christ,
our living Lord. **Amen.**

*The Lord's Prayer*

## HYMN *or* SPIRITUAL

## DISMISSAL

May the grace of the Lord Jesus Christ be with us all.    *Phil. 4:23*

**Amen.**

Bless the Lord.

**The Lord's name be praised.**

### EVENING PRAYER

## OPENING SENTENCES AT ENTRANCE OF THE LIGHT

Jesus Christ is risen from the dead.

**Alleluia, Alleluia, Alleluia!**

We are illumined by the brightness of his rising.

**Alleluia, Alleluia, Alleluia!**

Death has no more dominion over us.

**Alleluia, Alleluia, Alleluia!**

*Or*

O God, come to our assistance.

**O Lord, hasten to help us.**

*And*

By God's great mercy
we have been born anew to a living hope
through the resurrection of Jesus Christ from the dead.

**Blessed be God the Father of our Lord Jesus Christ.**     *1 Peter 1:3*

**HYMN OF LIGHT** *(4, 100\*) or other evening hymn or Easter hymn*

**THANKSGIVING FOR LIGHT**

The Lord be with you.

**And also with you.**

Let us give thanks to the Lord our God.

**It is right to give our thanks and praise.**

We praise and thank you, O God,
through your Son, Jesus Christ our Lord.
You have enlightened us
by revealing the light that never fades.
Dark death has been destroyed
and radiant life is everywhere restored.
What was promised is fulfilled:
we have been joined to God,
through renewed life in the Spirit of the risen Lord.

---

Glory and praise to you, our Father,
through Jesus your Son,
who lives and reigns with you and the Spirit,
in the kingdom of light eternal,
forever and ever. **Amen.**

## INCENSE

An angel, holding a golden censer full of incense,
stood before the altar.
The smoke of the incense went up before God,
mingled with the prayers of the people.                    *Rev. 8:3–4*

## EVENING PSALM Psalm 141

**PSALTER** *One or both of the following:* Psalms 23; 114

**SCRIPTURE READING** *followed by silent reflection*

**BIBLICAL SONG** *Song of Mary (2, 98\*), Christ Our Passover (23), Jesus
Christ Is Lord (20), Christ, the Head of All Creation (19), Worthy Is the
Lamb (25), Song of the Redeemed (16), or other New Testament song (15–25)*

## PRAYERS OF THANKSGIVING AND INTERCESSION

Let us walk in love, as Christ loved us and gave himself for us,

**a fragrant offering and sacrifice to God.**

*Free prayer (or prayer 67, 68, or 40)*

*Silent prayer*

*And*

Protect your people, O God,
and keep us safe
until the coming of your new dawn
and the establishment of your righteous rule.

By your Holy Spirit,
stir up within us a longing
for the light of your new day,
and guide us by the bright presence of Jesus Christ,
your Son, our risen Lord. **Amen.**

*The Lord's Prayer*

## HYMN *or* SPIRITUAL

## DISMISSAL

May the grace of the Lord Jesus Christ be with us all.     *Phil. 4:23*

**Amen.**

Bless the Lord.

**The Lord's name be praised.**

# PENTECOST

## THE DAY OF PENTECOST
### Morning Prayer

**OPENING SENTENCES**

O Lord, open my lips.

**And my mouth shall proclaim your praise.**

*And*

The Lord said:
You shall receive power
when the Holy Spirit has come upon you,
and you shall be my witnesses
to the ends of the earth.                                    *Acts 1:8*

**Come, Holy Spirit,**
**Fill the hearts of your faithful**
**and kindle in them the fire of your love. Alleluia!**

**MORNING PSALM** (95; 100; 63; or 51) *or* **MORNING HYMN** *or*
**PENTECOST HYMN**

**PSALTER** *One or both of the following:* Psalms 104; 150

**SCRIPTURE READING** *followed by silent reflection*

**BIBLICAL SONG** *Song of Zechariah (1, 97\*), Te Deum (5), Glory to God
(6), A Song for Pentecost (17), Song of Miriam and Moses (7), or Old
Testament song (7–14)*

**PRAYERS OF THANKSGIVING AND INTERCESSION**

Satisfy us with your love in the morning,

**and we will live this day in joy and praise.**

*Free prayer (or prayer 70)*

*Silent prayer*

*And*

True and only Light,
from whom comes every good gift,
send your Spirit into our lives
with the power of a mighty wind.
Open the horizons of our minds
by the flame of your wisdom.
Loosen our tongues to show your praise,
for only in your Spirit
can we voice your words of peace
and acclaim Jesus as Lord. **Amen.**

*The Lord's Prayer*

## HYMN *or* SPIRITUAL

## DISMISSAL

To God be honor and glory forever and ever!          *1 Tim. 1:17*
**Amen.**

Bless the Lord.

**The Lord's name be praised.**

*The liturgies for Ordinary Days (pp. 51–84) are used beginning on Monday following the Day of Pentecost.*

### EVENING PRAYER

## OPENING SENTENCES AT ENTRANCE OF THE LIGHT

Jesus Christ is risen from the dead.

**Alleluia, Alleluia, Alleluia!**

We are illumined by the brightness of his rising.

**Alleluia, Alleluia, Alleluia!**

Death has no more dominion over us.

**Alleluia, Alleluia, Alleluia!**

*Or*

O God, come to our assistance.

**O Lord, make haste to help us.**

*And*

Send forth your Spirit,

**and renew the face of the earth.**

Come, Creator Spirit,

**inflame our waiting hearts.**

**HYMN OF LIGHT** *(4, 100\*) or other evening hymn or Pentecost hymn*

**THANKSGIVING FOR LIGHT**

The Lord be with you.

**And also with you.**

Let us give thanks to the Lord our God.

**It is right to give our thanks and praise.**

Blessed are you,
O Lord, Redeemer God.
You destroyed the bonds of death
and from the darkness of the tomb
drew forth the light of the world.
Led through the waters of death,

we become the children of light
singing our Alleluia
and dancing to the music of new life.

Pour out your Spirit upon us
that dreams and visions
bring us ever closer to the kingdom of Jesus Christ,
our risen Savior.
Through him and in the Holy Spirit
all glory be to you, almighty Father,
this night and forever and ever. **Amen.**

## INCENSE

An angel, holding a golden censer full of incense,
stood before the altar.
The smoke of the incense went up before God,
mingled with the prayers of the people.                    *Rev. 8:3–4*

## EVENING PSALM Psalm 141

**PSALTER** *One or both of the following:* Psalms 29; 33

**SCRIPTURE READING** *followed by silent reflection*

**BIBLICAL SONG** *Song of Mary (2, 98\*), Te Deum (5), A Song for Pentecost (17), Song of the Redeemed (16), or other New Testament song (15–25)*

## PRAYERS OF THANKSGIVING AND INTERCESSION

Let us walk in love, as Christ loved us and gave himself up for us,

**a fragrant offering and sacrifice to God.**

*Free prayer (or prayer 71, 72, or 40)*

*Silent prayer*

*And*

Come, Holy Spirit!
Rain upon our dry and dusty lives.
Wash away our sin
and heal our wounded spirits.
Kindle within us the fire of your love
to burn away our apathy.
With your warmth bend our rigidity,
and guide our wandering feet. **Amen.**

*Or*

Almighty and everliving God,
you fulfilled the Easter promise
by sending us your Holy Spirit.
May that Spirit unite the races and nations on earth
to proclaim your glory.
Grant this through our Lord Jesus Christ, your Son,
who lives and reigns with you and the Holy Spirit,
one God, forever and ever. **Amen.**

*The Lord's Prayer*

**HYMN** *or* **SPIRITUAL**

**DISMISSAL**

To God be honor and glory forever and ever!          *1 Tim. 1:17*

**Amen.**

Praise the Lord.

**The Lord's name be praised.**

*The liturgies for Ordinary Days (pp. 51–84) are used during the Pente-*
*cost season, beginning on Monday following the Day of Pentecost.*

# MIDDAY AND
# NIGHT PRAYER

# MIDDAY PRAYER

## OPENING SENTENCES

Our help is in the name of the Lord,
**who made heaven and earth.**

*And*

The Lord is our God,
**whose commands are for all the world.**
Never forget God's covenant,
**which is made to last forever.**

*Or*

Like an eagle teaching her young to fly,
**catching them safely on her spreading wings,**
the Lord kept Israel from falling.                    *Deut. 32:11*
**The Lord's name be praised.**

*Or*

Even those who are young grow weak;
**the young can fall exhausted.**
But those who trust in the Lord for help
will find their strength renewed.
**They will rise on wings like eagles;**
they will run and not get weary;
**they will walk and not grow weak.**          *Isa. 40:30–31*

**HYMN** *Optionally, a hymn may be sung or read.*

## PSALTER SELECTION

### SUNDAY—PSALM 113

*Refrain:* **Praise the Lord who lifts up the poor.**
*Psalm Prayer*
From morning to evening we praise your name, great and wonderful God, for you lift us when we fall, and set us in high places with Jesus Christ, our Lord and Savior. **Amen.**

### MONDAY—PSALM 127

*Refrain:* **Let all our labor glorify God.**
*Psalm Prayer*
Almighty God, deliver us from empty work, and make all we do be for the service of Jesus Christ, that we may love with his love and show his justice in everything. **Amen.**

### TUESDAY—PSALM 126

*Refrain:* **The Lord has done great things for us,
and we are glad.**
*Psalm Prayer*
Eternal God, keep our eyes open this day that we may see your mighty hand at work in our world; give us always a vision of Christ that we may follow him closely in self-giving discipleship. **Amen.**

### WEDNESDAY—PSALM 121

*Refrain:* **Our help is from the Lord,
who made heaven and earth.**
*Psalm Prayer*
Keep watch, O God, over our lives this day. Guide us that we may not stumble into sin; protect us that we may not be overcome by evil; sustain us that we may do what is good and right and loving, in Jesus Christ. **Amen.**

## THURSDAY—PSALM 122

*Refrain:* **May the peace of God be with us all.**
*Psalm Prayer*
Great God, as we receive the peace you alone can give, fill us with your grace to share that peace wherever we are, and in whatever we do; in the name and for the sake of Jesus Christ our Redeemer. **Amen.**

## FRIDAY—PSALM 124

*Refrain:* **Our help is in the name of the Lord,**
**who made heaven and earth.**
*Psalm Prayer*
Over and over again, O God, we see your redeeming hand lifting us from the snares of wickedness, claiming us for your righteous work. Strengthen and sustain us by your Spirit, in Jesus Christ our Lord. **Amen.**

## SATURDAY—PSALM 128

*Refrain:* **Blessed are those who fear the Lord.**
*Psalm Prayer*
O God, bless the work of our hands today that we may reap the harvest of peace and show the fruits of love, as we labor with our Lord, Jesus Christ. **Amen.**

**SCRIPTURE READING** *followed by:*

This is the Word of the Lord.

**Thanks be to God.**

*Silent reflection*

## PRAYERS OF THE PEOPLE

*There may be a brief time of prayer, spoken and silent, in which the promises of God are claimed for individual and corporate needs and concerns, concluding with one of the following prayers:*

Eternal God,
send your Holy Spirit into our hearts,
to direct and rule us according to your will,
to comfort us in all our afflictions,
to defend us from all error,
and to lead us into all truth;
through Jesus Christ our Lord. **Amen.**

*Or*

New every morning is your love,
great God of light,
and all day long you are working for good in the world.
Stir up in us the desire to serve you,
to live peacefully with our neighbors,
and to devote each day to your Son,
our Savior, Jesus Christ the Lord. **Amen.**

*Or*

Creator God,
work is your gift to us,
a call to reach new heights
by using our talents for the good of all.
Guide us as we work,
and teach us to live
in the Spirit who made us your sons and daughters,
in the love that made us brothers and sisters,
through Jesus Christ our Lord. **Amen.**

*Or*

Eternal God,
you call us to ventures
of which we cannot see the ending,

by paths as yet untrodden,
through perils unknown.
Give us faith to go out with courage,
not knowing where we go,
but only that your hand is leading us
and your love supporting us;
through Jesus Christ our Lord. **Amen.**

*Or*

O God,
you are ever at work in the world for us
and for all humankind.
Guide and protect all who work to get a living.
Work through us,
and help us always to work for you;
in Jesus Christ our Lord. **Amen.**

*Noon*

Almighty Savior,
who at noonday called your servant Saint Paul
to be an apostle to the Gentiles:
We pray you to illumine the world with the radiance of your glory,
that all nations may come and worship you;
for you live and reign forever and ever. **Amen.**

*Noon*

Blessed Savior,
at this hour you hung upon the cross,
stretching out your loving arms:
Grant that all the peoples of the earth
may look to you and be saved;
for your tender mercy's sake. **Amen.**

*Noon*

God of mercy,
this midday moment of rest is your welcome gift.
Bless the work we have begun,
make good its defects,
and let us finish it in a way that pleases you.
Grant this through Christ our Lord. **Amen.**

*The Lord's Prayer*

**HYMN** *Optionally, a hymn may be sung or read.*

**DISMISSAL**

The God of peace be with us. *Phil. 4:9*

**Amen.**

Bless the Lord.

**The Lord's name be praised.**

# NIGHT PRAYER

OPENING SENTENCES *(Musical setting 110\*)*

O God, come to our assistance.

**O Lord, hasten to help us.**

The Lord Almighty grant us a restful night
and peace at the last.

**Amen.**

**HYMN** *Optionally, a hymn may be sung or read.*

**PRAYER OF CONFESSION**

> *Silent prayer*

> *And*

**Merciful God,
we confess that we have sinned against you
in thought, word, and deed.
We have not loved you
with our whole heart and mind and strength;
we have not loved our neighbors as ourselves.
In your mercy forgive what we have been,
help us amend what we are,
and direct what we shall be,
so that we may delight in your will
and walk in your ways,
to the glory of your holy name.**

> *Or*

**Eternal God,
in whom we live and move and have our being,**

your face is hidden from us by our sins,
and we forget your mercy in the blindness of our hearts.
Cleanse us from all our offenses,
and deliver us from proud thoughts and vain desires.
With lowliness and meekness
may we draw near to you,
confessing our faults,
confiding in your grace,
and finding in you our refuge and strength;
through Jesus Christ your Son.

*Or*

I confess to Almighty God,
in the communion of the saints of heaven and earth,
and to you, my brothers and sisters,
that I have sinned through my own fault,
in my thoughts and in my words,
in what I have done,
and in what I have failed to do.
So I ask you, my brothers and sisters,
to pray for me to the Lord our God.

*And*

May the almighty and merciful God
grant unto us pardon and remission of all our sins,
true repentance,
amendment of life,
and the grace and comfort of the Holy Spirit. **Amen.**

## PSALTER SELECTION

SUNDAY—PSALM 91

*Refrain:* **Night holds no terrors for me,
sleeping under God's wings.**
*Psalm Prayer*
Gracious God, let us live confident that nothing in life or death can
ever separate us from your love in Jesus Christ our Lord. **Amen.**

## MONDAY—PSALM 4

*Refrain:* **I will lie down in peace, O God,
for I dwell in your safety.**

*Psalm Prayer*

Mighty God, we ponder your mercy, for you redeem us in Jesus Christ, who delivers us from all fear and gives us his peace. **Amen.**

## TUESDAY—PSALM 134

*Refrain:* **Let your face shine upon us, O Lord.**

*Psalm Prayer*

Great God, we praise your holy name, and long to arrive at last at our home in your house, where Jesus Christ has prepared a place for us. **Amen.**

## WEDNESDAY—PSALM 139:1–12

*Refrain:* **You know me, O God, in my resting and my rising.**

*Psalm Prayer*

God of wonder, we are never beyond your reach, so we will rest securely by night and day in the confidence of your love in Jesus Christ. **Amen.**

## THURSDAY—PSALM 33

*Refrain:* **May your love be upon us, O God,
for we put our hope in you.**

*Psalm Prayer*

Loving God, we entrust ourselves to your keeping this night, confident of your power and peace revealed in Christ crucified and risen. **Amen.**

## FRIDAY—PSALM 34

*Refrain:* **God's praise is always on our lips.**

*Psalm Prayer*

Merciful God, in Jesus Christ you free us from the bondage of death, and call us to rest our weary souls in your forgiveness. Refresh us with righteousness, and raise us with the dawn to new life in Jesus Christ the Lord. **Amen.**

*Refrain:* **We give you thanks, O God;**
**your love endures forever!**

*Psalm Prayer*

Eternal God, persist in your love for us and all your children this night, to protect the helpless, comfort the sorrowing, give rest to the weary, and sustain all who serve with Christ our Savior. **Amen.**

## SCRIPTURE READING

*One of the following is read:*

The servants of the Lamb shall worship him; they shall see his face, and his name shall be on their foreheads. And night shall be no more; they need no light of lamp or sun, for the Lord God shall be their light, and they shall reign for ever and ever.     *Rev. 22:3c–5*

God has not destined us for wrath, but to obtain salvation through our Lord Jesus Christ, who died for us so that whether we wake or sleep we might live with him.     *1 Thess. 5:9–10*

Come to me, all who labor and are heavy laden, and I will give you rest. Take my yoke upon you, and learn from me; for I am gentle and lowly in heart, and you will find rest for your souls. For my yoke is easy, and my burden is light.     *Matt. 11:28–30*

May the God of peace sanctify you wholly; and may your spirit and soul and body be kept sound and blameless at the coming of our Lord Jesus Christ.     *1 Thess. 5:23*

You are in our midst, O Lord, and we are called by your name. Do not forsake us, O Lord our God.     *Jer. 14:9*

May the God of peace, who brought again from the dead our Lord Jesus, the great shepherd of the sheep, by the blood of the eternal covenant, equip you with everything good that you may do God's will, working in you that which is pleasing in God's sight, through Jesus Christ, to whom be glory for ever and ever.     *Heb. 13:20–21*

Peace I leave with you; my peace I give to you; not as the world gives do I give to you. Let not your hearts be troubled, neither let them be afraid. *John 14:27*

I am convinced that there is nothing in death or life, in the realm of spirits or superhuman powers, in the world as it is or the world as it shall be, in the forces of the universe, in heights or depths— nothing in all creation that can separate us from the love of God in Christ Jesus our Lord. *Rom. 8:38–39*

Remember this! The Lord—and the Lord alone—is our God. Love the Lord your God with all your heart, with all your soul, and with all your strength. Never forget these commands that I am giving you today. Teach them to your children. Repeat them when you are at home and when you are away, when you are resting and when you are working. *Deut. 6:4–7*

*Followed by:*

This is the Word of the Lord.

**Thanks be to God.**

*Silent reflection*

## PRAYERS OF THE PEOPLE *(Musical setting 111*)*

Into your hands, O Lord, I commend my spirit;

**for you have redeemed me, O Lord, O God of truth.**

Keep us, O Lord, as the apple of your eye;

**hide us under the shadow of your wings.**

In righteousness I shall see you;

**when I awake your presence shall give me joy.** *Ps. 31:5; 17:8, 15*

*There may be a brief time of prayer, silent or spoken, concluding with one of the following:*

O Lord, support us all the day long
of this troubled life,
until the shadows lengthen
and the evening comes,
and the busy world is hushed,
and the fever of life is over,
and our work is done.
Then, in your mercy,
grant us a safe lodging,
and a holy rest,
and peace at the last;
through Jesus Christ our Lord. **Amen.**

*Or*

O God,
you have designed this wonderful world,
and know all things good for us.
Give us such faith
that, by day and by night,
at all times and in all places,
we may without fear
entrust those who are dear to us
to your never-failing love,
in this life
and in the life to come;
through Jesus Christ our Lord. **Amen.**

*Or*

Keep watch, dear Lord,
with those who work or watch
or weep this night,
and give your angels charge over those who sleep.
Tend the sick, Lord Christ;
give rest to the weary,
bless the dying,
soothe the suffering,
pity the afflicted,
shield the joyous;
and all for your love's sake. **Amen.**

*Or*

O God,
who appointed the day for labor
and the night for rest:
Grant that we may rest in peace and quietness
during the coming night
so that tomorrow
we may go forth to our appointed labors.
Take us into your holy keeping,
that no evil may befall us
nor any ill come near our home.
When at last our days are ended
and our work is finished,
grant that we may depart in your peace,
in the sure hope of that glorious kingdom
where there is day without night,
light without darkness,
and life without shadow of death forever;
through Jesus Christ,
the Light of the world. **Amen.**

*Or*

Lord God,
send peaceful sleep to refresh our tired bodies.
May your help always renew us
and keep us strong in your service.
We ask this through Christ our Lord. **Amen.**

*Or*

Visit our dwellings, O Lord,
and drive from them all the snares of the enemy;
let your holy angels dwell with us
to preserve us in your peace;
and let your blessing be upon us always,
through Jesus Christ our Lord. **Amen.**

*Or*

Gracious Lord,
we give you thanks for the day,
especially for the good
we were permitted to give and to receive;
the day is now past
and we commit it to you.
We entrust to you the night;
we rest in surety,
for you are our help,
and you neither slumber nor sleep. **Amen.**

*Or*

Eternal God,
the hours both of day and night are yours,
and to you the darkness is no threat.
Be present, we pray,
with those who labor in these hours of night,
especially those who watch and work on behalf of others.
Grant them diligence in their watching,
faithfulness in their service,
courage in danger,
and competence in emergencies.
Help them to meet the needs of others
with confidence and compassion;
through Jesus Christ our Lord. **Amen.**

*Or*

Be our light in the darkness, O Lord,
and in your great mercy
defend us from all perils and dangers of this night;
for the love of your only Son,
our Savior Jesus Christ. **Amen.**

*Or*

Be present, O merciful God,
and protect us through the hours of this night,

so that we who are wearied
by the changes and chances of life
may rest in your eternal changelessness;
through Jesus Christ our Lord. **Amen.**

*Or*

Lord,
fill this night with your radiance.
May we sleep in peace and rise with joy
to welcome the light of a new day in your name.
We ask this through Christ our Lord. **Amen.**

*Or*

Lord,
give our bodies restful sleep
and let the work we have done today
bear fruit in eternal life.
We ask this through Christ our Lord. **Amen.**

*The Lord's Prayer*

**SONG OF SIMEON** *(3; Musical setting 112*)*

*Refrain:* **Guide us waking, O Lord,
and guard us sleeping;
that awake we may watch with Christ,
and asleep rest in his peace.**

**DISMISSAL** *(Musical setting 113*)*

May Almighty God bless, preserve, and keep us,
this night and forevermore.

**Amen.**

Bless the Lord.

**The Lord's name be praised.**

# SUPPLEMENTAL
# LITURGICAL TEXTS

# PSALM REFRAINS
# AND PSALM PRAYERS

PSALM 1

*Refrain:* **Happy are they who delight in the law of God.**
*Psalm Prayer*
We praise you, O God, that you reveal your will for our happiness.
As we reflect on this day, we thank you for your firm and loving
guidance in Jesus Christ, who is the way and truth and life. **Amen.**

PSALM 2

*Refrain:* **You are mine, this day have I begotten you.**
*Psalm Prayer*
Lord God, you gave the peoples of the world as an inheritance to
your Son. You crowned him to rule over Zion, your holy city, and
gave him your church as his bride. As he proclaims the way of your
eternal kingdom, may we serve him faithfully, and so know the
royal power of your Son, Jesus Christ our Lord. **Amen.**

PSALM 3

*Refrain:* **You alone, O God, will keep us in perfect safety.**
*Psalm Prayer*
Almighty God, you consoled Christ in his anguish and released
him from the darkness of the grave. Turn your face toward us, that
we may sleep in your peace and rise in your light; through Jesus
Christ our Lord. **Amen.**

PSALM 5

*Refrain:* **Hear our prayer in the morning, O God of justice.**

*Or, during Lent*

**Give ear to all my words,
give ear, O Lord.**

*Psalm Prayer*
You alone, O God, are holy and righteous, and we praise you for
your truth and mercy in Jesus Christ. Keep us safe from evil;
protect our souls. Let us honor you all day with our righteousness.
**Amen.**

*Or, during Lent*

God of justice and goodness, you hate evil and abhor lies. Lead us
in the path of justice, that all who hope in you may, with the
church, rejoice in Jesus Christ. **Amen.**

## PSALM 6

*Refrain:* **Show us your mercy, Lord,**
 **and keep us in your love.**

*Or, during Lent*

**Hear us, O God, for we cry out from the depths.**

*Psalm Prayer*
Lord God, you love mercy and tenderness; you give life and overcome death. Look upon our weakness and grief, and renew us by
your risen Son, that we may sing a new song in your praise,
through Jesus Christ our Lord. **Amen.**

*Or, during Lent*

Merciful God, you know our anguish, not from afar, but in the
suffering of Jesus Christ. Take all our grieving and sorrow, all our
pain and tears, and heal us according to your promises in Jesus our
Lord. **Amen.**

## PSALM 7

*Refrain:* **Sing praises to the God of justice!**
*Psalm Prayer*
O God, source of light and life, by the light of your truth let the
virtuous know your goodness and sinners know your mercy, that
together they may drink from the river of delight and rejoice now
and ever in Jesus Christ our Lord. **Amen.**

PSALM 8

*Refrain:* **How great is your name, O Lord, through all the earth.**
*Psalm Prayer*
Almighty Lord, amid the grandeur of your creation you sought us out, and by the coming of Christ you adorned us with glory and honor, raising us in him above the heavens. Enable us so to care for the earth that all creation may radiate the splendor of Jesus Christ our Lord. **Amen.**

PSALM 9

*Refrain:* **The Lord is a refuge for the oppressed,
a refuge in time of trouble.**

*Or, during Easter*

**I sing to your name, O Most High!**
*Psalm Prayer*
Almighty God, in Jesus Christ you rule the world with righteousness and judge the nations with justice. Bring down the haughty and lift up the lowly, and set us on the side of the needy that we may be close to Jesus Christ, our servant Lord. **Amen.**

*Or, during Easter*

Lord God, righteous judge, hear the cries of your oppressed people. Rescue them from their oppressors, and save them from the gates of death, so that we may always rejoice in your help and speak your praise in the gates of Zion; through Jesus Christ our Lord. **Amen.**

PSALM 12

*Refrain:* **Help us, O God, and keep us always safe.**
*Psalm Prayer*
O God, protector of your people, your light is true light and your truth shines like the day. Through your pure and life-giving words, direct us to salvation and give us the help we long for in Jesus Christ our Lord. **Amen.**

*Or*

Lord God, in Jesus Christ you championed the weak and be-
friended outcasts. In the shining light of his goodness you expose
hypocrisy. Give us the courage to do the same, that we may truly
follow our Lord, Jesus Christ. **Amen.**

## PSALM 14

*Refrain:* **God alone is righteous and true.**
*Psalm Prayer*
O God of justice and righteousness, deliver us from the foolishness
of ignoring you. Teach us the wisdom of your way in Jesus Christ,
that we may seek your goodness and act out your love to all your
people. **Amen.**

## PSALM 15

*Refrain:* **We would be righteous and true to you, our God.**

*Or*

**Blessed are the pure in heart,**
**for they shall see God.** *Matt. 5:8*

*Or*

**Be doers of the Word**
**and not hearers only.** *James 1:22*
*Psalm Prayer*
Heavenly Father, you adopted us as your children. Grant that we
may pass through this world with such integrity that no one will
have just complaint against us. At the end, may we inherit what
has been prepared for us in heaven; through Jesus Christ, our only
Savior. **Amen.**

*Or*

Lord Jesus, you chose to live among us, and in returning to your
Father you made an eternal home for us. Help us to walk in your

ways and bring us at last to the place reserved for us, where you live and reign with the Father and the Holy Spirit, one God, now and forever. **Amen.**

PSALM 16

*Refrain:* **In your presence, O Lord, is fullness of joy.**

*Or, during Advent*

**The Lord will show me the path of life.**
*Psalm Prayer*
Glorious God, we delight in prayer and rejoice that you always hold us secure in your thoughts. No pleasure approaches that which you so generously give: love and life and joy in Jesus Christ, our Lord and Savior. **Amen.**

*Or, during Advent*

Lord Jesus, uphold all who hope in you and give us your counsel, so that we may know the joy of your resurrection and share the blessedness of the saints at your right hand, where you live and reign with the Father and the Holy Spirit, one God, now and forever. **Amen.**

PSALM 17

*Refrain:* **Keep me as the apple of your eye;**
**hide me under the shadow of your wings.**
*Psalm Prayer*
Lord God, watch over your people as the apple of your eye, and guard our steps until we see your face; through Jesus Christ our Lord. **Amen.**

*Or*

Good Lord, you are the searcher of human hearts. When we are surrounded by dangers, show us your favor, without which we would perish. Let not our hearts be earthbound, but may we follow your commandments and aspire to heaven's joy, which is won for us by Jesus Christ, your Son. **Amen.**

PSALM 18:1–20

> *Refrain:* **I love you, O Lord, my strength,**
> **my rock, my fortress, my deliverer.**
>
> *Psalm Prayer*
> Lord God, our stronghold and salvation, set us aflame with your love that we may reach out to our neighbor without counting the cost, for the sake of Jesus Christ our Lord. **Amen.**

PSALM 19:1–6

> *Refrain:* **You are the bright star of morning, O Christ our Lord.**
> *Psalm Prayer*
> Faithful God, you sent us your Word as the sun of truth and justice to shine upon all the world. Open our eyes to see your glory in all your works, that, rejoicing in your whole creation, we may learn to serve you with gladness, for the sake of him through whom all things were made, Jesus Christ our Lord. **Amen.**

PSALM 19:7–14

> *Refrain:* **Let the words of my mouth**
> **and the thoughts of my heart**
> **find favor in your sight, O Lord.**
>
> *Psalm Prayer*
> You have spoken your Word of Wisdom, O God, in the person of Jesus Christ. In him we find your truth, the way to follow, and new life to live. May our words and work always be as worship, and announce the risen Christ bringing your love to the whole world. **Amen.**

PSALM 20

> *Refrain:* **All praise to Jesus Christ in victory!**
> *Psalm Prayer*
> Almighty God, you have given victory to your chosen one, Jesus the Christ. Do not allow us to stumble into lesser loyalties, but make us stand firm in trusting your power and peace. **Amen.**

PSALM 22

> *Refrain:* **Lord, hear my prayer,**
> **let my cry come to you.**

*Psalm Prayer*

Eternal God, when your Son was handed over to torture and felt abandoned by you, he cried out from the cross. Then death was destroyed, and life was restored. By his death and resurrection save the poor, lift up the downtrodden, break the chains of the oppressed, that your church may sing your praises. **Amen.**

## PSALM 23

*Refrain:* **Lead us in righteousness, Lord God,
that we may find rest in you.**

*Or*

**My shepherd is the Lord,
I shall not be in want.**

*Psalm Prayer*

Lord Jesus Christ, Shepherd of your church, you give us new birth in the waters of baptism; you anoint us with oil, and call us to salvation at your table. Dispel the terrors of death, and lead us along safe paths, that we may rest securely in you and dwell in the house of the Lord now and forever. **Amen.**

*Or*

Eternal God, bring us at last to our true home in your secure presence, where Christ has gone ahead to prepare a place for us. Strengthen us for another day along the way, following wherever Christ, our Shepherd, leads. **Amen.**

*Or*

Eternal and everlasting God, Source of all happiness, we praise you for making known our Shepherd and Defender. Grant that as we cast away all fear and terror of death, we may embrace and confess your truth revealed in your Son, our sovereign Master, Christ Jesus. **Amen.**

## PSALM 24

*Refrain:* **Fling wide the gates.
Open the ancient doors,
and the Holy One will come in!**

*Psalm Prayer*
Lord of all creation, open our hearts that the Holy One may enter
and rule our lives. Give us clean hands and pure hearts, that we
may stand in your presence and receive your blessing in Jesus
Christ our Lord. **Amen.**

## PSALM 25

*Refrain:* **Remember me, O Lord, according to your love.**

*Or, during Advent*

**To you, O Lord, I lift my soul.**

*Or, during Lent*

**Lead me in your truth, O Lord, and teach me.**

*Psalm Prayer*
God our Savior, teach us your ways that we may live according to
your truth. You alone can forgive our sins and lead us into righteousness. Strengthen our trust in you that we may follow in the
way of Jesus Christ. **Amen.**

*Or, during Advent*

Lord, our God, you show us your ways of compassion and love,
and you spare sinners. Remember not our sins; relieve our misery;
satisfy the longing of your people; and fulfill all our hopes for
eternal peace through Jesus Christ our Lord. **Amen.**

*Or, during Lent*

Good and gracious God, you desire nothing but our salvation.
Give us your mercy, and put our sins out of your sight, that we
may be governed by your Holy Spirit and walk in your commandments without wavering, to come at last to the joy obtained for us
in Christ Jesus. **Amen.**

## PSALM 26

*Refrain:* **O God, be merciful to us and save us.**

*Psalm Prayer*

Jesus, Lamb of God, you take away the sins of the world. Give us grace to avoid sin, and strength to be faithful to you. Lead us to the place where God dwells in glory, that we may join with all the saints to praise God with joy now and forever. **Amen.**

## PSALM 27

*Refrain:* **The Lord is my light and my salvation; whom shall I fear?**

*Psalm Prayer*

O God, you are the guardian and guide of all your people. Protect and lead us through times of trouble, establishing our faith firmly on the rock of Jesus Christ, who is the way, the truth, and the life. **Amen.**

*Or*

Fountain of all goodness, help us in our affliction and do not withdraw from us when we are in danger. Whatever happens to us, strengthen our hearts, O God, that we may hope continually in your promises made to us in Jesus Christ our Lord. **Amen.**

*Or*

O Lord, you are the refuge of our life, for we find our safety in you. Do not forsake us in times of trouble, but let us see your face and follow your way revealed to us in Jesus Christ, our Lord and Savior. **Amen.**

## PSALM 28

*Refrain:* **My heart trusts in the Lord who protects and defends me.**

*Psalm Prayer*

Strong Shepherd of your people, when Jesus stretched out his arms on the cross, you heard him and he did not become like those who go down into the pit. By his resurrection strengthen your people to offer you thanks for the mighty works that you have done, and make our hearts dance for joy; through Jesus Christ our Lord. **Amen.**

PSALM 29

*Refrain:* **Give us your strength, O God,
and bless us with your peace.**

*Or, for Baptism of the Lord*

**Today the heavens are opened,
and the voice of the Father is heard:
This is my beloved Son.**

*Or, for Pentecost*

**The God of glory thunders!
The Lord flashes forth flames of fire!**

*Psalm Prayer*
O God, your voice is full of power and majesty, and we worship
you with all praise and glory. Bless your people with strength and
peace, that we may honor you with our songs and our service, in
the name of Jesus Christ. **Amen.**

*Or, for Baptism of the Lord*

Sovereign God, your voice sounds over the waters as you reign
above the flood. Help us, born again by water and the Holy Spirit,
to praise your wonderful deeds in your holy temple; through Jesus
Christ our Lord. **Amen.**

*Or, for Pentecost*

God of creation, your Spirit hovered over the waters in the beginning of creation and brought forth life. May the same Creator Spirit
create and inspire us anew until the whole world can sing with us:
Glory to God! **Amen.**

PSALM 30

*Refrain:* **Weeping lasts but a night;
joy comes with the morning.**

*Psalm Prayer*
Loving God, turn our mourning into dancing, our despair into celebration. Lift us out of our distress that we may tell of your faithfulness and your great love for all people in Jesus Christ our Lord. **Amen.**

## PSALM 31

*Refrain:* **In you, O Lord, have I taken refuge.**
*Psalm Prayer*
O God, our refuge and our strength, you protect us in the mighty fortress of your constant love. Keep us strong in the victory of Jesus Christ, and fill us with hope, that we may serve as his courageous disciples. **Amen.**

*Or*

Eternal God, you know our weakness and infirmities. Be our protector and defender against all who might do us mischief or harm, and give us all good gifts promised in Jesus Christ. **Amen.**

## PSALM 32

*Refrain:* **Happy are those whose sins are forgiven!**

*Or, during Lent*

**I acknowledge my sin to you
and you forgive me all my guilt.**
*Psalm Prayer*
We confess, O merciful God, we have squandered your blessings and turned our backs on your love. Help us repent and return to you, our home, confident that you will welcome us as your sons and daughters in Jesus Christ. **Amen.**

*Or*

Merciful God, you desire not the death but the life of the sinner. Bury all our iniquities, that being guarded by your goodness, we may rejoice in your righteousness, according to the teaching of your Son, Jesus Christ. **Amen.**

*Or, during Lent*

O God, you alone can forgive our guilt and take away our sin. Bless us with candor in confession, that we may be safe in your salvation and follow in your way, in Jesus Christ, Redeemer of us all. **Amen.**

PSALM 33

*Refrain:* **Let your constant love be with us, Lord, as we put our hope in you.**

*Or, during Pentecost*

**The Spirit of the Lord fills the whole world. Alleluia!**

*Psalm Prayer*

Creator and Redeemer of the world, write your Word in our hearts, that we may know your will, witness to your love, and herald your glory, for the sake of Jesus Christ our Lord. **Amen.**

*Or, during Advent*

Lord God, with your Son you made heaven and earth; through him you continue to accomplish your purpose for creation. Strengthen us to witness to your truth among the nations, and herald your glory in the heavens, for the sake of Jesus Christ our Lord. **Amen.**

*Or, during Pentecost*

O heavenly Ruler, Comforter, Spirit of truth, everywhere present and filling all things, Treasury of blessings and Giver of life: Come dwell in us, cleanse us of every stain, and save us. **Amen.**

PSALM 34

*Refrain:* **Taste and see the goodness of the Lord.**

*Psalm Prayer*

Graciously hear us, Lord, for we seek you alone. Quiet us with the peace which passes understanding, and make us radiant with joy, through Jesus Christ our Lord. **Amen.**

PSALM 36

*Refrain:* **You give us life, O God,**
**and light to see your way.**

*Psalm Prayer*

Eternal God, you satisfy our hunger by feeding us with the bread of life, and you quench our thirst for righteousness by your mighty acts. Nourish us always by your Spirit, that we may grow into the stature of Jesus Christ. **Amen.**

PSALM 40

*Refrain:* **Great is the Lord, our help and deliverer.**

*Or*

**I love to do your will, O God.**

*Psalm Prayer*

Lord Jesus Christ, you became obedient to death and your name was exalted above all others. Teach us always to do God's will, so that, made holy by your obedience and united to your sacrifice, we may know your great love in times of sorrow and sing a new song to our God now and forever. **Amen.**

*Or*

There is none to compare with you, O God, for you have done wondrous things and worked salvation for all people. We sing your praises and tell your story, which we know in Jesus Christ our Redeemer. **Amen.**

PSALM 42

*Refrain:* **We hope in God, who is our help.**

*Or, during Lent*

**My soul thirsts for the Lord,**
**for the living God.**

*Psalm Prayer*

Mighty God, remind us that you do not forget us, nor have you neglected your promises made and kept in Jesus Christ. Kindle hope within us that we may warmly welcome Christ into our hearts and serve him with burning zeal. **Amen.**

*Or*

Lord God, fountain of life, through the waters of baptism you called us from the depths of sin to the depths of your mercy. From the refreshing springs of your Word satisfy our thirst for you, that we may come rejoicing to your holy mountain, where you live and reign now and forever. **Amen.**

## PSALM 43

*Refrain:* **My hope is in my God, my hope is not in vain.**
*Psalm Prayer*
Eternal God, you created us to glorify your name. Show us your favor and fulfill your promises, that we may render to you all honor and glory, through your Son, Jesus Christ. **Amen.**

## PSALM 45

*Refrain:* **Your throne, O God, endures forever.**
*Psalm Prayer*
Holy God, you have formed the holy church to be the bride of Christ. Grant to your church the faith and peace she will need to do your will and to show your glory, through Jesus Christ our Lord. **Amen.**

## PSALM 46

*Refrain:* **God is our refuge and strength.**

*Or*

**The mighty Lord is with us,**
**the God of Jacob is our refuge.**
*Psalm Prayer*
God, our refuge and strength, when the floods of this world rise up against your holy city, watch over it and keep it safe. By the river that flows from the throne of the Lamb, purify your church, for you are with us, our stronghold now and forever. **Amen.**

*Or*

O God, you are the only refuge of all who trust you. Fortify us with your goodness to live in quietness of spirit, that we may serve you all our days, through Jesus Christ, your Son. **Amen.**

*Or, for Epiphany*

Though you are mightier than all rulers of earth, O God, and you govern the universe, still you are with us. So we rejoice and sing your praises, for you came to us in Jesus Christ, and you stay with us still in our risen Lord, by the power of your Holy Spirit. **Amen.**

## PSALM 47

*Refrain:* **We praise you, great God, ruler over all!**

> *Or, during Easter*
>
> **God has gone up with shouts of joy
> and the blast of trumpets.**

*Psalm Prayer*
God of power and righteousness, you stand in authority over all authorities, and you rule over all governments. Let the peoples rejoice and the leaders of nations follow the way of Jesus Christ, the Prince of peace. **Amen.**

*Or, during Easter*

Lord Jesus, the dominion of the universe is yours, for you have ascended on high and are seated on the throne prepared for you by the Father. Gather all people into your church and make them a holy nation, a royal priesthood, your own chosen heritage, to praise and adore you now and forever. **Amen.**

## PSALM 48

*Refrain:* **Great is the Lord,
and worthy to be praised in the city of our God.**

*Psalm Prayer*
Almighty God, in Jesus Christ you have loved us beyond all deserving, and in him you call us to new commitment. Give us grace to respond to your love with our loyalty, and keep us always in your powerful peace. **Amen.**

PSALM 49

*Refrain:* **From the grasp of death,
God has ransomed my life. Alleluia!**
*Psalm Prayer*
O God, giver of all wisdom, deliver us from the folly of giving up
our eternal birthright for that which is only temporary. Teach us
to hold firmly to you so that we may not treasure things, but show
the imperishable riches of your love in Jesus Christ. **Amen.**

PSALM 50

*Refrain:* **Out of Zion, perfect in beauty, God shines in glory.**
*Psalm Prayer*
Almighty Lord and God, because Jesus your servant became obe-
dient to death, his sacrifice was greater than all the sacrifices of old.
Accept our sacrifice of praise, and help us to do your will, until our
whole life becomes worship in spirit and truth; through Jesus
Christ our Lord. **Amen.**

PSALM 51

*Refrain:* **Since we are saved by faith,
we have peace with God through Jesus Christ our Lord.**

*Or, during Lent*

**The sacrifice you accept, O God, is a humble spirit.**
*Psalm Prayer*
Eternal God, you know us better than we know ourselves, and still
you love us. Purify our desires that we may seek your will and
follow closely on the way of our Lord Jesus Christ. **Amen.**

*Or, during Lent*

God of mercy, you forgive us even before our lips form the words
to ask for pardon. Wash us from all our sins; create in us clean
hearts and strengthen us by your Holy Spirit that we may give you
praise. **Amen.**

## PSALM 53

*Refrain:* **Our God in heaven is watching over us.**

*Psalm Prayer*

Holy God, apart from you nothing is true, nothing is holy. Take away our sins and give us strength in our weakness, so that all who believe in Christ may rejoice in his glory now and forever. **Amen.**

## PSALM 54

*Refrain:* **I will call upon God,
and the Lord will deliver me.**

*Psalm Prayer*

O God, hear our prayer and come to the aid of your church. Deliver us from evil, so that from the rising of the sun to its setting we may offer you our sacrifice of praise; through Jesus Christ our Lord. **Amen.**

## PSALM 56

*Refrain:* **We trust in God,
and will not be afraid.**

*Psalm Prayer*

O God, in the midst of this day's difficulties, stay close to your people to give us courage. Remind us that we belong to you in baptism, for you have claimed us in Jesus Christ to be servants with him. Keep us upright all the day long. **Amen.**

## PSALM 57

*Refrain:* **Awake, lyre and harp,
with praise let us awake the dawn.**

*Psalm Prayer*

You alone, great God, are our refuge, our only hope in living and our only salvation in dying. Keep us in your care that we may always praise you and faithfully proclaim your name before the nations; in Jesus Christ our Lord. **Amen.**

## PSALM 62

*Refrain:* **For God alone, my soul in silence waits.**
*Psalm Prayer*
We wait for you, O God, in our worship; we wait upon you in our work. Give us patience to be quiet and listen for your Word; give us patience to be diligent and to labor according to your will; in Jesus Christ. **Amen.**

*Or*

Lord God, in a confusing world we look to you as our rock of hope. Hear us as we pour out our hearts to you, and give us your grace and secure protection; through Jesus Christ our Lord. **Amen.**

## PSALM 63

*Refrain:* **O God, you are my God;**
**eagerly I seek you.**
*Psalm Prayer*
Deep within our hearts, creating God, there is a yearning for your presence, a hunger and thirst for your righteousness. Satisfy us by the power of your Spirit, yet keep us restless to seek your will as we follow where Christ may lead. **Amen.**

## PSALM 65

*Refrain:* **You are worthy of praise, O God.**
*Psalm Prayer*
Great God, from sunrise to sunset you sustain this earth, and abundantly provide for all your creatures. As you have kept your pledge in Jesus Christ, so we dare pledge ourselves to you in following him who is Redeemer of all. **Amen.**

## PSALM 66

*Refrain:* **All earth, shout with joy to God!**
*Psalm Prayer*
Almighty God, in the death and resurrection of Jesus you brought us through the waters of baptism to the shores of new life. Accept the sacrifice of our lives, and let us enter your house, where we shall praise your unfailing love and power. **Amen.**

*Or*

Almighty God, you have redeemed your people through all ages, and you rescue us even now. Deliver us from the bondage of sin and death, that we may fulfill our vows of service and always give you praise, in Jesus Christ our Lord. **Amen.**

## PSALM 67

*Refrain:* **Let the people praise you, O God.
Let all the people praise you.**

*Or, during Epiphany*

**Let all the nations praise you, O God.**

*Psalm Prayer*
Holy God, through your power the earth has brought forth the tree of the cross. Unite all people in its embrace, and feed them with its fruit, everlasting life through Jesus Christ our Lord. **Amen.**

*Or, during Advent*

Be gracious and bless us, Lord, and let your face shed its light on us, so that we may make you known with reverence and bring forth a harvest of justice. **Amen.**

*Or, for Epiphany*

Light of the world, you have come into the world's darkness and the darkness cannot overwhelm the light. Let your holy name be known through all the earth, that all people and nations may praise you and walk in your ways, through Jesus Christ our Lord. **Amen.**

## PSALM 68

*Refrain:* **My lips are filled with your praise,
with your glory all the day long.**

*Psalm Prayer*
Lord Jesus, you came to us in our bondage, and led us to freedom by the cross and resurrection. May our lives praise you, and our lips proclaim your mighty power to all people that they may find their hope in you. **Amen.**

PSALM 72

*Refrain:* **Justice shall flourish,**
**and peace shall abound forever.**

*Or, for Epiphany*

**All rulers shall bow before him,**
**and all nations serve him.**

*Psalm Prayer*
Almighty God, you gave the kingdom of justice and peace to David
and to his descendant, our Lord Jesus Christ. Extend the reign of
Christ to every nation, so that the poor may receive justice, the
destitute relief, and the people of the earth peace in the name of
him who lives and reigns with you and the Holy Spirit, one God,
now and forever. **Amen.**

*Or, for Epiphany*

We bless you, O God, for you rule over all nations and people.
Establish your Son, Jesus Christ, on the throne of this world, that
all will bow to his authority, and the cause of the needy will be
upheld. **Amen.**

PSALM 73

*Refrain:* **It is good to be near to God,**
**to proclaim God's mighty acts.**

*Psalm Prayer*
Almighty God, you alone are great, for you alone are good. Deliver
us from chasing after illusions of power and prestige, that we may
follow instead the true way to eternal life, in Jesus Christ our Lord.
**Amen.**

PSALM 80

*Refrain:* **Restore us, O God, and we shall be saved.**

*Psalm Prayer*

Lord God, you so tend the vine you planted that now it extends its branches throughout the world. Keep us in Christ as branches on the vine, that, grafted firmly in your love, we may show the whole world your great power and bear the fruit of righteousness; through Jesus Christ our Lord. **Amen.**

## PSALM 81

*Refrain:* **Sing with joy to God our strength;**
**shout to the God of Jacob.**

*Psalm Prayer*

You rescue us daily, our God, and set us in places of safety, for we are your people. Let us listen always to your voice, that we may be filled with goodness and nourished by your Spirit, strong to serve with Jesus Christ, our Servant Lord. **Amen.**

## PSALM 82

*Refrain:* **Holy God, holy and mighty,**
**holy immortal One, have mercy upon us.**

*Psalm Prayer*

Jesus, our Lord and our God, by your death you give life to the dead; by your resurrection you give strength to the weak. Rise up to rule the earth, and at the end of the world, when the secrets of the heart are revealed, make us glad to celebrate your justice now and forever. **Amen.**

## PSALM 84

*Refrain:* **How lovely is your dwelling place,**
**Lord, God of hosts.**

*Or, during Lent*

**I love the beauty of your house, O Lord,**
**the place where your glory dwells.**

*Psalm Prayer*

Guide us, great God, that at the end of our restless journey on earth, we may come at last to our heavenly home. We are glad for the promise of a place prepared for us, where we shall enjoy the hospitality of Christ and the peace of your Spirit. **Amen.**

*Or, during Lent*

Holy God, you call us together to invoke your name, and to hear and embrace your Word. Increase our love of your church, that with all the faithful we may behold your splendor seen in Jesus Christ, and praise your name forever. **Amen.**

## PSALM 85

*Refrain:* **Let righteousness and peace embrace in our life.**

*Or, during Advent*

**Show us your love and mercy, Lord,**
**and give us your saving help.**
*Psalm Prayer*
God of peace, rule in our world and in our hearts, that we may abandon warfare within our souls and throughout the world. Revive us and restore us to righteousness as disciples of Jesus Christ, Redeemer of all people. **Amen.**

*Or, during Advent*

God of love and faithfulness, you so loved the world that you gave your only Son to be our Savior. Help us to receive him as both Lord and brother, and freely celebrate him as our gracious Redeemer now and forever. **Amen.**

## PSALM 86

*Refrain:* **How great is your constant love for us, O God!**
*Psalm Prayer*
Eternal God, in every time and place and circumstance your people call on you, rejoicing in your love and cherishing your truth. Hear the prayers of our hearts that we may be protected from sin and delivered from evil, in Jesus Christ. **Amen.**

## PSALM 88

*Refrain:* **Every day we call to you, O God,**
**and lift our hands in prayer.**

*Psalm Prayer*
O Lord, our God, we lift up our lives to you in prayer and call upon you for our salvation. Redeem us from death and show us your steadfast love, that we may rejoice in your resurrection and serve our risen Lord, Jesus Christ. **Amen.**

## PSALM 89:1–18

*Refrain:* **Your love, O Lord, will I sing forever.**
*Psalm Prayer*
O God, you alone are wise and good. You never cease to show us the greatness of your love and favor. Above all, you gave us a King and Savior, Jesus Christ, your only Son, to assure us of the truth of your promises. Grant us your grace, that obeying you, we may know the joy of your salvation. **Amen.**

## PSALM 89:19–52

*Refrain:* **I have made a covenant with David, my servant;**
 **I will establish his throne forever.**
*Psalm Prayer*
Mighty God, you fulfilled the promise you made to David, by coming in Jesus of Nazareth to establish a lasting covenant. You anointed him and raised him higher than all the rulers of earth. Remember your covenant with us, that we may sing of your mercies forever; through Jesus Christ our Lord. **Amen.**

## PSALM 90

*Refrain:* **Each morning, Lord, you fill us with your kindness.**

*Or*

**Teach us to number our days,**
**that we may gain wisdom of heart.**
*Psalm Prayer*
Eternal God, you alone are constant in this changing world. As each new day begins, fill us with your never-failing love, grant us true wisdom of heart and guide us in serving you all the days of our life; through Jesus Christ our Lord. **Amen.**

*Or*

Eternal God, though our lives are but a breath, we are in your hands, now and always. Keep us alert to your love each day, that we may see your promises coming true in Jesus Christ our Lord. **Amen.**

PSALM 91

*Refrain:* **Be our defender, O God,
and show us your salvation.**

*Or*

**God is my refuge and my strength,
the one in whom I put my trust.**

*Psalm Prayer*

You have come to us, O God, to keep our souls safe from the destruction of death. In Jesus Christ you keep your promises of redemption. Make us confident of your present protection, that we may be disciples of Jesus Christ our Lord. **Amen.**

*Or*

O God, to know you is to live, to serve you is to reign. Defend us from every enemy, that trusting in your protective care we may have no fear; through the power of Jesus Christ our Lord. **Amen.**

PSALM 92

*Refrain:* **It is good to give thanks to you, Lord,
and to celebrate your name, O Most High!**

*Psalm Prayer*

Take away our shame, O Christ, and make us rejoice in your saving acts, that we may abound in works of faith, hope, and love in your service. **Amen.**

PSALM 93

*Refrain:* **We worship you, God of glory!**

*Or*

**Praise the Lord, praise the name of the Lord.**

*Psalm Prayer*

Eternal God, you have raised Jesus from death to rule eternally from heaven. Keep us steadfast in serving our Lord, that your will may be done on earth as it is in heaven, and that all people may come to worship you. **Amen.**

*Or*

Omnipotent God, your glory is incomprehensible, your majesty infinite, and your power incomparable. Settle us on the certainty of your promises, that no matter what happens, we may be firm in faith and live uprightly in your church, bought by the blood of Jesus Christ. **Amen.**

## PSALM 94

*Refrain:* **Happy are those you teach, O Lord.**

*Psalm Prayer*

Faithful God, you do not abandon your people to the power of evil. Grant that those who suffer for the sake of justice may find strength in the cross of Jesus and be filled with your peace now and forever. **Amen.**

## PSALM 95

*Refrain:* **Let us shout for joy to the rock of our salvation. Alleluia!**

*Or*

**Harden not your hearts, as those before you did in the wilderness.**

*Psalm Prayer*

O Lord, our protector and our strength, you guide us as the sheep of your fold. In your goodness sustain us, that our hearts may never be hardened through unbelief of your holy Word, but that we may serve you in true and living faith and so enter into your heavenly rest. **Amen.**

PSALM 96

*Refrain:* **We bless you, O God, almighty Creator.**

*Or*

**Our God in heaven is watching over us.**

*Or, during Christmas*

**Let the heavens be glad
and the earth rejoice,
for the Lord has come.**

*Or, during Easter*

**Sing a new song to the Lord, all the earth.**

*Psalm Prayer*
Day by day, O God, we announce your goodness and proclaim your power. For we have seen your righteousness in Jesus Christ, crucified and risen, and we know your wondrous love for all the world. **Amen.**

*Or, during Christmas*

Ever-living God, the heavens were glad and the earth rejoiced when you sent your Son, the incarnate Word, to dwell among us. Help us to proclaim your glory to those who do not know you, until the whole earth sings a new song to you now and forever. **Amen.**

*Or, during Easter*

Lord Jesus Christ, victorious ruler, your triumph over death and hell is the new song sung by all the world. Extend your gentle rule over all nations and prepare them for your coming in glory and might, for you live and reign forever and ever. **Amen.**

PSALM 97

*Refrain:* **Rejoice in the Lord,
and give thanks to God's holy name.**

*Or, during Christmas*

**A prince from the day of your birth;
from the womb before daybreak, have I begotten you.**

*Or, for Epiphany*

**People of every race
shall walk in the splendor of your sunrise. Alleluia!**

*Or, during Easter*

**The Lord rules, let earth rejoice.**

*Psalm Prayer*

O God, you clothe the sky with light, and ocean depths with
darkness. You work your mighty wonders among us. Claim us for
your purposes, that we may be among those who see your glory
and give you praise. **Amen.**

*Or*

O God, all glory and honor belong to you. By your Word enlighten
the whole world to put away idolatry and superstition, that all may
come to praise your name and give thanks for your benefits received through Jesus Christ, your Son. **Amen.**

## PSALM 98

*Refrain:* **We sing to our God,
who has done wonderful things.**

*Or, during Christmas and Easter*

**All the ends of the earth
have seen the victory of our God. Alleluia!**

*Psalm Prayer*

Almighty God, we celebrate the victory over death and destruction
accomplished in Jesus Christ. Use the praise of our lives to proclaim
your love to all people, that the world may rejoice that you are
God. **Amen.**

*Or, during Christmas*

Eternal God, you redeemed humanity by sending your only Son in fulfillment of your promises of old. Let the truth and power of your salvation be known in all places of the earth, that all nations may give you praise, honor, and glory, through Jesus Christ your Son. **Amen.**

*Or, during Easter*

Lord, we sing to you a new song, for your victory is ever new. In the empty tomb you have given us a glimpse of your future. In your victory over death you have shown us how we shall overcome the last enemy. As the seas roar and the hills sing together, we too will praise you for your great triumph, Father, Son, and Holy Spirit, now and forever. **Amen.**

## PSALM 99

*Refrain:* **The Lord our God is holy!**

*Or, during Easter*

**Holy, holy, holy are you, Lord God of hosts;
your glory fills the earth.**
*Psalm Prayer*
God of might and mercy, you have kept your promises to your people in Jesus Christ. Strengthen us to worship you with works of righteousness and to proclaim your greatness with the praises of our lips. **Amen.**

*Or, during Easter*

Holy God, Ruler of the universe, you love what is right and true. Lead us in your ways that we may live to praise you and proclaim your greatness in Jesus Christ our Lord. **Amen.**

## PSALM 100

*Refrain:* **Your love is eternal, O God;
your faithfulness lasts forever.**

*Or, for Epiphany*

**Shout for joy to the Lord, all the earth.**
*Psalm Prayer*
Gracious God, you are the source of our life. Make us grow today
in our understanding of your goodness, truth, and mercy, that we
may join with your whole creation in praising your name, through
Jesus Christ our Lord. **Amen.**

*Or, for Epiphany*

Loving God, by your power you created us, and by your goodness
you call us to be your people. Accept the offering of our worship
that every race and nation may enter your courts praising you in
song. **Amen.**

PSALM 102

*Refrain:* **You, O Lord, will abide forever;**
**your name endures from age to age.**

*Or, during Lent*

**Lord, you are my strength;**
**hasten to help me.**
*Psalm Prayer*
Almighty and awesome God, you have come down in Jesus Christ
to free the prisoners of sin and death. Protect and preserve your
people now, that all generations will praise your holy name. **Amen.**

*Or, during Lent*

Lord, while our days vanish like shadows and our lives wear out
like a garment, you are eternal. Although our earthly lives come to
an end, help us to live in Christ's endless life and at length attain
our home, the heavenly Jerusalem. **Amen.**

PSALM 103

*Refrain:* **Bless the Lord, my soul;**
**never forget what God has done.**

*Psalm Prayer*

God of might and mercy, you bring us to new life each day, and nurture us in your tender love. Keep us far from all sinfulness, that our lives may be a blessing to you, in Jesus Christ our Lord. **Amen.**

## PSALM 104

*Refrain:* **Lord, you are clothed with majesty and splendor; you wrap yourself with light as with a cloak.**

*Or, for Baptism of the Lord*

**In the beginning, when God created the heavens and the earth, the spirit of God moved over the face of the waters. Alleluia!**

*Or, on Pentecost*

**When you give them breath, they live; you give new life to the earth. Alleluia!**

*Psalm Prayer*

God of majesty, we are constantly surrounded by your gifts and touched by your grace; our words of praise do not approach the wonders of your love. Send forth your Spirit again, that our lives may be refreshed and the whole world may be renewed, in Jesus Christ our Lord. **Amen.**

*Or, for Baptism of the Lord*

O living and eternal source of life, the waters of Jordan parted to embrace Christ your Son, your Holy Spirit descended as a dove, and the Father's voice was heard: This is my beloved Son. We praise you that he in whom all things exist, and in whom there is no sin, should be revealed to sinners. Glory to you. **Amen.**

*Or, on Pentecost*

Creator of all that is, Giver of life: On the first Pentecost you poured out your Spirit upon those who believed in Jesus. By the same Spirit, show us what is right and true, and give us continually a sense of your presence and power. **Amen.**

## PSALM 105

*Refrain:* **Tell out the deeds of the Lord;
proclaim the wonders God has wrought.**

*Psalm Prayer*

Just and righteous God, you have chosen your church to show forth your holy name, and you have mercifully received us into that fellowship. Grant that we may know the sweetness of your mercies and assist us in times of trouble, that we may celebrate your power and goodness which you have declared in Jesus Christ. **Amen.**

## PSALM 107

*Refrain:* **They cried to the Lord in their trouble,
and were delivered from their distress.**

*Psalm Prayer*

Holy God, you fill the hungry with good things and break the sinner's chains. Hear your people who call to you in their need, and lead your church from the shadows of death. Gather us from sunset to sunrise, that we may grow together in faith and love, and may give thanks for your kindness in Jesus Christ our Lord. **Amen.**

## PSALM 108

*Refrain:* **My soul awakes to praise God among the peoples!**
*Psalm Prayer*

Your love endures, O God, beyond cross and grave, for we have seen the risen Christ. Help us in times of trouble, that his victory may be ours, and your name be exalted over all the earth. **Amen.**

## PSALM 110

*Refrain:* **The Lord will come on the clouds of heaven
with power and great glory. Alleluia!**

*Psalm Prayer*

Almighty God, make known in every place the perfect offering of your Son, the eternal high priest of the new Jerusalem, and so consecrate all nations to be your holy people, that the kingdom of Christ, your anointed One, may come in its fullness; and to you, Father, Son, and Holy Spirit, be all honor and praise now and forever. **Amen.**

## PSALM 111

*Refrain:* **You have sent deliverance to your people.**
**Holy is your name.**

*Psalm Prayer*
Faithful God, you have nourished us in your holy covenant with the food and drink of Christ's love. Keep us firm in our faith and loyal in our love, that we may obediently serve as disciples of Jesus Christ, our Lord and Savior. **Amen.**

## PSALM 112

*Refrain:* **Blessed are all who fear you, O Lord,**
**who delight in your commandments.**

*Psalm Prayer*
Eternal God, in the order of your creation you have given righteousness, justice, peace, and love for the enlightenment of all people. Keep us always illumined by Jesus Christ, that we may reflect his brightness throughout our lives. **Amen.**

## PSALM 113

*Refrain:* **From the rising of the sun to its setting,**
**the name of the Lord be praised. Alleluia!**

*Or, during Easter*

**Our God, who is high above all nations,**
**has raised us up with Christ Jesus. Alleluia!**

*Psalm Prayer*
God of creation, in Jesus Christ you come to lift the lowly and give riches to the needy. Help us to praise the name of the Lord, in all times and all places, that we may be faithful servants of Jesus Christ, Savior of all. **Amen.**

*Or, during Easter*

O God, you alone are worthy of all glory and majesty. We pray you will illumine our hearts and take away all pride, that we may be obedient to your Word and bring forth the fruits of good works, to the glory of your name, in Jesus Christ our Lord. **Amen.**

## PSALM 114

*Refrain:* **Tremble, O earth, at the presence of God. Alleluia!**
*Psalm Prayer*
Great and gracious God, by your mighty power you led your people out of the slavery of Egypt, and raised the dead Christ to life. Bring us continually by your power from slavery to freedom and from death to life. **Amen.**

## PSALM 115

*Refrain:* **To your name be glory. Alleluia!**
*Psalm Prayer*
Lord God, creator and ruler of the universe, you have entrusted the care of the earth to its peoples. Grant that your children, surrounded by signs of your presence, may live continually in Christ, praising you through him and with him. **Amen.**

## PSALM 116

*Refrain:* **We raise the cup of salvation in praise of our Lord.**

*Or, during Easter*

**The Lord has rescued my life from death. Alleluia!**
*Psalm Prayer*
While we were helpless, O God, you came to save us in Jesus Christ. Give us rest in him that our lives may be renewed and we will fulfill our vows to Christ, as you have kept all promises in him. **Amen.**

*Or, during Easter*

God our Redeemer, you have delivered us from death in the resurrection of Jesus Christ and brought us to new life by the power of your Spirit. Give us grace to keep our promises to praise and serve you all our days; through Christ our Lord. **Amen.**

PSALM 117

*Refrain:* **The faithfulness of the Lord is eternal. Alleluia!**

*Or, during Easter*

**Sing praise to the Lord!**
**Let all the nations praise our God!**

*Psalm Prayer*
Great God, your love is constant and your loyalty endures forever.
Send us to show your love, that we may share with all in praising
you; through Jesus Christ our Lord. **Amen.**

*Or, during Easter*

Lord God, you have revealed your kindness to all people. Gather
all nations to yourself, that in all the various tongues of the earth
one hymn of praise may rise to you; through Jesus Christ our Lord.
**Amen.**

PSALM 118

*Refrain:* **Give thanks to God, whose love is eternal.**

*Or, during Easter*

**This is the day the Lord has made. Alleluia!**

*Psalm Prayer*
Faithful God, you persist in caring for your people, and bring us
finally to victory in Jesus Christ. Save us anew, and give us success
in serving our Lord, the Savior of the world. **Amen.**

*Or, during Easter*

Lord God, your Son, rejected by the builders, has become the
cornerstone of the church. Shed rays of your glory throughout the
earth that all may shout with joy in celebration of the wonder of
Christ's resurrection, now and forever. **Amen.**

## PSALM 119:1–24

*Refrain:* **Blessed are you, O Lord.**
**Teach me your statutes.**

*Psalm Prayer*

Holy God, you are just in all your ways and your commandments
are the greatest of treasures. Give us understanding of your law
and direct us according to your will that we may be faithful in
serving you. **Amen.**

## PSALM 119:73–80

*Refrain:* **Lead me in the path of your commandments,**
**for your law is my delight.**

*Psalm Prayer*

Merciful God, Author of all that is good, you gave us your holy
commandments to direct our lives. Imprint your Holy Spirit in our
hearts, that we may turn from evil and find pleasure in your law.
Govern us by your Word, lead us to that eternal salvation promised
through Jesus Christ. **Amen.**

## PSALM 121

*Refrain:* **Our help comes from the Lord,**
**the maker of heaven and earth.**

*Psalm Prayer*

God our Protector, teach us to hold confidently to your grace, that
in times of fear and danger we may know you are near and depend
on you, our sure deliverer. **Amen.**

## PSALM 122

*Refrain:* **I rejoiced when I heard them say:**
**Let us go to the house of God.**

*Or, during Advent*

**The desire of all human hearts comes**
**and will dwell in resplendent glory. Alleluia!**

*Psalm Prayer*

Eternal God, may we know the peace of your presence wherever
we may be, in our homes, at work, in our churches, or at play, that
every place may be sacred and every action as worship in the name
of Christ. **Amen.**

Lord Jesus, give us the peace of the new Jerusalem. Bring all nations into your kingdom to share your gifts, that they may render thanks to you without end and may come to your eternal city, where you live and reign with the Father and the Holy Spirit, now and forever. **Amen.**

## PSALM 123

*Refrain:* **We look to you, O Lord our God. Have mercy on us.**
*Psalm Prayer*
O God, we are your servants and we look up to you for direction. Bless us by your mercy, that we may endure all oppression and danger for the sake of Jesus Christ our Lord. **Amen.**

## PSALM 124

*Refrain:* **People of God, sing this song. Alleluia!**
*Psalm Prayer*
Lord Jesus, you told your disciples that they would be despised because of your name, yet you number the very hairs of their heads. In times of persecution, defend and revive us by the power and comfort of the Holy Spirit, that we may be free from our enemies and praise your saving help now and forever. **Amen.**

## PSALM 125

*Refrain:* **Surround your people with strength, O Lord.**
*Psalm Prayer*
Almighty God, surround us with your power and defend us from the forces of evil. Keep us standing on the solid rock of your Word, that we may not fall, but remain upright in your presence, through the Lord Jesus Christ. **Amen.**

## PSALM 126

*Refrain:* **Those who sow in tears will reap in joy.**

*Psalm Prayer*

Faithful God, let the seeds of justice, which we have sown in tears, grow and increase in your sight. May we reap in joy the harvest for which we patiently hope, in Jesus Christ our Lord. **Amen.**

*Or, during Lent*

Lord Jesus, our life and our resurrection, the tears you sowed in the sorrow of your suffering and death brought the earth to flower on Easter morning. Renew in us the wonders of your power, so that after the sorrows of our exile, we may come home to you in gladness and praise you now and forever. **Amen.**

## PSALM 130

*Refrain:* **With the Lord there is mercy,
and fullness of redemption.**

*Or, during Advent*

**We watch for God's dawn bringing a new day.**

*Or, during Lent*

**Out of the depths I cry to you, O Lord.**

*Psalm Prayer*

O God, you have come to us in the depths of our darkest despair, in the suffering of Jesus Christ. By the rising of your Son, give us new light to live by, that we may always praise your holy name. **Amen.**

*Or, during Advent and Lent*

God of might and compassion, you sent your Word into the world as one who watches for the morning to announce the dawn of salvation. Do not leave us in the depths of our sins, but bring us into the fullness of your redeeming grace; through Jesus Christ our Lord. **Amen.**

## PSALM 132

*Refrain:* **Let us rejoice with all God's people.**

*Psalm Prayer*
Mighty One, we remember your promises to David, and how you
kept them in Jesus Christ. Come to dwell among us in Christ, that
we at last may come to dwell with you forever. **Amen.**

## PSALM 133

*Refrain:* **We are one in Christ, one in the Spirit.**
*Psalm Prayer*
We praise you, wonderful God, that we are your children brought
together by your love shown in Christ, bound together by the
power of your Spirit. Let us live that unity and witness to your
mighty love for all the world. **Amen.**

## PSALM 134

*Refrain:* **Lift up your hands and bless the Lord.**
*Psalm Prayer*
Lord Christ, where two or three gather in your name, you have
promised to be with them and share their fellowship. Look upon
your family gathered in your name, and graciously pour out your
blessing upon us. **Amen.**

## PSALM 135

*Refrain:* **You have chosen us, O God,**
        **to be your own possession.**
*Psalm Prayer*
Deliver us, O God, from the tyranny of human idols, for they are
dumb and blind and deaf, and they lead in the way of death. Make
us your own and lead us in the Way, the Truth, and the Life, Jesus
Christ. **Amen.**

## PSALM 136

*Refrain:* **Give thanks to God, whose love endures forever.**
*Psalm Prayer*
God of everlasting love, through your Word you made all things
in heaven and on earth. You have opened to us the path from
death to life. Listen to the song of the universe, the hymn of
resurrection, sung by your church and give us your blessing;
through Jesus Christ our Lord. **Amen.**

# PSALM 138

*Refrain:* **Thanks be to God, who is steadfast and faithful.**

*Or*

**Your love, O Lord, is eternal.**

*Psalm Prayer*

Great and wonderful God, you have claimed us for your purpose and preserved us for your work. Increase in us strength and compassion, that we may be able servants of Jesus Christ, our Lord and Savior. **Amen.**

*Or*

Holy God, you keep the proud at a distance and look upon the lowly with favor. Stretch out your hand to us in our suffering, perfect in us the work of your love, and bring us to life in Jesus Christ our Lord. **Amen.**

# PSALM 139

*Refrain:* **Search me, O God, and know my heart; test me and know my thoughts.**

*Psalm Prayer*

Almighty God, Creator of the universe, we are awed by your wondrous works and overwhelmed by your infinite wisdom. For all your majesty we praise you; yet even more we rejoice that you do not forget us, that you want to know us, that you come to care for us, sisters and brothers of Jesus Christ, your Son. **Amen.**

# PSALM 141

*Refrain:* **Let my prayer rise before you as incense, the lifting of my hands as the evening sacrifice.**

*Or*

**Be our refuge and our rest, O Lord, our God.**

*Psalm Prayer*

Holy God, let the incense of our repentant prayer ascend before you, and let your loving-kindness descend upon us, that with purified minds we may sing your praises with the church on earth and the whole heavenly host, and glorify you forever and ever. **Amen.**

*Or*

We bring to you the weariness of this day, O God, that we might be refreshed and relieved of all burdens. Fill us with your peace, descending in us gently by your Spirit, and still our souls with the secure love of Jesus Christ. **Amen.**

## PSALM 142

*Refrain:* **You are my refuge, Lord;**
       **you are all I desire in life.**
*Psalm Prayer*
Lord Jesus, hanging on the cross and left alone by your disciples, you called on your Father with a mighty cry as you gave up your spirit. Deliver us from the prison of affliction, and be yourself our inheritance in the land of the living, where with the Father and the Holy Spirit you are blessed now and forever. **Amen.**

## PSALM 143

*Refrain:* **Teach me to do your will, for you are my God.**

*Or, during Lent*

**Do not hide your face from me,**
**in you I put my trust.**
*Psalm Prayer*
Remind us of your love, O God, that our trust in you may remain firm. Let Christ be our teacher and your Spirit be our guide, today and all our days. **Amen.**

*Or, during Lent*

Hear our prayer, O God. Do not bring us to judgment, for before you no one can stand. Teach us to do your will. In your kindness lead us along a safe path, for the sake of Jesus Christ our Lord. **Amen.**

PSALM 145

*Refrain:* **I will bless you day after day**
**and praise your name forever.**

*Or*

**Your reign is everlasting,**
**and endures from age to age.**

*Psalm Prayer*

Merciful Lord, you are faithful in all your promises, and just in all your ways. Govern us, for we are weak; strengthen us, for we are failing; refresh us, for we are famished; abundantly bestow your gifts upon us. Defend us from evil, that we be not tempted from your way, but may praise your name forever. **Amen.**

*Or, during Advent*

Loving God, you are faithful in your promises and tender in your compassion. Listen to our hymn of joy, and continue to satisfy the needs of all your creatures, that all flesh may bless your name in your everlasting kingdom, where with your Son and the Holy Spirit you live and reign, now and forever. **Amen.**

*Or, during Christmas and Epiphany*

Lord God, unite our voices with the praise of all creation, that we may worthily magnify your excellent greatness; through Jesus Christ our Lord, who lives and reigns with you and the Holy Spirit, one God, now and forever. **Amen.**

*Or, during Lent and Easter*

You are close to us, O God, present in our midst in the risen Christ. By his death and rising again, you promise our salvation. Direct us today in his righteous way, until we come at last before your throne of grace. **Amen.**

## PSALM 146

*Refrain:* **I will praise the Lord as long as I live. Alleluia!**

*Or*

**Praise the Lord, my soul!**
**Praise the Lord!**

*Or, during Advent*

**Tell it out among the nations;**
**Behold our God and Savior comes. Alleluia!**

*Psalm Prayer*

God of all mercy, you have kept faith with us, reaching out to redeem us in Jesus Christ. Keep us faithful to you, that we may reach out to lift the lowly, as we have been raised to new life in Christ our Lord. **Amen.**

*Or, during Advent*

God of might and majesty, Strength of those who hope in you, rescue the troubled and afflicted, set us free from our sin, and preserve us in your truth; through Christ our Lord. **Amen.**

*Or, during Christmas and Epiphany*

O Christ, your coming floods the world with light, for you are Light of light, the very radiance of the Father. Let everything that breathes praise you in song, for you are the image of the Father's glory rising upon our darkness from the Virgin's womb. O Lord, glory to you. **Amen.**

*Or, during Lent and Easter*

Happy are those who put their trust in you, O God, our sure rock and refuge. Guard us from giving to any other the allegiance which belongs only to you. Shine upon us with the brightness of your light, that we may love you with a pure heart and praise you forever. **Amen.**

PSALM 147:1–11

*Refrain:* **It is always right to praise you, our gracious God.**

*Or, during Advent*

**In that day, the mountains shall drip sweet wine,
and the hills shall flow with milk and honey. Alleluia!**

*Or, during Christmas and Epiphany*

**The Lord shall reign forever. Alleluia!**

*Or, during Lent*

**Great and mighty is our Lord,
whose wisdom cannot be measured.**

*Or, during Easter*

**With joy let us praise the Lord our God.**

*Psalm Prayer*
Creator God, you have given us life and called us each by name as
you give us new life in Jesus Christ. Sustain us by your Spirit
through all our days, that you may take pleasure in us, and we
may hope in your steadfast love. **Amen.**

*Or, during Advent, Christmas, and Epiphany*

Lord God, unite our voices with the praise of all creation, that we
may worthily magnify your excellent greatness; through Jesus
Christ our Lord, who lives and reigns with you and the Holy Spirit,
one God, now and forever. **Amen.**

*Or, during Lent*

Loving God, great builder of the heavenly Jerusalem, you know
the number of the stars and call them by name. Heal hearts that
are broken, gather those who have been scattered, and enrich us
all from the fullness of your eternal wisdom, Jesus Christ our Lord.
**Amen.**

*Or, during Easter*

God of all creation, you lift the lowly by your mighty hand, and in Jesus Christ you have restored your people to yourself. By his resurrection, lift us to new life that we may with joy praise your holy name. **Amen.**

PSALM 147:12–20

*Refrain:* **We praise you, O God, for your mercy and care.**

*Or*

**Alleluia! Alleluia!**

*Or, during Advent*

**Praise the Lord, O Jerusalem!**
**O Zion, praise your God!**

*Or, during Lent*

**We do not live by bread alone,**
**but by every word that comes from the mouth of God.**

*Psalm Prayer*
O Lord, marvelous is your might by which you cast down the proud and lift up the humble. Restore and rebuild your church. Gather your scattered sheep and nourish us by your holy Word, that we may follow your will and come at last to the heritage prepared for us in Christ Jesus. **Amen.**

*Or*

O God, your word commands snow and ice to cover the earth, and your wind melts the waters so that streams flow. Speak your word in Jesus Christ to command our lives, and move us by your Spirit to serve your purpose. **Amen.**

*Or, during Advent, Christmas, and Epiphany*

O Christ, your coming floods the world with light, for you are Light of light, the very radiance of the Father. Let everything that breathes praise you in song, for you are the image of the Father's glory rising upon our darkness from the Virgin's womb. O Lord, glory to you. **Amen.**

*Or, during Lent*

Great and wonderful God, you send us in peace, secure in your protecting love. Lead us in the way of service, confident in Christ, who is your redeeming Word for us and the whole human family. **Amen.**

## PSALM 148

*Refrain:* **We raise our voices to praise our God!**

*Or*

**Praise the name of the Lord. Alleluia!**

*Or, during Christmas and Epiphany*

**The Lord shall reign forever. Alleluia!**

*Psalm Prayer*

Great is your majesty, mighty God, for you created all things and keep them in your care. Your glory shines in all you have made, in heaven and earth and in the sea. Unite our voices with all creation to praise the glory of your name. **Amen.**

*Or*

God most high, by your Word you created a wondrous universe, and through your Spirit you breathed into it your breath of life. Accept creation's hymn of praise from our lips, and let the praise that is sung in heaven resound in the heart of every creature on earth, to your glory, Father, Son, and Holy Spirit, now and forever. **Amen.**

*Or, during Christmas and Epiphany*

Lord God, unite our voices with the praise of all creation, that we may worthily magnify your excellent greatness; through Jesus Christ our Lord, who lives and reigns with you and the Holy Spirit, one God, now and forever. **Amen.**

*Or, during Lent*

Make our souls attentive, O God, that we may hear your praises sung in all creation and join our lives in giving you glory, with all your saints and servants of Jesus Christ, our Lord. **Amen.**

*Or, during Easter*

God of majesty and might, we join our praise with the celebrations of all your creatures in heaven and on earth. Come close to us in the risen Christ, that we may always be close to you in prayer and praise, in witness and work. **Amen.**

PSALM 149

*Refrain:* **Sing to the Lord a new song.**

*Or, during Advent*

**Christ will come again to save those who wait for him.**

*Or, during Christmas, Epiphany, and Easter*

**Alleluia! Alleluia! Alleluia!**

*Or, during Lent*

**Let the faithful rejoice in their maker.**

*Psalm Prayer*

O God, you delight in the humble praise of your people. Receive the words of our mouths as songs, and the works of our hands as worship, that we may know your triumph in Jesus Christ our Savior. **Amen.**

*Or, during Advent*

Eternal God, let your people rejoice in you and acknowledge you as creator and redeemer. In your loving-kindness embrace us now, that we may proclaim the wonderful truths of salvation with your saints in glory; through your Son, Jesus Christ our Lord. **Amen.**

*Or, during Christmas and Epiphany*

O Christ, your coming floods the world with light, for you are Light of light, the very radiance of the Eternal One. Let everything that breathes praise you in song, for you are the image of the Father's glory rising upon our darkness from the Virgin's womb. O Lord, glory to you. **Amen.**

*Or, during Lent*

Almighty God, you place on the lowly your crown of victory. Accept our service in the name of Jesus Christ, that you may be praised and honored in the church, and proclaimed as Redeemer throughout the earth. **Amen.**

*Or, during Easter*

Your name be praised, great God, for the victory of Jesus Christ over the powers of death! May your praise be always on our lips, and your power always in our lives, that we may fearlessly follow our risen Lord. **Amen.**

PSALM 150

*Refrain:* **Alleluia! We praise our God!**

*Or*

**Praise the Lord, Alleluia!
Let all people praise the Lord.**

*Or, during Lent*

## Let everything that has breath praise the Lord!
*Psalm Prayer*
O good and gracious God, we praise you for our glorious redemption, purchased for us by your Son Christ Jesus. Give us your Holy Spirit, that all things that breathe with life may praise you as the true life of all, through Jesus Christ, who reigns with you and the Holy Spirit, one God forever. **Amen.**

*Or, during Advent, Christmas, and Epiphany*

O Christ, your coming floods the world with light, for you are Light of light, the very radiance of the Father. Let everything that breathes praise you in song, for you are the image of the Father's glory rising upon our darkness from the Virgin's womb. O Lord, glory to you. **Amen.**

*Or, during Lent*

You are worthy of all praise, mighty God. In your wisdom you created us, in Jesus Christ you came to redeem us, and through your Holy Spirit you guide and sanctify us. Let everything that breathes praise you as the true life of all creation. **Amen.**

*Or, during Easter and Pentecost*

Great and glorious God, you have redeemed us in Jesus Christ. By your Spirit, give us breath to sing of your majesty, and raise us to new life in Christ to honor you as followers of our risen Lord. **Amen.**

# BIBLICAL SONGS
# AND ANCIENT HYMNS: A LIST

In addition to the psalms, there are many other biblical texts that lend themselves to song. Biblical songs other than the psalms are called canticles. Ancient hymns such as the *Te Deum* are also called canticles. Any of the canticles for which texts are given (nos. 1–25), or which are listed below, may be used at any time, as provided in the daily services. It is traditional to sing the Song of Zechariah in the morning, the Song of Mary in the evening, and the Song of Simeon in Night Prayer, as suggested in the daily services. Other texts are provided as alternatives to the traditional canticles. A Song of Creation, A Song of Praise, and the *Te Deum* ("We Praise You, O God") are especially appropriate for use on Sundays and festivals. Canticles particularly suitable for various festivals and seasons are indicated below.

## ADVENT

### OLD TESTAMENT

Deut. 32:1–12
Isa. 2:2–5
Isa. 11:1–9
Isa. 12:2–6 (*Song of Thanksgiving*)
Isa. 25:6–9
Isa. 35:1–7ab, 10
Isa. 40:3–11
Isa. 42:10–16
Isa. 55:1–5
Isa. 55:6–11 (*Seek the Lord*)
Isa. 55:12–13
Isa. 60:1–3, 19–20 (*The New Jerusalem*)
Jer. 31:10–14
Micah 5:2–5a
Zeph. 3:14–18

### NEW TESTAMENT

Eph. 3:1–10
Phil. 2:5c–11 (*Jesus Christ Is Lord*)
Col. 1:15–20 (*Christ, the Head of All Creation*)
Rev. 15:3–4 (*Song of the Redeemed*)
Rev. 19:1b–2a, 5b, 6b–8
Rev. 22:12–13, 16–17, 20

### APOCRYPHA

Song of the Three Young Men 29–34 (*A Song of Praise*)
Song of the Three Young Men 35–65, 34 (*A Song of Creation*)

# CHRISTMAS

*We Praise You, O God*
*Glory to God*

### NEW TESTAMENT

John 1:1–5, 10–12, 14
Eph. 1:3–10
Phil. 2:5c–11 (*Jesus Christ Is Lord*)
Col. 1:15–20 (*Christ, the Head of All Creation*)

### APOCRYPHA

Song of the Three Young Men 29–34 (*A Song of Praise*)
Song of the Three Young Men 35–65, 34 (*A Song of Creation*)

# EPIPHANY

*We Praise You, O God*
*Glory to God*

### OLD TESTAMENT

Isa. 40:9–11
Isa. 60:4–9
Isa. 60:1–3, 19–20 (*The New Jerusalem*)

### NEW TESTAMENT

Phil. 2:5c–11 (*Jesus Christ Is Lord*)
Col. 1:15–20 (*Christ, the Head of All Creation*)
1 Tim. 3:16b
Rev. 15:3–4 (*Song of the Redeemed*)

# BAPTISM OF THE LORD

### OLD TESTAMENT

Isa. 11:1–5
Isa. 42:1–8

### NEW TESTAMENT

Rom. 6:3–5

# LENT

### OLD TESTAMENT

Isa. 38:10–20
Isa. 53:1–6
Isa. 53:6–12
Isa. 55:1–5
Isa. 55:6–11 (*Seek the Lord*)
Jer. 31:31–34
Ezek. 36:24–28

### NEW TESTAMENT

Matt. 5:3–12 (*The Beatitudes*)
Phil. 2:5c–11 (*Jesus Christ Is Lord*)
1 Peter 2:21–25 (*Christ the Servant*)
Rev. 15:3–4 (*Song of the Redeemed*)

### APOCRYPHA

Prayer of Manasseh 1–2, 4, 6–7, 11–15 (*A Song of Penitence*)

## MAUNDY THURSDAY

NEW TESTAMENT

John 15:4–5, 9–10, 12–14

## GOOD FRIDAY

OLD TESTAMENT

Hab. 3:2–4, 13a, 15–19

NEW TESTAMENT

Phil. 2:5c–11 (*Jesus Christ Is Lord*)

## HOLY SATURDAY

OLD TESTAMENT

Isa. 38:10–14, 17–20

NEW TESTAMENT

Phil. 2:5c–11 (*Jesus Christ Is Lord*)

## EASTER

*We Praise You, O God*
*Glory to God*

OLD TESTAMENT

Ex. 15:1–6, 11–13, 17–18 (*Song of Miriam and Moses*)
1 Sam. 2:1–10
1 Chron. 29:10–13 (*Song of David*)
Isa. 12:2–6 (*Song of Thanksgiving*)
Isa. 38:10–14, 17–20
Isa. 42:10–16
Isa. 66:10–14a
Jer. 31:10–14
Hos. 6:1–3

NEW TESTAMENT

1 Cor. 5:7–8; Rom. 6:9–11; 1 Cor. 15:20–22 (*Christ Our Passover*)
2 Cor. 4:6–11, 14
Eph. 1:3–10

Phil. 2:5c–11 (*Jesus Christ Is Lord*)
Col. 1:15–20 (*Christ, the Head of All Creation*)
1 Peter 1:3–4, 18–21
1 Peter 2:4–10
Rev. 4:11; 5:9–10, 13 (*A Song to the Lamb*)
Rev. 5:9–10, 12, 13b (*Worthy Is the Lamb*)
Rev. 11:17–18; 12:10b–12a
Rev. 15:3–4 (*Song of the Redeemed*)
Rev. 19:1b–2a, 5b, 6b–8

APOCRYPHA

Judith 16:13–17
Song of the Three Young Men 29–34 (*A Song of Praise*)
Song of the Three Young Men 35–65, 34 (*A Song of Creation*)

## ASCENSION (those for Easter, and the following:)

OLD TESTAMENT

Isa. 42:10–13

NEW TESTAMENT

1 Tim. 3:16
Rev. 11:17–18; 12:10b–12a

## PENTECOST

*We Praise You, O God*
*Glory to God*

OLD TESTAMENT

Ex. 15:1–6, 11–13, 17–18 (*Song of Miriam and Moses*)
Isa. 61:1–4, 8–11
Ezek. 36:24–28

NEW TESTAMENT

Rev. 15:3–4 (*Song of the Redeemed*)

BOTH TESTAMENTS

Joel 2:28; John 14:16; 16:13a; 14:26; Acts 2:2, 4a; Rom. 8:26 (*A Song for Pentecost*)

## TRINITY SUNDAY

NEW TESTAMENT

Eph. 1:3–10
Rev. 4:8, 11 (*Holy, Holy, Holy Is the Lord*)
Rev. 15:3–4 (*Song of the Redeemed*)

## ALL SAINTS' DAY

NEW TESTAMENT

Rev. 1:8, 17c–18; 2 Tim. 2:11–13; Rom. 8:17
Rev. 2:8b, 7b, 10c, 17bc, 26; 3:5, 7b, 12, 21, 14b

## CHRIST THE KING

NEW TESTAMENT

Rev. 4:11; 5:9–10, 13 (*A Song to the Lamb*)

# OTHER CANTICLES FOR GENERAL USE

### OLD TESTAMENT

Deut. 12:1–12
1 Sam. 2:1b–10
1 Chron. 29:10–13 (*Song of David*)
Isa. 26:1b–4, 7–8, 12
Isa. 40:10–17
Isa. 40:28–31
Isa. 41:17–20
Isa. 45:5–8, 18, 21–25
Isa. 61:10–62:5
Isa. 66:10–14a
Jer. 14:17–21
Jonah 2:2–9

### NEW TESTAMENT

Matt. 5:3–10
Luke 1:46–55 (*Song of Mary*)
Luke 1:68–79 (*Song of Zechariah*)
Luke 2:29–32 (*Song of Simeon*)
Rom. 8:28, 31–35, 37–39
1 Tim. 3:16; 4:10; 1:17
1 John 4:7–8; 1 Cor. 13:4–10, 12–13
   (*A Song of Love*)
Rev. 5:9–10, 12, 13b (*Worthy Is the Lamb*)
Rev. 19:1b–2a, 5b, 6b–8

### APOCRYPHA

Song of the Three Young Men 29–34 (*A Song of Praise*)
Song of the Three Young Men 35–65, 34 (*A Song of Creation*)
Judith 16:13–17
Wisdom 9:1–6, 9–11

# BIBLICAL SONGS
# AND ANCIENT HYMNS: TEXTS

## SONG OF ZECHARIAH
*Benedictus*

**1**

Blessed are you, Lord, the God of Israel,
you have come to your people and set them free.
You have raised up for us a mighty Savior
born of the house of your servant David.*

Through your holy prophets, you promised of old
to save us from our enemies,
from the hands of all who hate us,
to show mercy to our forebears,
and to remember your holy covenant.*

This was the oath you swore to our father Abraham:
to set us free from the hands of our enemies,
free to worship you without fear,
holy and righteous before you,
all the days of our life.*

And you, child, shall be called the prophet of the Most High,
for you will go before the Lord to prepare the way,
to give God's people knowledge of salvation
by the forgiveness of their sins.*

In the tender compassion of our God
the dawn from on high shall break upon us,
to shine on those who dwell in darkness and the shadow of death,
and to guide our feet into the way of peace.*      *Luke 1:68–79*

*Refrain:* **You have come to your people and set them free.**

*Or*

**In the tender compassion of our God
the dawn from on high shall break upon us.**

*For Advent*

**The Lord proclaims:**
**Repent, the kingdom of God is upon you. Alleluia!**

*For Christmas–Epiphany*

**You have raised up for us a mighty Savior,**
**born of the house of David. Alleluia!**

*For Lent*

**God has given us knowledge of salvation**
**by the forgiveness of our sins.**

*For Easter*

**The Lord, the God of Israel, has set us free. Alleluia!**

## SONG OF MARY
### *Magnificat*

2

My soul proclaims the greatness of the Lord,
my spirit rejoices in God my Savior,
for you, Lord, have looked with favor on your lowly servant.*

From this day all generations will call me blessed:
you, the Almighty, have done great things for me
and holy is your name.
You have mercy on those who fear you,
from generation to generation.*

You have shown strength with your arm
and scattered the proud in their conceit,
casting down the mighty from their thrones
and lifting up the lowly.
You have filled the hungry with good things
and sent the rich away empty.*

You have come to the aid of your servant Israel,
to remember the promise of mercy,

the promise made to our forebears,
to Abraham and his children for ever.*                    *Luke 1:46–55*

*Refrain:* **You have done great things for me,**
**and holy is your name.**

> *Or*

**My spirit rejoices in God my Savior.**

> *Or*

**You have come to the aid of your servant Israel,**
**to remember the promise of mercy.**

> *For Advent*

**Fear not, Mary, you have found favor with the Lord;**
**Behold, you shall conceive and bear a Son. Alleluia!**

*The traditional refrains for December 17–23 are incorporated in a litany
(no. 45). These refrains are the basis for the well-known Advent hymn
"O Come, O Come, Emmanuel." Since the Middle Ages, they have been
used on the following days:*

| | | | |
|---|---|---|---|
| *Dec. 17* | *"O Wisdom . . ."* | *Dec. 21* | *"O Radiant Dawn . . ."* |
| *Dec. 18* | *"O Adonai . . ."* | *Dec. 22* | *"O Ruler . . ."* |
| *Dec. 19* | *"O Root . . ."* | *Dec. 23* | *"O Emmanuel . . ."* |
| *Dec. 20* | *"O Key . . ."* | | |

> *For Christmas–Epiphany*

**The Word was made flesh and dwelt among us,**
**and we beheld his glory. Alleluia!**                    *John 1:14*

> *For Lent*

**Let justice roll down like waters,**
**and righteousness like an ever-flowing stream.**
                                        *Amos 5:24*

*For Easter*

**This is the day the Lord has made. Alleluia!**
**Let us rejoice and be glad in it.**                  *Ps. 118:24*

### SONG OF SIMEON
*Nunc Dimittis*

3

*Now, Lord, you let your servant go in peace:
your word has been fulfilled.
My own eyes have seen the salvation
which you have prepared in the sight of every people:
a light to reveal you to the nations
and the glory of your people Israel.*                  *Luke 2:29–32*

*Refrain for use with Night Prayer (before and after the Song of Simeon):*

**Guide us waking, O Lord,**
**and guard us sleeping;**
**that awake we may watch with Christ,**
**and asleep rest in his peace.**

### HYMN OF LIGHT
*Phos Hilaron*

4

O radiant Light, O Sun divine,
of God the Father's deathless face,
O image of the Light sublime,
that fills the heavenly dwelling place.

O Son of God, the source of life,
praise is your due by night and day.
Our happy lips must raise the strain
of your esteemed and splendid name.

Lord Jesus Christ, as daylight fades,
as shine the lights of eventide,
we praise the Father with the Son,
the Spirit blest and with them one.

*This ancient hymn is found in many hymnals as "O Gladsome Light."*

# WE PRAISE YOU, O GOD
*Te Deum Laudamus*

**5**

We praise you, O God,
we acclaim you as Lord;
all creation worships you,
the Father everlasting.
To you all angels, all the powers of heaven,
the cherubim and seraphim, sing in endless praise:
Holy, holy, holy Lord, God of power and might,
heaven and earth are full of your glory.
The glorious company of apostles praise you.
The noble fellowship of prophets praise you.
The white-robed army of martyrs praise you.
Throughout the world the holy church acclaims you:
Father, of majesty unbounded,
your true and only Son, worthy of all praise,
the Holy Spirit, advocate and guide.

You, Christ, are the king of glory,
the eternal Son of the Father.
When you took our flesh to set us free
you humbly chose the Virgin's womb.
You overcame the sting of death
and opened the kingdom of heaven to all believers.
You are seated at God's right hand in glory.
We believe that you will come, and be our judge.
Come then, Lord, and help your people,
bought with the price of your own blood,
and bring us with your saints
to glory everlasting.

*Versicles and Responses after the Te Deum:*

Save your people, Lord, and bless your inheritance.

**Govern and uphold them now and always.**

Day by day we bless you.

**We praise your name forever.**

Keep us today, Lord, from all sin.

**Have mercy on us, Lord, have mercy,**

Lord, show us your love and mercy;

**for we have put our trust in you.**

In you, Lord, is our hope:

**let us never be put to shame.**

*A metrical setting of the Te Deum is found in many hymnals: "Holy God, We Praise Your Name."*

### GLORY TO GOD
*Gloria in Excelsis*

6

Glory to God in the highest,
and peace to God's people on earth.

Lord God, heavenly King,
almighty God and Father,
we worship you, we give you thanks,
we praise you for your glory.

Lord Jesus Christ, only Son of the Father,
Lord God, Lamb of God,
you take away the sin of the world:
have mercy on us;
you are seated at the right hand of the Father:
receive our prayer.

For you alone are the Holy One,
you alone are the Lord,
you alone are the Most High,
Jesus Christ,
with the Holy Spirit,
in the glory of God the Father.

I will sing to the Lord, so lofty and uplifted;
the horse and its rider have been hurled into the sea.
The Lord is my strength and my refuge;
the Lord has become my Savior.*

This is my God whom I will praise,
the God of my people whom I will exalt.
The Lord is a mighty warrior;
whose name is Yahweh.*

The chariots of Pharaoh and his army
have been hurled into the sea;
the finest of those who bear armor
have been drowned in the Red Sea.
The fathomless deep has overwhelmed them;
they sank into the depths like a stone.*

Your right hand, O Lord, is glorious in might;
your right hand, O Lord, has overthrown the enemy.
Who can be compared with you, O Lord, among the gods?
who is like you, glorious in holiness,
awesome in renown, and worker of wonders?*

You stretched forth your right hand;
the earth swallowed them up.
With your constant love you led the people you redeemed;
with your might you brought them in safety to your holy dwelling.*

You will bring them in and plant them
on the mount of your possession,
the resting place you have made for yourself, O Lord,
the sanctuary, O Lord, that your hand has established.
The Lord shall reign
for ever and ever.*                                   *Ex. 15:1–6, 11–13, 17–18*

*Refrain:* **I will sing to the Lord;**
          **the Lord has risen up in might.**

## SONG OF THANKSGIVING
### First Song of Isaiah

**8**

Surely, it is God who saves me;
ever trusting I will not be afraid.
For the Lord is my stronghold and my sure defense,
and God will be my Savior.*

Therefore you shall draw water with rejoicing
from the springs of salvation.
And on that day you shall say,
Give thanks to the Lord and call upon that holy Name.*

Make the Lord's deeds known among the peoples;
see that they remember and that God's name is exalted.
Sing the praises of the Lord, who has done great things;
this is known in all the world.*

Cry aloud, inhabitants of Zion,
ring out your joy,
for the great one in the midst of you
is the Holy One of Israel.*

*Isa. 12:2–6*

*Refrain:* **Sing the praises of the Lord, who has done great things.**


## SEEK THE LORD
### Second Song of Isaiah

**9**

Seek the Lord while the Lord may be found;
call upon God, while God is near.
Let the wicked forsake their ways
and the unrighteous their thoughts;
and let them return to the Lord, who will have compassion,
and to our God, who will abundantly pardon.*

For my thoughts are not your thoughts,
nor your ways my ways, says the Lord.
For as the heavens are higher than the earth,
so are my ways higher than your ways,
and my thoughts than your thoughts.*

For as rain and snow fall from the heavens,
and return not again, but water the earth,

bringing forth life and giving growth,
seed for sowing and bread for eating,
so is my word that goes forth from my mouth;
it will not return to me empty;
but it will accomplish that which I have purposed,
and prosper in that for which I sent it.*    *Isa. 55:6–11*

*Refrain:* **You are full of compassion and mercy, O Lord,
for you will abundantly pardon.**

### THE NEW JERUSALEM
Third Song of Isaiah

**10**

Arise, shine, for your light has come,
and the glory of the Lord has dawned upon you.
For behold, darkness covers the land;
deep gloom enshrouds the peoples.*

But over you the Lord will rise,
and the splendor of God will appear upon you.
Nations will stream to your light,
and rulers to the brightness of your dawning.*

Your gates will always be open;
by day or night they will never be shut.
They will call you, The City of the Lord,
The Zion of the Holy One of Israel.*

Violence will no more be heard in your land,
ruin or destruction within your borders.
You will name your walls, Salvation,
and all your portals, Praise.*

The sun will no more be your light by day;
by night you will not need the brightness of the moon.
The Lord will be your everlasting light;
and your God will be your glory.*    *Isa. 60:1–3, 11a, 14c, 18–19*

*Refrain:* **Zion, sing, break into song!
For within you is the Lord with saving power.**

All you works of the Lord, bless the Lord!
The Lord be exalted above all, and praised forevermore!

Bless the Lord, angels and all the hosts of the Lord!
O heavens and all waters above the heavens, bless the Lord!
The Lord be exalted above all, and praised forevermore!

Bless the Lord, sun and moon and stars of the sky!
Every shower of rain and fall of dew, bless the Lord!
The Lord be exalted above all, and praised forevermore!

Bless the Lord, every breeze and gusting wind!
Each drop of dew and flake of snow, bless the Lord!
The Lord be exalted above all, and praised forevermore!

Bless the Lord, fire and heat, cold and chill!
Nights and days, light and darkness, bless the Lord!
The Lord be exalted above all, and praised forevermore!

Bless the Lord, frost and cold, ice and sleet!
Thunderclouds and lightning flashes, bless the Lord!
The Lord be exalted above all, and praised forevermore!

Bless the Lord, O Earth!
Mountains and hills, and all that grows from the earth, bless the
    Lord!
The Lord be exalted above all, and praised forevermore!

Bless the Lord, O springs of water, seas and rivers!
Whales and all that swim in the depths of the seas, bless the Lord!
The Lord be exalted above all, and praised forevermore!

Bless the Lord, all birds of the air!
Beasts of the wild, flocks and herds, bless the Lord!
The Lord be exalted above all, and praised forevermore!

Bless the Lord, men and women, children and youth!
All people everywhere, bless the Lord!
The Lord be exalted above all, and praised forevermore!

Bless the Lord, people of God!
Priests and all who serve the Lord, bless the Lord!
The Lord be exalted above all, and praised forevermore!

Bless the Lord, all who are upright in spirit!
All who are holy and humble of heart, bless the Lord!
   The Lord be exalted above all, and praised forevermore!

Praise the Lord: Father, Son, and Holy Spirit!
Blessed are you, O Lord, in the vast expanse of heaven!
   The Lord be exalted above all, and praised forevermore!
                    *Song of the Three Young Men 35–65, 34*


## A SONG OF PRAISE
12

Glory to you, Lord God of those before us;
   you are worthy of praise; glory to you.
Glory to you for the radiance of your holy name;
   we will praise you and highly exalt you forever.

Glory to you in the splendor of your temple;
   on the throne of your majesty, glory to you.
Glory to you, seated between the cherubim;
   we will praise you and highly exalt you forever.

Glory to you, beholding the depths;
   in the high vault of heaven, glory to you.
Glory to you, Father, Son, and Holy Spirit;
   we will praise you and highly exalt you forever.
                    *Song of the Three Young Men 29–34*


## A SONG OF PENITENCE
13

O Lord and Ruler of the hosts of heaven,
God of Abraham, Isaac, and Jacob,
and of all their righteous offspring;
You made the heavens and the earth,
with all their vast array.
All things quake with fear at your presence;
they tremble because of your power.
But your merciful promise is beyond all measure;
it surpasses all that our minds can fathom.*

O Lord, you are full of compassion,
most patient, and abounding in mercy.
You hold back your hand;
you do not punish as we deserve.
In your great goodness, Lord,
you have promised forgiveness to sinners,
that they may repent of their sin and be saved.*

And now, O Lord, I bend the knee of my heart,
and make my appeal, sure of your gracious goodness.
I have sinned, O Lord, I have sinned,
and I know my wickedness all too well.
Therefore I make my prayer to you:
Forgive me, Lord, forgive me.
Do not let me perish in my sin,
nor condemn me to the depths of the earth.*

For you, O Lord, are the God of those who repent,
and in me you will show forth your goodness.
Unworthy as I am, you will save me,
in accordance with your great mercy,
and I will praise you without ceasing all the days of my life.
For all the powers of heaven sing your praises,
and yours is the glory to ages of ages. Amen.*

*Prayer of Manasseh 1–2, 4, 6–7, 11–15*

*Refrain:* **O Lord, you are full of compassion,
long-suffering, and abounding in mercy.**


## Song of David

**14**

Blessed are you, O Lord,
God of Israel our father,
from eternity to eternity.

Yours, O Lord, are grandeur and power,
majesty, splendor, and glory.

For all in the heavens and on the earth is yours;
yours, O Lord, is the sovereignty.
You are exalted as head above all.

Riches and honor come from you,
and you rule over all.
In your hand are power and might;
it is yours to make great and to give strength to all.

And now we thank you, our God,
and praise your glorious name.                    *1 Chron. 29:10–13*

## A Song to the Lamb
**15**

Splendor and honor and sovereign power
are yours by right, O Lord our God,
For you created everything that is,
and by your will they were created and have their being;*

They are yours by right, O Lamb that was slain,
for with your blood you have redeemed for God,
From every family, language, and nation,
a dominion of priests to serve our God.*

And so, to God who sits upon the throne,
and to Christ the Lamb,
be worship and praise, dominion and splendor,
forever and forevermore.*                    *Rev. 4:11; 5:9–10, 13*

*Refrain:* **Worthy is the Lamb that was slain**
**to receive glory and honor.**

## Song of the Redeemed
**16**

O Ruler of the universe, Lord God,
great deeds are they that you have done,
surpassing human understanding.
Your ways are ways of righteousness and truth,
O Sovereign of all the ages.*

Who can fail to do you homage, Lord,
and sing the praises of your name?
for you only are the Holy One.

All nations will draw near and fall down before you,
because your just and holy works have been revealed.*

Rev. 15:3–4

*Refrain: **Your ways are ways of righteousness and truth,**
        **O Sovereign of all the ages.**

## A Song for Pentecost

**17**

I will pray the Father,
who will give you another Counselor,
to be with you forever.
The Spirit of truth, having come,
will guide you into all truth.*

The Counselor, the Holy Spirit,
whom the Father will send in my name,
will teach you all things,
and bring to remembrance
all that I have said to you.*

And suddenly a sound came from heaven
like the rush of a mighty wind,
and it filled all the house where they were sitting,
and they were all filled with the Holy Spirit.*

The Spirit helps us in our weakness;
for we do not know how we ought to pray,
but the Spirit pleads for us
with sighs too deep for words.*     *John 14:16; 16:13a; 14:26;*
Acts 2:2, 4a; Rom. 8:26

*Refrain: **I will pour out my Spirit on all flesh.**
        **Your sons and your daughters shall prophesy,**
        **your old shall dream dreams**
        **and your young shall see visions.**     *Joel 2:28*

**18**

Beloved, let us love one another,
for love is of God.
All who love are born of God and know God;
all who do not love do not know God.*

Love does not insist on its own way,
is not quick to take offense;
it does not rejoice at wrong, but rejoices in the right.*

Love is patient and kind;
love is not jealous or boastful;
it is not arrogant or rude.
Love bears all things and believes all things.
Love hopes and endures all things.
Love will never come to an end.*

Prophecies will vanish; tongues will cease;
and knowledge will pass away.
For our knowledge and our prophecy are imperfect,
but when the perfect comes, the imperfect will pass away.*

Now I know in part,
then I shall understand fully,
even as I have been fully understood.

There are three things that last forever: faith, hope, and love;
but the greatest of these is love.*

*1 John 4:7–8; 1 Cor. 13:4–10, 12–13*

*Refrain:* **Faith, hope, and love abide,**
**but the greatest of these is love.**

## CHRIST, THE HEAD OF ALL CREATION

**19**

Christ is the image of the invisible God,
the first-born of all creation.
In him all things in heaven and on earth were created,
things visible and invisible.*

All things were created through him and for him.
Christ is before all things,
the one in whom all things hold together.*

Christ is head of the body, the church;
he is the beginning, the first-born of the dead,
so that he may be first in everything.*

In Christ all the fullness of God was pleased to dwell,
and, through Christ to reconcile all things,
whether on earth or in heaven,
making peace by the blood of his cross.*                    *Col. 1:15–20*

*Refrain:* **Glory to you, the first-born of the dead!**

### JESUS CHRIST IS LORD
20

Christ Jesus,
though he was in the form of God,
did not count equality with God
a thing to be grasped,
but emptied himself,
taking the form of a servant,
being born in human likeness.

And being found in human form,
he humbled himself,
and became obedient unto death,
even death on a cross.

Therefore God has highly exalted him
and bestowed on him the name which is above all names,
that at the name of Jesus
every knee should bow—
in heaven, on earth, and under the earth—
and every tongue confess to the glory of God:
Jesus Christ is Lord!                                    *Phil. 2:5c–11*

**21**

Blessed are the poor in spirit,
for theirs is the dominion of heaven.

Blessed are those who mourn,
for they shall be comforted.

Blessed are the meek,
for they shall inherit the earth.

Blessed are those who hunger and thirst for righteousness,
for they shall be satisfied.

Blessed are the merciful,
for they shall obtain mercy.

Blessed are the pure in heart,
for they shall see God.

Blessed are the peacemakers,
for they shall be called children of God.

Blessed are those who are persecuted for righteousness' sake,
for theirs is the dominion of heaven.

Blessed are you when you are reviled and persecuted
and all kinds of evil are uttered against you on my account.

Rejoice and be glad,
for your reward is great in heaven.                    *Matt. 5:3–12*

## CHRIST THE SERVANT

**22**

Jesus Christ suffered for you, leaving you an example:
that you should follow in his steps.
Christ committed no sin, no guile was found on his lips.
When reviled, he did not revile in return;
when suffering, he did not threaten;
but he trusted the One who judges justly.*

Christ bore our sins in his body on the tree,
that we might die to sin and live to righteousness.
By his wounds you have been healed.

For you were straying like sheep,
but have now returned
to the Shepherd and Guardian of your souls.*        *1 Peter 2:21–25*

*Refrain:* **By his wounds we are healed.**

## CHRIST OUR PASSOVER
23

Alleluia!
Christ our Passover has been sacrificed for us;
therefore let us keep the feast,
not with the old leaven, the leaven of malice and evil,
but with the unleavened bread of sincerity and truth. Alleluia!

Christ being raised from the dead will never die again;
death no longer has dominion over him.
The death that he died, he died to sin, once for all;
but the life he lives, he lives to God.
So also consider yourselves dead to sin
and alive to God in Jesus Christ our Lord. Alleluia!

Christ has been raised from death,
the first fruits of those who have fallen asleep.
For since by one human came death,
by one human has come also the resurrection of the dead.
For as in Adam all die,
so also in Christ shall all be made alive. Alleluia!
                    *1 Cor. 5:7–8; Rom. 6:9–11; 1 Cor. 15:20–22*

## HOLY, HOLY, HOLY IS THE LORD
24

Holy, holy, holy is the Lord God Almighty,
who was, who is, and who is to come!

You are worthy, our Lord and God,
to receive glory, honor, and power.
For you created all things,
and by your will they were given existence and life.    *Rev. 4:8, 11*

**25**

You are worthy to take the scroll
and to break open its seals.
For you were slain,
and by your blood you bought for God
people from every tribe, race, language, and nation.
You made them a kingdom of priests to serve our God,
and they shall rule on earth.

Worthy is the Lamb,
the Lamb who was slain,
to receive power and wealth,
wisdom and strength,
honor and glory and praise!

To him who sits on the throne and to the Lamb,
be praise and honor, glory and might,
forever and ever!                     *Rev. 5:9–10, 12, 13b*

# PRAYERS OF THANKSGIVING
# AND INTERCESSION

*After each of the following prayers (26–72) there may be silent prayer.
The prayers conclude with the appointed petition in the daily services
(or a similar prayer) and the Lord's Prayer.*

**26**

**SUNDAY/Morning Prayer**

Mighty God of mercy, we thank you for the resurrection dawn bringing the glory of our risen Lord who makes every day new. Especially
we thank you for
    the beauty of your creation . . .
    the new creation in Christ and all gifts of healing and forgiveness . . .
    the sustaining love of family and friends . . .
    the fellowship of faith in your church. . . .
Merciful God of might, renew this weary world, heal the hurts of all
your children, and bring about your peace for all in Christ Jesus, the
living Lord. Especially we pray for
    those who govern nations of the world . . .
    the people of countries where there is strife or warfare . . .
    all who work for peace and international harmony . . .
    the church of Jesus Christ in every land. . . .

    *Silent prayer—Concluding petition—The Lord's Prayer*

**27**

**SUNDAY/Evening Prayer**

We lift our voices in prayers of praise, great God, for you have lifted
us to new life in Jesus Christ, and your blessings come in generous
measure. Especially we thank you for
    the privilege of worship and service in this congregation . . .
    the good news of the gospel of Jesus Christ for us . . .
    food and drink to share in the Lord's name . . .
    our calling to discipleship. . . .
We hold up before you human needs, God of compassion, for you
have come to us in Jesus Christ and shared our life so we may share

his resurrection. Especially we pray for
　the healing of those who are sick . . .
　the comfort of the dying . . .
　the renewal of those who despair . . .
　the Spirit's power in the church. . . .

*Silent prayer—Concluding petition—The Lord's Prayer*

## 28

### MONDAY/Morning Prayer

We praise you, God our creator, for your handiwork in shaping and
sustaining your wondrous creation. Especially we thank you for
　the miracle of life and the wonder of living . . .
　particular blessings coming to us in this day . . .
　the resources of the earth . . .
　gifts of creative vision and skillful craft . . .
　the treasure stored in every human life. . . .
We dare to pray for others, God our Savior, claiming your love in
Jesus Christ for the whole world, committing ourselves to care for
those around us in his name. Especially we pray for
　those who work for the benefit of others . . .
　those who cannot work today . . .
　those who teach and those who learn . . .
　people who are poor . . .
　the church in Europe. . . .

*Silent prayer—Concluding petition—The Lord's Prayer*

## 29

### MONDAY/Evening Prayer

We rejoice in your generous goodness, O God, and celebrate your
lavish gifts to us this day, for you have shown your love in giving
Jesus Christ for the salvation of the world. Especially we give thanks
for
　the labors of those who have served us today . . .
　friends with whom we have shared . . .
　those whom we love and have loved us . . .

opportunities for our work to help others . . .
all beauty that delights us. . . .
Gracious God, we know you are close to all in need, and by our
prayers for others we come closer to you. We are bold to claim for
others your promises of new life in Jesus Christ, as we claim them
for ourselves. Especially we pray for
those in dangerous occupations . . .
physicians and nurses . . .
those who are ill or confined to nursing homes . . .
those who mourn . . .
the Roman Catholic Church. . . .

*Silent prayer—Concluding petition—The Lord's Prayer*

## 30

**TUESDAY/Morning Prayer**

Eternal God, we rejoice this morning in the gift of life, which we have
received by your grace, and the new life you give in Jesus Christ.
Especially we thank you for
the love of our families . . .
the affection of our friends . . .
strength and abilities to serve your purpose today . . .
this community in which we live . . .
opportunities to give as we have received. . . .
God of grace, we offer our prayers for the needs of others and
commit ourselves to serve them even as we have been served in Jesus
Christ. Especially we pray for
those closest to us, families, friends, neighbors . . .
refugees and homeless men, women and children . . .
the outcast and persecuted . . .
those from whom we are estranged . . .
the church in Africa. . . .

*Silent prayer—Concluding petition—The Lord's Prayer*

## 31

**TUESDAY/Evening Prayer**

Generous God, we thank you for being with us today,
and for every sign of your truth and love in Jesus Christ.

*Prayers of Thanksgiving and Intercession 281*

Especially we thank you for
  the gift of peace in Christ . . .
  reconciliation in our relationships . . .
  each new insight into your love . . .
  energy and courage to share your love . . .
  the ministries of the church. . . .
Gracious God, we remember in our own hearts the needs of others,
that we may reach up to claim your love for them, and reach out to
give your love in the name of Christ. Especially we pray for
  racial harmony and justice . . .
  those imprisoned . . .
  strangers we have met today . . .
  friends who are bereaved . . .
  Orthodox and Coptic churches. . . .

  *Silent prayer—Concluding petition—The Lord's Prayer*


**32**

**WEDNESDAY/Morning Prayer**

God of all mercies, we praise you that you have brought us to this
new day, brightening our lives with the dawn of promise and hope
in Jesus Christ. Especially we thank you for
  the warmth of sunlight, the wetness of rain and snow, and all that
    nourishes the earth . . .
  the presence and power of your Spirit . . .
  the support and encouragement we receive from others . . .
  those who provide for public safety and well-being . . .
  the mission of your church around the world. . . .
Merciful God, strengthen us in prayer that we may lift up the broken-
ness of this world for your healing, and share in the saving love of
Jesus Christ. Especially we pray for
  those in positions of authority over others . . .
  the lonely and forgotten . . .
  children without families or homes . . .
  agents of caring and relief . . .
  the church in Asia and the Middle East. . . .

  *Silent prayer—Concluding petition—The Lord's Prayer*

**33**

## WEDNESDAY/Evening Prayer

Give us your peace, O God, that we may rejoice in your goodness to
us and to all your children, and be thankful for your love revealed in
Jesus Christ. Especially we thank you for
  people who reveal your truth and righteousness . . .
  courage to be bold disciples . . .
  those who show hospitality . . .
  surprises that have blessed us . . .
  the unity of the church of Jesus Christ. . . .
Give us your peace, O God, that we may be confident of your care
for us and all your children, as we remember the needs of others.
Especially we pray for
  friends and relatives who are far away . . .
  neighbors in special need . . .
  those who suffer hunger and thirst . . .
  those who work at night while others sleep . . .
  Episcopal and Methodist churches. . . .

  *Silent prayer—Concluding petition—Lord's Prayer*


**34**

## THURSDAY/Morning Prayer

Loving God, as the rising sun chases away the night, so you have
scattered the power of death in the rising of Jesus Christ, and you
bring us all blessings in him. Especially we thank you for
  the community of faith in our church . . .
  those with whom we work or share common concerns . . .
  the diversity of your children . . .
  indications of your love at work in the world . . .
  those who work for reconciliation. . . .
Mighty God, with the dawn of your love you reveal your victory
over all that would destroy or harm, and you brighten the lives of all
who need you. Especially we pray for
  families suffering separation . . .
  people different from ourselves . . .
  those isolated by sickness or sorrow . . .

the victims of violence or warfare . . .
the church in the Pacific region. . . .

*Silent prayer—Concluding petition—The Lord's Prayer*

## 35

### THURSDAY/Evening Prayer

We give you our praise and thanks, O God, for all gifts of love we have received from you, and for your persistent mercy in Jesus Christ. Especially we thank you for
work we have accomplished pleasing to you . . .
the faithful witness of Christian people . . .
the example of righteousness we see in parents and teachers . . .
the innocence and openness we see in children . . .
all works of Christian compassion. . . .
We give you our cares and concerns, O God, because we know you are kind and care for your children in every circumstance. Especially we pray for
those who struggle with doubt and despair . . .
people afflicted with disease . . .
those called to special ministries . . .
people neglected or abused . . .
Baptist and other free churches. . . .

*Silent prayer—Concluding petition—The Lord's Prayer*

## 36

### FRIDAY/Morning Prayer

Eternal God, we praise you for your mighty love given in Christ's sacrifice on the cross, and the new life we have received by his resurrection. Especially we thank you for
the presence of Christ in our weakness and suffering . . .
the ministry of Word and Sacrament . . .
all who work to help and heal . . .
sacrifices made for our benefit . . .
opportunities for our generous giving. . . .
God of grace, let our concern for others reflect something of Christ's self-giving love, not only in our prayers, but in our practice as well.

Especially we pray for
　those subjected to tyranny and oppression . . .
　wounded and injured people . . .
　those who face death . . .
　those who may be our enemies . . .
　the church in Latin America. . . .

*Silent prayer—Concluding petition—The Lord's Prayer*

## 37

### FRIDAY/Evening Prayer

Merciful God, we praise you that you give strength for every weakness, forgiveness for our failures, and new beginnings in Jesus Christ. Especially we thank you for
　the guidance of your Spirit through this day . . .
　signs of new life and hope . . .
　people who have helped us . . .
　those who struggle for justice . . .
　expressions of love unexpected or undeserved. . . .
Almighty God, you know all needs before we speak our prayers, yet you welcome our concerns for others in Jesus Christ. Especially we pray for
　those who keep watch over the sick and dying . . .
　those who weep with the grieving . . .
　those who are without faith and cannot accept your love . . .
　those who grow old . . .
　Reformed, Presbyterian, and Lutheran churches. . . .

*Silent prayer—Concluding petition—The Lord's Prayer*

## 38

### SATURDAY/Morning Prayer

Great and wonderful God, we praise and thank you for the gift of renewal in Jesus Christ. Especially we thank you for
　opportunities for rest and recreation . . .
　the regenerating gifts of the Holy Spirit . . .
　activities shared by young and old . . .
　fun and laughter . . .

every service that proclaims your love. . . .

You make all things new, O God, and we offer our prayers for the renewal of the whole world and the healing of its wounds. Especially we pray for

those who have no leisure . . .

people enslaved by addictions . . .

those who would entertain and enlighten . . .

those confronted with temptation . . .

the church in North America. . . .

*Silent prayer—Concluding petition—The Lord's Prayer*

## 39

### SATURDAY/Evening Prayer

God of glory, we praise you for your presence in our lives, and for all goodness that you shower upon your children in Jesus Christ. Especially we thank you for

promises kept and hope for tomorrow . . .

the enjoyment of friends . . .

the wonders of your creation . . .

love from our parents, our sisters and brothers, our spouses and children . . .

pleasures of living. . . .

God of grace, we are one with all your children, for we are sisters and brothers of Jesus Christ, and we offer our prayers for all whom you love. Especially we pray for

those we too often forget . . .

people who have lost hope . . .

victims of tragedy and disaster . . .

those who suffer mental anguish . . .

ecumenical councils and church agencies. . . .

*Silent prayer—Concluding petition—The Lord's Prayer*

*This Litany is based on litanies from the Eastern liturgies of St. Basil and St. John Chrysostom. It may be sung using the following musical setting.*

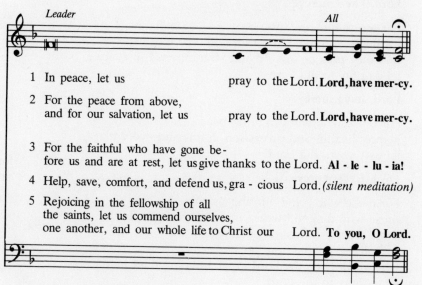

1  In peace, let us                    pray to the Lord. **Lord, have mer-cy.**

2  For the peace from above,
   and for our salvation, let us        pray to the Lord. **Lord, have mer-cy.**

3  For the faithful who have gone be-
   fore us and are at rest, let us give thanks to the Lord. **Al - le - lu - ia!**

4  Help, save, comfort, and defend us, gra - cious Lord. *(silent meditation)*

5  Rejoicing in the fellowship of all
   the saints, let us commend ourselves,
   one another, and our whole life to Christ our     Lord. **To you, O Lord.**

[1]In peace, let us pray to the Lord.

**Lord, have mercy.**

[2]For the peace from above,
and for our salvation,
let us pray to the Lord.

**Lord, have mercy.**

For the peace of the whole world,
for the well-being of the church of God,
and for the unity of all,
let us pray to the Lord.

**Lord, have mercy.**

For this holy house,
and for all who offer here their worship and praise,
let us pray to the Lord.

**Lord, have mercy.**

*Prayers of Thanksgiving and Intercession   287*

For _____ , for our *pastor(s)* in Christ,
for all servants of the church,
and for all the people,
let us pray to the Lord.

**Lord, have mercy.**

For our public servants,
for the government and those who protect us,
that they may be upheld and strengthened in every good deed,
let us pray to the Lord.

**Lord, have mercy.**

For those who work to bring peace,
justice, health, and protection in this and every place,
let us pray to the Lord.

**Lord, have mercy.**

For those who bring offerings,
those who do good works in this congregation,
those who toil, those who sing,
and all the people here present
who await from the Lord great and abundant mercy,
let us pray to the Lord.

**Lord, have mercy.**

For favorable weather,
for an abundance of the fruits of the earth,
and for peaceful times,
let us pray to the Lord.

**Lord, have mercy.**

For our deliverance from all affliction,
wrath, danger, and need,
let us pray to the Lord.

**Lord, have mercy.**

[3]For the faithful who have gone before us
and are at rest,
let us give thanks to the Lord.

**Alleluia!**

<sup>4</sup>Help, save, comfort, and defend us, gracious Lord.

*Silence for meditation*

<sup>5</sup>Rejoicing in the fellowship of all the saints,
let us commend ourselves,
one another,
and our whole life to Christ our Lord.

**To you, O Lord.**

O God, from whom come all holy desires,
all good counsels, and all just works.
Give to us, your servants,
that peace which the world cannot give,
that our hearts may be set to obey your commandments;
and also that we,
being defended from the fear of our enemies,
may live in peace and quietness;
through the merits of Jesus Christ our Savior,
who lives and reigns with you and the Holy Spirit,
God forever.

**Amen.**


## THE GREAT LITANY

41

*The Great Litany is appropriate for times of special petition or supplication. It may be sung or said. In daily prayer, there is a tradition that it be used as a separate service on all Wednesdays and Fridays of Lent beginning the Friday after Ash Wednesday until Palm Sunday. If the entire litany is not used, the Prayer of Approach to God and the Concluding Prayers are used, but a selection of appropriate petitions may be made from remaining sections.*


*Prayer of Approach to God*

O God the Father, creator of heaven and earth,

**Have mercy on us.**

O God the Son, redeemer of the world,

**Have mercy on us.**

O God the Holy Spirit, advocate and guide,

**Have mercy on us.**

Holy, blessed, and glorious Trinity,
three persons and one God,

**Have mercy on us.**

*Prayers for Deliverance*

Remember not, Lord Christ, our offenses,
nor the offenses of our forebears.
Spare us, good Lord,
spare your people whom you have redeemed with your precious
 blood.

**Spare us, good Lord.**

From all spiritual blindness;
from pride, vainglory, and hypocrisy;
from envy, hatred, and malice;
and from all want of charity,

**Good Lord, deliver us.**

From all deadly sin;
and from the deceits of the world,
the flesh, and the devil,

**Good Lord, deliver us.**

From all false doctrine, heresy, and schism;
from hardness of heart,
and contempt for your Word and commandments,

**Good Lord, deliver us.**

From earthquake and tempest;
from drought, fire, and flood;
from civil strife and violence;
from war and murder;
and from dying suddenly and unprepared,

**Good Lord, deliver us.**

By the mystery of your holy incarnation,
by your baptism, fasting, and temptation;
and by your proclamation of the kingdom,

**Good Lord, deliver us.**

By your bloody sweat and bitter grief;
by your cross and suffering;
and by your precious death and burial,

**Good Lord, deliver us.**

By your mighty resurrection;
by your glorious ascension;
and by the coming of the Holy Spirit,

**Good Lord, deliver us.**

In our times of trouble;
in our times of prosperity;
in the hour of death,
and on the day of judgment,

**Good Lord, deliver us.**

*Prayers of Intercession*

Receive our prayers, O Lord our God.

**Hear us, good Lord.**

*For the church*

Govern and direct your holy church;
fill it with love and truth;
and grant it that unity which is your will.

**Hear us, good Lord.**

Enlighten all ministers
with true knowledge and understanding of your Word,
that by their preaching and living
they may declare it clearly
and show its truth.

**Hear us, good Lord.**

Encourage and prosper your servants
who spread the gospel in all the world,
and send out laborers into the harvest.

**Hear us, good Lord.**

Bless and keep your people,
that all may find and follow their true vocation and ministry.

**Hear us, good Lord.**

Give us a heart to love and reverence you,
that we may diligently live according to your commandments.

**Hear us, good Lord.**

To all your people
give grace to hear and receive your Word,
and to bring forth the fruit of the Spirit.

**Hear us, good Lord.**

Strengthen those who stand firm in the faith,
encourage the fainthearted,
raise up those who fall,
and finally give us the victory.

**Hear us, good Lord.**


*For our country*

Rule the hearts of your servants,
the President of the United States (*or* of this nation),
and all others in authority,
that they may do justice, and love mercy,
and walk in the ways of truth.

**Hear us, good Lord.**

Bless and defend all who strive for our safety and protection,
and shield them in all dangers and adversities.

**Hear us, good Lord.**

Grant wisdom and insight to those who govern us,
and to judges and magistrates the grace to execute justice with
   mercy.

**Hear us, good Lord.**

*For all people*

To all nations grant unity, peace, and concord,
and to all people give dignity, food, and shelter.

**Hear us, good Lord.**

Grant us abundant harvests,
strength and skill to conserve the resources of the earth,
and wisdom to use them well.

**Hear us, good Lord.**

Enlighten with your Spirit all who teach
and all who learn.

**Hear us, good Lord.**

Come to the help of all who are in danger, necessity, and trouble;
protect all who travel by land, air, or water;
and show your pity on all prisoners and captives.

**Hear us, good Lord.**

Strengthen and preserve all women who are in childbirth,
and all young children,
and comfort the aged, the bereaved, and the lonely.

**Hear us, good Lord.**

Defend and provide for the widowed and the orphaned,
the refugees and the homeless,
the unemployed,
and all who are desolate and oppressed.

**Hear us, good Lord.**

Heal those who are sick in body or mind,
and give skill and compassion to all who care for them.

**Hear us, good Lord.**

Grant us true repentance,
forgive our sins,
and strengthen us by your Holy Spirit
to amend our lives according to your Holy Word.

**Hear us, good Lord.**

*Concluding Prayers*

Son of God, we ask you to hear us.

**Son of God, we ask you to hear us.**

Lamb of God, you take away the sin of the world,

**have mercy on us.**

Lamb of God, you take away the sin of the world,

**have mercy on us.**

Lamb of God, you take away the sin of the world,

**grant us peace.**

Lord, have mercy on us.

**Christ, have mercy on us.**

Lord, have mercy on us.

*The Lord's Prayer is said.*

*The Litany concludes with the following or some other collect.*

Let us pray.

Almighty God,
you have given us grace at this time with one accord
to make our common supplication to you;
and you have promised through your well-beloved Son
that when two or three are gathered together in his name
you will be in the midst of them.
Fulfill now, O Lord, our desires and petitions
as may be best for us;
granting us in this world knowledge of your truth,
and in the age to come life everlasting. **Amen.**

## 42

## ADVENT/Morning Prayer 1

God of the ages, we praise you, for in the dawn of time you created the world, sending light by your Word to dispel darkness. In Jesus Christ you began a new creation, sending him to be the Light of the world, to drive away fear and despair, and to rule in peace and justice, holiness and love. Especially we thank you for

the order and beauty of your creation . . .

coming in Jesus Christ to share our human life . . .

the place you give us in your continuing creation . . .

the promise of peace among nations, and justice for all peoples . . .

the church as the sign of your coming kingdom. . . .

Mighty God, prepare the world for your rule, for we long for the day when there shall be no more crying or tears, and death will be destroyed. Help us to share the ministry of Christ and be agents of his compassion. Especially we pray for

the nations of the earth and peace in the world . . .

victims of violence . . .

those who are sick and suffering . . .

our families and friends . . .

the church and those who serve in Christ's name. . . .

*Silent prayer—Concluding petition—The Lord's Prayer*

*Or*

## 43

## ADVENT/Morning Prayer 2

God of peace and justice,
come as the Ruler of our world,
so full of war.
Silence the shouts of hatred,
govern the nations with love.

**Come, Lord Jesus, and set us free.**

You alone are the key
that opens the door to joy.

You alone can lock up
all that threatens to ruin our lives.

**Come, Lord Jesus, and set us free.**

You are the Light of the world,
the dawning of a new day.
Turn the darkness of our despair
into the radiant brightness of your light.

**Come, Lord Jesus, and set us free.**

Come to enlighten our lives,
that all may see your goodness and give you glory.

**Come, Lord Jesus, and set us free.**

*Silent prayer—Concluding petition—The Lord's Prayer*

**44**

**ADVENT/Evening Prayer 1**

God of power and splendor, we praise you for your great gift in
sending Jesus Christ to be one with us. Keep us alert in this season
as we await with joyful hope our Savior's coming again, to be thank-
ful always for every blessing that announces your constant love.
Especially we thank you for
    the good news your church is to proclaim . . .
    blessings of love and kindness we have received . . .
    promises kept and signs of hope for the future . . .
    opportunities to show your love . . .
    those who act out the compassion of Christ. . . .
Ever-present God, you are always at work in the world to overcome
evil with good. As you have come to us in Jesus Christ, enable us to
go to others in ministries of caring and healing. Especially we pray for
    peacemakers in the councils of nations . . .
    the homes of those single or married . . .
    the poor and needy, the oppressed and outcast . . .
    those in mental or physical pain . . .
    those who grieve and mourn . . .
    Christ's church in particular need . . .
    and in this place. . . .

*Silent prayer—Concluding petition—The Lord's Prayer*

*Or*

**45**

**ADVENT/Evening Prayer 2**

O Wisdom,
coming forth from the mouth of the Most High,
pervading and permeating all creation,
you order all things with strength and gentleness:
come now and teach us the way to salvation.

**Come, Lord Jesus.**

O Adonai,
Ruler of the house of Israel,
you appeared in the burning bush to Moses
and gave him the Law on Sinai:
come with outstretched arm to save us.

**Come, Lord Jesus.**

O Root of Jesse,
rising as a sign for all the peoples,
before you earthly rulers will keep silent,
and nations give you honor:
come quickly to deliver us.

**Come, Lord Jesus.**

O Key of David,
Scepter over the house of Israel,
you open and no one can close,
you close and no one can open:
come to set free the prisoners
who live in darkness and the shadow of death.

**Come, Lord Jesus.**

O Radiant Dawn,
splendor of eternal light,
Sun of Justice:

come, shine on those who live in darkness
and in the shadow of death.

**Come, Lord Jesus.**

O Ruler of the nations,
Monarch for whom the people long,
you are the Cornerstone uniting all humanity:
come, save us all,
whom you formed out of clay.

**Come, Lord Jesus.**

O Emmanuel,
our Sovereign and Lawgiver,
desire of the nations and Savior of all:
come and save us, O Lord our God.

**Come, Lord Jesus.**

*Silent prayer—Concluding petition—The Lord's Prayer*

**46**

**CHRISTMAS/Morning Prayer 1**

Eternal God, we rejoice with all creation at the birth of Christ Jesus,
for he is the daystar from on high, the light dawning on those who
have walked in darkness, and the presence of new life for a weary
world. By the light of this gift of our Savior, we see how generous
all your blessings are to us. Especially we thank you for
    those whom we love and who love us . . .
    freedom to worship you and serve our God . . .
    forgiveness and healing to begin life anew . . .
    the preciousness of human life . . .
    the innocence of children, the wisdom of the aged, and all human
        hopes for peace and righteousness . . .
    the church as the cradle of the mystery of your Word become
        flesh. . . .
Gracious God, you bring light to chase away the gloom. Kindle a
flame in our hearts to warm our love for others even as you love
this world enough to send your Son. Especially we pray for
    those in families, children and parents . . .
    those who are alone, the bereaved, the outcast, the abandoned . . .

the homeless and refugees . . .
those burdened by despair . . .
all who care for the helpless and defend the weak . . .
the church as the home for all your children. . . .

*Silent prayer—Concluding petition—The Lord's Prayer*

*Or*

## 47

## CHRISTMAS/Morning Prayer 2

All the ends of the earth
have seen the salvation of our God. Alleluia!

**Shout to the Lord, all the earth. Alleluia!**

O Christ, splendor of God's eternal glory,
sustaining the universe by your mighty Word,
renew our lives by your presence.

**Lord, have mercy.**

O Christ, born into the world in the fullness of time
for the liberation of all creation,
let all come to their rightful freedom.

**Lord, have mercy.**

O Christ, begotten of the Father before all time,
born in the stable at Bethlehem,
may your church be a sign of hope and joy.

**Lord, have mercy.**

O Christ, truly God and truly human,
born to a people in fulfillment of their expectations,
fulfill our desires in you.

**Lord, have mercy.**

O Christ, born of the Virgin Mary,
child of wonder and splendor,
mighty God of all ages, Prince of peace,
may the whole world live in peace and justice.

**Lord, have mercy.**

*Silent prayer—Concluding petition—The Lord's Prayer*

**48**

**CHRISTMAS/Evening Prayer 1**

Holy God, heaven and earth are met this day in the newborn Child, Savior of the world. We celebrate his birth, for in him you come to be close to us that we might be close to you. Especially we give thanks for
the birth, life, death and resurrection of our Lord Jesus Christ and all he means to us . . .
prospects of peace in the world . . .
confidence in your almighty love . . .
those who generously give . . .
those who graciously receive . . .
the church's nurturing us in the faith. . . .
God of all mercy, as you have come in Jesus Christ to be our guest, inspire our hearts to a hospitality that welcomes all your children in his name. Especially we pray for
those who have not heard your good news . . .
the sick and suffering . . .
those who know no laughter, only tears . . .
those who govern and rule . . .
those enslaved by tyranny . . .
prisoners of addiction or abuse . . .
the church as a refuge for the needy. . . .

*Silent prayer—Concluding petition—The Lord's Prayer*

*Or*

**49**

**CHRISTMAS/Evening Prayer 2**

The Word was made flesh,

**Alleluia, Alleluia!**

and dwelt among us,

**Alleluia, Alleluia!**

Jesus, Son of the living God, splendor of the Father, Light eternal:

**Glory to you, O Lord!**

Jesus, King of glory, Sun of righteousness, born of the Virgin Mary:

**Glory to you, O Lord!**

Jesus, Wonderful Counselor, mighty God, everlasting Lord:

**Glory to you, O Lord!**

Jesus, Prince of peace, Source of life, perfect in holiness:

**Glory to you, O Lord!**

Jesus, Friend of all, Protector of the poor, Treasure of the faithful:

**Glory to you, O Lord!**

Jesus, Good Shepherd, inexhaustible Wisdom, our Way, our Truth, and our Life:

**Glory to you, O Lord!**

Jesus, joy of the angels, and crown of all the saints:

**Glory to you, O Lord!**

*Silent prayer—Concluding petition—The Lord's Prayer*

**50**

**EPIPHANY/Morning Prayer 1**

Ruler of the universe, your light shines to guide all people in the way of Jesus Christ. We rejoice that in him you have revealed your great love for everyone, and we praise you for every blessing to us and to all. Especially we thank you for
the unity we have with all Christians in Jesus Christ . . .
the proclamation of your Word in every corner of the world . . .
those who exemplify to us your love in Jesus Christ . . .
opportunities to witness to your love in our lives. . . .
God of wisdom, your brilliant light attracted the worship of the wise, and shows us all the way of humility and service in Jesus Christ.

Illumine our hearts that we may see clearly the needs of those around
us and how to respond with your love. Especially we pray for
  monarchs and magistrates of every nation . . .
  agents of reconciliation . . .
  those who stand for justice and truth . . .
  the poor and exploited . . .
  Christians who are persecuted. . . .

  *Silent prayer—Concluding petition—The Lord's Prayer*

  *Or*

## 51

## EPIPHANY/Morning Prayer 2

O Christ,
by your epiphany your light shines upon us
giving us the fullness of salvation.
Help us show your light to all we meet today.

**Lord, have mercy.**

O Christ of glory,
you humbled yourself to be baptized,
showing us the way of humility.
Strengthen us to serve you in humility all the days of our life.

**Lord, have mercy.**

O Christ,
by your baptism you cleansed us from our sin,
making us children of your Father.
Give the grace of being a child of God to all who seek you.

**Lord, have mercy.**

O Christ,
by your baptism you sanctified creation
and opened the door of repentance
to all who are baptized.
Make us servants of your gospel in the world.

**Lord, have mercy.**

O Christ,
by your baptism you revealed to us the glorious Trinity
when the voice from heaven proclaimed, "This is my beloved Son,"
and the Holy Spirit descended upon you like a dove.
Renew a heart of worship within all the baptized.

**Lord, have mercy.**

*Silent prayer—Concluding petition—The Lord's Prayer*

## 52

### EPIPHANY/Evening Prayer 1

God of glory, in Jesus Christ you have put on our humanity and
blessed all life in him. We rejoice in your love for us and for all
people, and that you should come to us and bring happiness and
hope. Especially we thank you for
    the joy of love and the laughter it brings to our hearts . . .
    our baptisms in Jesus Christ and cleansing from sin . . .
    Christ's witness to the world of your huge love for all people . . .
    freedom from fear . . .
    the faithfulness of your church. . . .
God of grace, in Jesus Christ you have known all human joys and
sorrows. Keep us alert to those around us that we may share life with
them as your children, sisters and brothers of Jesus Christ. Especially
we pray for
    those who share your love in marriage . . .
    the widowed, divorced, and single . . .
    those beginning new ventures in life . . .
    peace among nations . . .
    unity in your church. . . .

*Silent prayer—Concluding petition—The Lord's Prayer*

*Or*

## 53

### EPIPHANY/Evening Prayer 2

All the ends of the earth
have seen the salvation of our God, Alleluia!

**Shout to the Lord, all the earth, Alleluia!**

With joy let us pray to our Savior,
the Son of God who became one of us, saying:

**The grace of God be with us all.**

O Christ,
let your gospel shine in every place
where the Word of life is not yet received.
Draw the whole creation to yourself,
that your salvation may be known through all the earth.

**The grace of God be with us all.**

O Christ, Savior and Lord,
extend your church to every place.
Make it a place of welcome for people of every race and tongue.

**The grace of God be with us all.**

O Christ, Ruler of rulers,
direct the work and thoughts of the leaders of nations,
that they may seek justice
and further peace and freedom for all.

**The grace of God be with us all.**

O Christ, Master of all,
support of the weak and comfort of the afflicted,
strengthen the tempted and raise the fallen.
Watch over the lonely and those in danger.
Give hope to the despairing
and sustain the faith of the persecuted.

**The grace of God be with us all.**

*Silent prayer—Concluding petition—The Lord's Prayer*

## 54

### ASH WEDNESDAY/Morning Prayer

Creator God, you made us for life, not death, and we praise you for new life given in Jesus Christ, and all your goodness to us, your wayward children. Especially we thank you for
this season of reflection on your love . . .

forgiveness for our failures . . .
time to make amends and corrections . . .
restoration of broken or injured relationships . . .
support of Christian friends and those who love us. . . .
Merciful God, you have been patient with our shortcomings and generous in meeting our needs by your love revealed in Jesus Christ. We offer to you the needs of a sinful and hurting world. Especially we pray for
those who live in danger . . .
people who care for the sick and dying . . .
victims of greed and warfare . . .
those who would be delivered from their sin . . .
your church in welcoming all sinners. . . .

*Silent prayer—Concluding petition—The Lord's Prayer*

## 55

## ASH WEDNESDAY/Evening Prayer

God of mercy, you have given us rest along the way as we journey with Christ and carry his yoke. We praise you for every refreshment for our souls and all good gifts of life. Especially we thank you for
the privilege of prayer . . .
the nourishment of scripture . . .
encouragement from our friends in faith . . .
your Spirit of renewal in our lives . . .
your strength in living and comfort in dying. . . .
Eternal God, we pray not only for ourselves but for all your children who, like us, need your help and healing in their lives. Especially we pray for
those who are wearied by their labors . . .
those worn out by grief and sorrow . . .
those who would lay down the burden of guilt . . .
people struggling with suffering in body or mind . . .
all who reach out with gentle love. . . .

*Silent prayer—Concluding petition—The Lord's Prayer*

## 56

## OTHER DAYS IN LENT/Morning Prayer 1

Mighty God, you raise the sun from its grave of night, and gather your people to celebrate the dawn, for in Jesus Christ you have destroyed death and set us free from its bondage. We praise your might and majesty, great God, and thank you for all good gifts of your salvation. Especially we thank you for
loving families and forgiving friends . . .
promises of newness in our lives . . .
blessings of nourishment and shelter and safety . . .
the community of Christians in which we worship. . . .
God our deliverer, you bring us from death to life and preserve us from all evil. Stir up in us concern for others that in serving them we may be close to Christ, who is our servant Lord. Especially we pray for
those who are ravaged by disease . . .
victims of prejudice . . .
the cynical who mock your love . . .
the hungry and homeless . . .
all who give of themselves in serving others. . . .

*Silent prayer—Concluding petition—The Lord's Prayer*

*Or*

## 57

## OTHER DAYS IN LENT/Morning Prayer 2

Jesus, remember us when you come into your kingdom.
Hear our intercessions.

For your church around the world,

**we ask for new life.**

For all who carry out ministries in your church,

**we ask grace and wisdom.**

For people who have accepted spiritual disciplines,

**we ask inspired discipleship.**

For Christians of every land,

**we ask new unity in your name.**

For Jews and Muslims and people of other faiths,

**we ask your divine blessing.**

For those who cannot believe,

**we ask your faithful love.**

For governors and rulers in every land,

**we ask your guidance.**

For people who suffer and sorrow,

**we ask your healing peace.**

*Silent prayer—Concluding petition—The Lord's Prayer*

**58**

**OTHER DAYS IN LENT/Evening Prayer 1**

Faithful God, by your strong hand we are led through the dark valleys of life kept safe in the security of your eternal love. You have rescued us all in Jesus Christ, and lead us on to your promised land. We praise you for every redemptive blessing we receive in Jesus Christ. Especially we thank you for

> our co-workers and colleagues . . .
> work accomplished this day . . .
> those who feed the hungry . . .
> house the homeless . . .
> clothe the naked . . .
> visit the imprisoned . . .
> new beginnings in our lives . . .
> our call to discipleship with Christ. . . .

Loving God, by your tender touch we are healed and comforted in Jesus Christ. Your Spirit makes the wounded whole and breathes new life into dry bones. Hear our prayers for the needs of others, that all may receive what you alone can give. Especially we pray for

> those deprived of dignity . . .
> people confined by disability or illness . . .
> those who wrestle with doubt or despair . . .

those confronting the mystery of death . . .
the church's ministries of compassion. . . .

*Silent prayer—Concluding petition—The Lord's Prayer*

*Or*

**59**

## OTHER DAYS IN LENT/Evening Prayer 2

O Christ,
out of your fullness we have all received grace upon grace.
You are our eternal hope;
you are patient and full of mercy;
you are generous to all who call upon you.

**Save us, Lord.**

O Christ, fountain of life and holiness,
you have taken away our sins.
On the cross you were wounded for our transgressions
and were bruised for our iniquities.

**Save us, Lord.**

O Christ, obedient unto death,
source of all comfort,
our life and our resurrection,
our peace and reconciliation:

**Save us, Lord.**

O Christ, Savior of all who trust in you,
hope of all who die in you,
and joy of all the saints:

**Save us, Lord.**

Jesus, Lamb of God,

**have mercy on us.**

Jesus, bearer of our sins,

**have mercy on us.**

Jesus, redeemer of the world,

**grant us peace.**

*Silent prayer—Concluding petition—The Lord's Prayer*

**60**

**MAUNDY THURSDAY/Morning Prayer**

God our provider, you feed us with the bread of life and lift for us the cup of salvation, and all we have is from your generous love in Jesus Christ. We praise you for every blessing of life in his name. Especially we thank you for
the loyalty of friends . . .
the love of families . . .
worship shared with your people in the church . . .
the mystery of life itself. . . .
God our Redeemer, you invite all to your feast, but not all can taste of life's joys. We remember before you, therefore, those in special need. Especially we pray for
those who feel unwanted or unloved . . .
people alone and forgotten . . .
the dying and those who wait with them . . .
those imprisoned . . .
Christians who suffer in the service of Christ. . . .

*Silent prayer—Concluding petition—The Lord's Prayer*

**61**

**MAUNDY THURSDAY/Evening Prayer**

Great God, in Jesus Christ you brought us to your royal banquet, where he is our host. We praise you for the sacrament of his love and for every blessing we have received. Especially we thank you for
those who have sacrificed for our benefit . . .
people who have gone before us in faith . . .
the community of your church, one in Jesus Christ. . . .
Generous God, you feed all who hunger and thirst after righteousness, and you care for all your children in Jesus Christ. We pray for people who would be fed by your grace. Especially we pray for
those who are widowed and orphaned . . .

people outside the Christian community . . .
those who need strength to minister in Christ's name. . . .

*Silent prayer—Concluding petition—The Lord's Prayer*

## 62

### GOOD FRIDAY AND HOLY SATURDAY/Morning Prayer

Our Redeemer suffered death,
was buried and rose again for our sake.
With love let us adore him, aware of our needs.

Christ our teacher,
for us you were obedient, even to death:

**Teach us to obey God's will in all things.**

Christ our life,
by dying on the cross
you destroyed the power of evil and death:

**Enable us to die with you, and to rise with you in glory.**

Christ our strength,
you were despised,
and humiliated as a condemned criminal:

**Teach us the humility by which you saved the world.**

Christ our salvation,
you gave your life out of love for us:

**Help us to love one another.**

Christ our Savior,
on the cross you embraced all time
with your outstretched arms:

**Gather all the scattered children of God into your realm.**

Jesus, Lamb of God,

**have mercy on us.**

Jesus, bearer of our sins,

**have mercy on us.**

Jesus, redeemer of the world,

**grant us peace.**

*Silent prayer—Concluding petition—The Lord's Prayer*

**63**

**GOOD FRIDAY/Evening Prayer**

Master, you are lifted up,
and we bow before your cross to receive your blessings:

"Father, forgive them—they know not what they do."

**We are humbled by your forgiveness.**

"Today you will be with me in paradise."

**We are awed by your promise.**

"Mother, he is your son—and she is your mother."

**We would love each other as you have loved us.**

"My God, my God, why have you forsaken me?"

**Stay with us, God, that we may stand by all in need.**

"I am thirsty."

**Make us generous to share with those who hunger and thirst.**

"It is finished."

**Complete your work in us, and use us according to your will.**

"Father, into your hands I commend my spirit."

**We give ourselves to you in trust and peace.**

*Silent prayer—Concluding petition—The Lord's Prayer*

**64**

**HOLY SATURDAY/Evening Prayer**

O crucified Jesus,
Son of the Father,
conceived by the Holy Spirit,

born of the Virgin Mary,
eternal Word of God,

**We worship you.**

O crucified Jesus,
holy temple of God,
dwelling place of the Most High,
gate of heaven,
burning flame of love,

**We worship you.**

O crucified Jesus,
sanctuary of justice and love,
full of kindness,
source of all faithfulness,

**We worship you.**

O crucified Jesus,
ruler of every heart,
in you are all the treasures of wisdom and knowledge,
in you dwells all the fullness of the godhead,

**We worship you.**

Jesus, Lamb of God,

**have mercy on us.**

Jesus, bearer of our sins,

**have mercy on us.**

Jesus, redeemer of the world,

**grant us peace.**

*Silent prayer—Concluding petition—The Lord's Prayer*

## 65

### EASTER/Morning Prayer 1

God of power and majesty, with the rising of the sun you have raised
Jesus Christ and delivered him and us all from death's destruction.
We praise you on this bright day for all your gifts of new life.

Especially we thank you for
all victories over sin and evil in our lives . . .
loyalty and love of friends and family . . .
the newborn, the newly baptized, and those now in your eternal
home . . .
the renewal of nature . . .
the continuing witness of the church of Christ. . . .
God of eternity, you are present with us because of Christ's rising
from the dead, and you persist in lifting us to new life in him. We
bring to you our prayers for this world in need of resurrection.
Especially we pray for
nations and peoples in strife . . .
the poor and impoverished, at home and abroad . . .
those we know in particular circumstances of distress . . .
the diseased and the dying . . .
all who follow the risen Christ. . . .

*Silent prayer—Concluding petition—The Lord's Prayer*

*Or*

## 66

## EASTER/Morning Prayer 2

O Christ, in your resurrection
the heavens and the earth rejoice. Alleluia!

By your resurrection you broke open the gates of hell,
and destroyed sin and death.

**Keep us victorious over sin.**

By your resurrection you raised the dead,
and brought us from death to life.

**Guide us in the way of eternal life.**

By your resurrection you confounded your guards and
executioners,
and filled the disciples with joy.

**Give us joy in your service.**

By your resurrection you proclaimed good news to the women and
   apostles,
and brought salvation to the whole world.

**Direct our lives as your new creation.**

*Silent prayer—Concluding petition—The Lord's Prayer*

**67**

**EASTER/Evening Prayer 1**

God of all life, we celebrate the works of your hands and rejoice in
your redemption of all humankind. Your victory over death is ours
in Jesus Christ, and we praise you for all blessings given in him.
Especially we thank you for
   glimpses of the risen Christ today . . .
   signs of life victorious over death . . .
   the comfort of friends and the kindness of strangers. . . .
God of peace, in Jesus Christ you have restored the whole world to
yourself, affirming your love for all people. We offer our prayers for
the needs of others. Especially we pray for
   those who suffer pain and sorrow . . .
   people bold in witness and brave in service . . .
   our parents, our children, our brothers and sisters . . .
   those who weary in doing well. . . .

*Silent prayer—Concluding petition—The Lord's Prayer*

*Or*

**68**

**EASTER/Evening Prayer 2**

O Christ,
after your resurrection you appeared to your disciples;
you breathed on them,
that they might receive the Holy Spirit.
You gave joy and exultation to the whole creation.
Through your victory, we pray to you:

**Hear us, Lord of glory.**

O Christ,
after your resurrection you sent out your disciples
to teach all nations
and to baptize them in the name of the Father, and of the Son, and
 of the Holy Spirit;
you promised to be with them
and us until the end of the world.
Through your victory, we pray to you:

**Hear us, Lord of glory.**

O Christ,
through your resurrection you have lifted us up and filled us with
 rejoicing.
Through your salvation you enrich us with your gifts
and renew our lives and fill our hearts with joy.
Through your victory, we pray to you:

**Hear us, Lord of glory.**

O Christ,
you are glorified by angels in heaven,
and worshiped on earth.
On the glorious feast of your resurrection,
we pray to you:

**Hear us, Lord of glory.**

Save us, O Christ our Lord, in your goodness,
extend your mercy to your people who await the resurrection,
and have mercy on us.

**Hear us, Lord of glory.**

O merciful God, you raised your beloved Son,
and in your love you established him as head of your church
and ruler of the universe.
By your goodness we pray:

**Hear us, Lord of glory.**

*Silent prayer—Concluding petition—The Lord's Prayer*

**ASCENSION DAY/Morning and Evening Prayer**

Arise, O Lord, in your strength.

**We will praise you for your glory!**

Let us pray with joy to Christ at the right hand of God, saying:

**You are the king of glory!**

You have raised the weakness of our flesh.
Heal us from our sins,
and restore to us the full dignity of life.

**You are the king of glory!**

May our faith lead us to the Father
as we follow the road you trod.

**You are the king of glory!**

You have promised to draw all people to yourself.
Let no one of us be separate from your body.

**You are the king of glory!**

Grant that by our longing we may join you in your kingdom,
where your humanity and ours is glorified.

**You are the king of glory!**

You are true God, and you will be our judge.
So lead us to contemplate your tender mercy.

**You are the king of glory!**

*Silent prayer—Concluding petition—The Lord's Prayer*

**70**

**THE DAY OF PENTECOST/Morning Prayer**

Eternal God, by your Holy Spirit you have given life to this earth, and brought new life to Christ's church. You have blessed your people with wonderful gifts, and we praise you for all you share with us. Especially we thank you for
those who proclaim your Word and administer the sacraments . . .

those who rule in your church . . .
those who wait on others in need . . .
those who teach and share wisdom and truth . . .
those who represent the church in civil matters . . .
those who provide music and art . . .
those who work for unity in the church . . .
those who do menial tasks . . .
those who care for children . . .
those who visit the lonely . . .
those who serve in other ways. . . .

Merciful God, by your Holy Spirit you have claimed us to be your people in this world, and you have empowered us to show your love. We pray for all whom we would serve in Christ's name. Especially we pray for
those who are poor and hungry and homeless . . .
those who are suffering from sickness . . .
nations torn by strife and warfare . . .
refugees and victims of oppression . . .
those who are bereaved and sorrowing . . .
people imprisoned or confined . . .
the illiterate and ignorant . . .
those who are abandoned and outcast . . .
those burdened by responsibility to govern . . .
those persecuted for their loyalty to Christ . . .
any and all who need our ministries in Christ's name. . . .

*Silent prayer—Concluding petition—The Lord's Prayer*

## 71

## PENTECOST/Evening Prayer 1

The Spirit helps us in our weakness. Alleluia!

**And intercedes for us with sighs too deep for words. Alleluia!**

Christ has gathered the church in unity through the Spirit.
With sure hope, let us pray:

Maker of all things,
in the beginning, you created heaven and earth.
In the fullness of time, you restored all things in Christ.
Renew our world, in this day, with your grace and mercy.

**Lord, hear our prayer.**

Life of the world,
you breathed life into the flesh you created.
Now, by your Spirit, breathe new life into the children of earth.
Turn hatred into love, sorrow into joy, and war into peace.

**Lord, hear our prayer.**

Lover of concord,
you desire the unity of all Christians.
Set aflame the whole church with the fire of your Spirit.
Unite us to stand in the world as a sign of your love.

**Lord, hear our prayer.**

God of compassion,
through your Spirit you supply every human need.
Heal the sick, and comfort the distressed.
Befriend the friendless, and help the helpless.

**Lord, hear our prayer.**

Source of peace,
your Spirit restores our anxious spirits.
In our labor, give us rest;
in our temptation, strength;
in our sadness, consolation.

**Lord, hear our prayer.**

*Silent prayer—Concluding petition—The Lord's Prayer*

*Or*

**72**

**PENTECOST/Evening Prayer 2**

God's Spirit joins with our spirits, Alleluia,

**to declare that we are children of God. Alleluia!**

Come, Spirit of wisdom,
and teach us to value the highest gifts.

**Come, Holy Spirit.**

Come, Spirit of understanding,
and show us all things in the light of eternity.

**Come, Holy Spirit.**

Come, Spirit of counsel,
and guide us along the straight and narrow path to our heavenly
home.

**Come, Holy Spirit.**

Come, Spirit of might,
and strengthen us against every evil spirit and interest
which would separate us from you.

**Come, Holy Spirit.**

Come, Spirit of knowledge,
and teach us the shortness of life and the length of eternity.

**Come, Holy Spirit.**

Come, Spirit of godliness,
and stir up our minds and hearts
to love and serve the Lord our God all our days.

**Come, Holy Spirit.**

Come, Spirit of fear of the Lord,
and make us tremble with awe and reverence
before your divine majesty.

**Come, Holy Spirit.**

*Silent prayer—Concluding petition—The Lord's Prayer*

# GRACE AT MEALS

**73**

God of grace,
sustain our bodies with this food,
our hearts with true friendship,
and our souls with your truth,
for Christ's sake. **Amen.**

**74**

Give us grateful hearts, O God, for all your mercies,
and make us mindful of the needs of others;
through Jesus Christ our Lord. **Amen.**

**75**

Lord Jesus, be our holy guest,
our morning joy, our evening rest;
and with our daily bread impart
your love and peace to every heart. **Amen.**

**76**

Bless us, O Lord, and these your gifts
which we are about to receive from your goodness,
through Christ our Lord. **Amen.**

*—Roman Catholic*

**77**

The eyes of all wait upon you, O Lord,
and you give them their food in due season.
You open your hand,
and fill all living things with plenteousness. **Amen.**

*—An Eastern Orthodox prayer before a meal*

**78**

Blessed are you, Lord.
You have fed us from our earliest days;
you give food to every living creature.
Fill our hearts with joy and delight.
Let us always have enough
and something to spare for works of mercy
in honor of Christ Jesus, our Lord.
Through him may glory, honor, and power be yours forever. **Amen.**

*—Fourth-century prayer*

**79**

Blessed are you, O Lord our God,
Ruler of the universe,
for you give us food to sustain our lives
    and make our hearts glad. **Amen.**

*—Jewish blessing*

**80**

Blessed are you, Lord, God of all creation,
for you feed the whole world with your goodness,
with grace, with loving-kindness and tender mercy.
You give food to all creatures,
and your loving-kindness endures forever.
Because of your great goodness, food has never failed us;
O may it not fail us forever and ever,
for the sake of your great name.
You nourish and sustain all creatures
and do good to all.
Blessed are you, O Lord, for you give food to all. **Amen.**

*—Jewish blessing*

**81**

Lord, you clothe the lilies,
you feed the birds of the sky,
you lead the lambs to pasture,
and the deer to the waterside,
you multiplied loaves and fishes,
and changed the water to wine;

come to our table as giver,
and as our guest to dine. **Amen.**

*As a sign of reverence, some fold hands for prayer before the meal. Others, standing about the table, lift hands as a sign of praise. Others join hands around the table as a sign of peace and unity. Still others make the sign of the cross after the prayer.*

## A Mealtime Blessing

**82**

*The following grace is based upon Jewish and Christian table blessings. The actions are signs of gratitude to God for the joy of food and drink and for the presence of those about the table. If circumstances do not allow for blessings over both wine and bread, a blessing may be said over either.*

*A person at the table takes a glass of wine, or appropriate beverage, lifts it, and says:*

Blessed are you, O Lord our God,
Ruler of all creation,
for you give us the fruit of the vine. **Amen.**

*The glass is passed and each person at the table drinks from it. The same person, or another, takes bread, holds it up for all to see, and says:*

Blessed are you, O Lord our God,
Ruler of all creation,
for you bring forth bread from the earth. **Amen.**

*The bread is broken and passed to those about the table for each one to eat of it.*

# MUSIC FOR
# DAILY PRAYER

Music © 1984 Hal H. Hopson.

## SINGING THE OPENING SENTENCES

O Lord, open ǀ my lips.*

**And my mouth shall proclaim ǀ your praise. ǁ**

Thanks ǀ be to God,*

**who gives us the victory through our Lord ǀ Jesus Christ. ǁ**

By our baptism we were buried with Christ and ǀ shared his death,*

**so that as Christ was raised from the dead,**

**we too might live ǀ a new life.**

Each versicle or response is sung to one measure of the tone. In the example above, a syllable indicated by a point ( ǀ ) preceding it is to be sung to the black note so marked. Most of the opening sentences have three couplets that correspond to the (A), (B), and (C) parts of this triple tone. If there are only two couplets, sing (A) and (C). When there are four, repeat (C) to accommodate the fourth couplet.

# PSALM REFRAINS AND PSALM TONES

## 1 ALLELUIA

Al-le - lu - ia! Al-le - lu - ia! Al-le - lu - ia!

Tone 1

## 2 PRAISE

Psalm 67:3

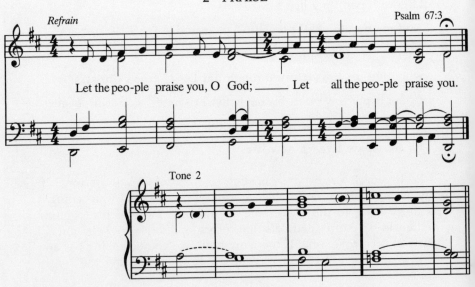

Let the peo-ple praise you, O God; ____ Let all the peo-ple praise you.

Tone 2

TEXT:  Hal H. Hopson
MUSIC:  Hal H. Hopson

# 3  LORDSHIP

# 4  SALVATION HISTORY

## 5  GOD'S LAW

Psalm 119:174

O  Lord, my de - light, _____ my de - light is in your  law.

Tone 5

## 6  TRUST

Psalm 46:1

God  is  our  ref - uge;  God  is  our  strength.

Tone 6

## 7  PENITENTIAL

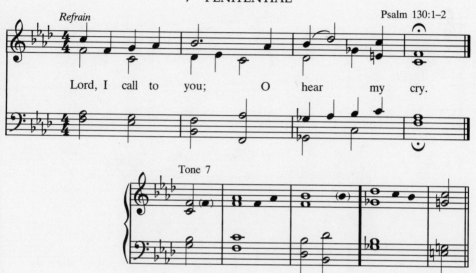

Psalm 130:1–2

*Refrain*

Lord, I call to you;  O  hear  my  cry.

Tone 7

## 8  LAMENT

Psalm 22:19

*Refrain*

Lord, you  are  my  strength,  has - ten to help  me.

Tone 8

# PSALM 51

*Unison*

1 God of all mer-cy, Lord a - bove, Show your com-
2 Be - fore you I con - fess my wrong, And pray you
3 God of all mer-cy, hear my prayer, And keep me
4 Sal - va-tion's joy to me re - store; From death now

pas - sion, show your love. O wash me clean from ev - ery
make my spir - it strong. My sin is e - vil in your
in your lov - ing care. Sus - tain in me a will - ing
save me ev - er - more. In - spire my tongue to speak your

sin, And make my heart re - newed with - in.
sight; Be kind to judge my heart con - trite.
heart, And let your Spir - it ne'er de - part.
praise And sing your mer - cy all my days.

TEXT: John Dunn; para. of Psalm 51
MUSIC: Graham George

THE KING'S MAJESTY
LM

Text copyright © by John Dunn.
Music copyright © 1941 by H. W. Gray Co., Inc. Copyright renewed. Used
by permission.

*Unison*

1 O Lord, you are my God, for you I long: Show me your
2 My spir-it seeks your glo-rious maj-es-ty: Show me your
3 I pray to you and in your help con-fide: Show me your

face. Your life with-in me makes my spir-it strong: Lord
face. Your con-stant love gives more than life to me: Lord
face. You feed my soul and I am sat-is-fied: Lord

of all grace. For you I thirst like des-erts parched and
of all grace. Thus will I bless your name through all my
of all grace. O keep me in the shel-ter of your

dried. With-in your care my soul is sat-is-fied.
days; And lift my hands to you in thank-ful praise.
throne; To you I cling, my joy, my God a-lone.

TEXT: John Dunn; para. of Psalm 63:1–8
MUSIC: W. H. Harris, 1930

ALBERTA
10 4 10 4 10 4 6

## PSALM 95
### (Verses 1–7)

1 Come, let us sing to the Lord; let us shout for

2 Lord is a great God, and a great

3 It is God who rules the seas, whose hands have

4 For this great one is our God, who choos - es a

1 joy to the Rock of our sal - va - tion. Let us come be - fore God's

2 [ omit ] rul - er o'er all gods. It is God who holds the

3 [ omit ] mold - ed the dry land. Come, let us bow

4 [ omit ] peo - ple and tends them, and whose hand will

*play this measure first time only*

TEXT: *The Book of Common Prayer*, 1977, alt.
MUSIC: Jack Noble White

# PSALM 100

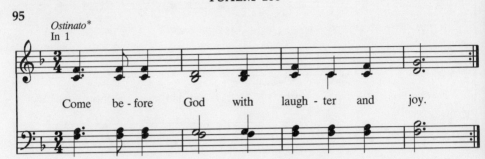

## 95

*Ostinato**
In 1

Come be-fore God with laugh-ter and joy.

*The ostinato (S.A.T.B.) continues as it provides an accompaniment to the verses.*

*rit.*        *(Sung the last time)*

Come be-fore God with joy.

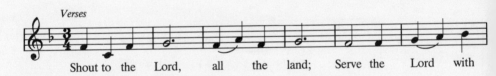

*Verses*

Shout to the Lord, all the land; Serve the Lord with

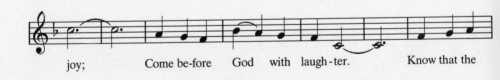

joy;        Come be-fore God with laugh-ter.        Know that the

TEXT: Psalm 100; tr. Gary Chamberlain
MUSIC: Hal H. Hopson

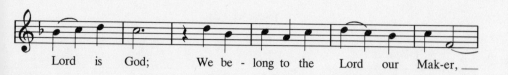

Lord is God; We be - long to the Lord our Mak-er, ___

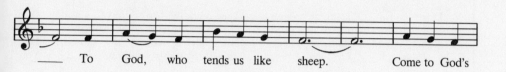

___ To God, who tends us like sheep. Come to God's

gates with thanks; Come to God's courts with praise; ___

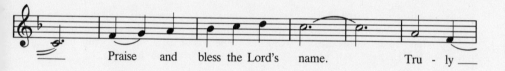

___ Praise and bless the Lord's name. Tru - ly ___

___ the Lord is good; God is al - ways gra-cious,

God is faith - ful from age to age.

*Unison*

1 I call, O Lord, on you: Come quick-ly to my aid; From
2 Lord, let my prayer as - cend Like in - cense in your sight; Lord,
3 Set, Lord, a guard to keep Close watch up - on my mouth; Let
4 Have pit - y, Lord, on me; You are my strength, my shield: You

heaven a - bove with pit - y hear My cry of deep dis - tress.
see in hands to heaven up-raised My eve-ning sac - ri - fice.
no re - bel-lious word es-cape Your seal up - on my lips.
are my ref - uge in all ills; I turn in trust to you.

TEXT: James Quinn, S.J., alt.                                     BAYLOR
MUSIC: Hal H. Hopson                                              SM
       Alternate tune: SOUTHWELL

# SONG OF ZECHARIAH

*Benedictus*

Unison

1 Blest be the God of Is - rael, who comes to set us free;
2 God from the house of Da - vid a child of grace has given;
3 On pris - on - ers of dark - ness the sun be - gins to rise,

Who vis - its and re - deems us, who grants us lib - er - ty.
A Sav - ior comes a - mong us to raise us up to heaven.
The dawn - ing of for - give - ness up - on the sin - ner's eyes.

The proph - ets spoke of mer - cy, of free - dom and re - lease;
Be - fore him goes the her - ald, fore - run - ner in the way,
God guides the feet of pil - grims a - long the paths of peace.

God shall ful - fill that prom - ise and bring the peo - ple peace.
The proph - et of sal - va - tion, the har - bin - ger of Day.
O bless our God and Sav - ior with songs that nev - er cease!

TEXT: Michael A. Perry, alt.
MUSIC: Hal H. Hopson
Alternate tune: LLANGLOFFAN

MERLE'S TUNE
76 76 D

# SONG OF MARY
*Magnificat*

1 O praise, my soul, the Lord! O glo - ri - fy that name!
2 From heaven God looked on me, A low - ly ser - vant maid:
3 The Lord of won - drous power Has done great things for me;
4 God's mer - cy is re - vealed To those who fear God's name;
5 That one is strong to save Who scat - ters all the proud,
6 God fills the hun - gry poor With bless-ings from a - bove;

In God my spir - it thrills with joy, My Sav - ior and my God!
Be - hold, all a - ges yet to come Shall call me blest of God!
For - ev - er bless - ed be that name Who is the ho - ly One!
From age to age the love of God Shall end-less - ly en - dure!
Who casts the might - y from their thrones, And rais - es up the meek!
The rich are stripped of wealth and power And emp - ty sent a - way!

7 God's mighty hand has grasped
The hand of Israel,
The servant son, beloved by God
With never-failing love!

8 Now is God's promise kept,
Once made to Abraham,
That in his seed should all be blest
For all eternity!

TEXT: James Quinn, S.J., alt.
MUSIC: Edgar M. Deale

EDWIN
SM

# SONG OF SIMEON
## *Nunc Dimittis*

1 Lord, bid your ser - vant go in peace, Your
2 This is the Sav - ior of the world, The

word is now ful - filled. These eyes have seen sal -
Gen - tiles' prom - ised light, God's glo - ry dwell - ing

va - tion's dawn, This child so long fore - told.
in our midst, The joy of Is - ra - el.

TEXT: James Quinn, S.J., alt.
MUSIC: Folk song, adapted as American folk hymn; arr. by
　　　　Annabel Morris Buchanan, 1938.

LAND OF REST
CM

# HYMN OF LIGHT
*Phos Hilaron*

1. O gra-cious Light, pure brightness of the everliving Fa - ther in

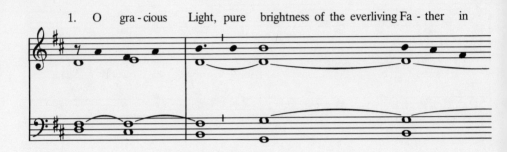

heav - en, O Je - sus Christ, ho - ly and blessed!

2. Now as we come to the setting of the sun, and our

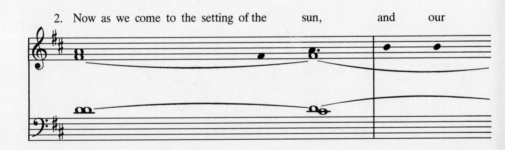

TEXT:  Second- or third-century hymn; *The Book of Common Prayer,* 1977
MUSIC:  Saint Meinrad, Mode 5, alt.; melody by Columba Kelly, O.S.B.;
harmonization by Samuel Weber, O.S.B.

eyes behold the ves - per light, we sing your prais - es, O God:

Father, Son, and Ho - ly Spir - it. 3. You are worthy at all times to be

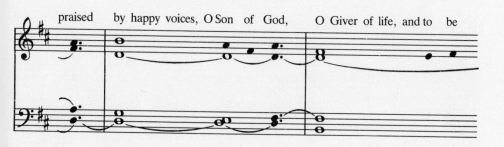

praised by happy voices, O Son of God, O Giver of life, and to be

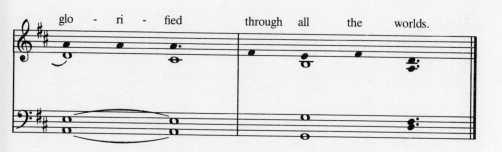

glo - ri - fied through all the worlds.

## 101

# THE LORD'S PRAYER

Our Fa - ther in heav - en, hal - lowed be your name,

your king - dom come, your will be done,

on earth as in heav - en. Give us to - day our

dai - ly bread. For - give us our sins as

TEXT: English Language Liturgical Consultation
MUSIC: Lutheran Book of Worship, 1978

Je - sus Christ is the    Light of the world, **the**

**light**    **no dark-ness can**    **o - ver-come.**      Stay with us, Lord, for

TEXT: *Lutheran Book of Worship,* 1978
MUSIC: John Weaver, 1985

it is eve-ning, **and the day is** al - most o - ver. Let your light

scat-ter the dark - ness **and il - lu-mine your church.**

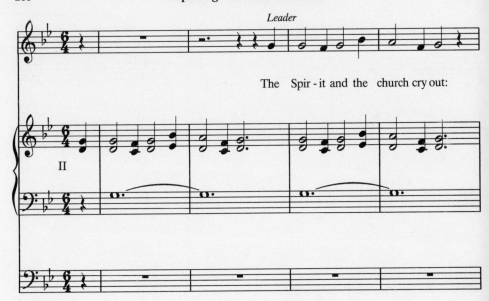

The Spir-it and the church cry out:

Come, Lord Je - sus. All those who a - wait his ap -

TEXT: *Lutheran Book of Worship,* 1978
MUSIC: John Weaver, 1985

pear - ance pray: Come, Lord Je - sus.

*All*

I

*Leader* *All*

The whole cre - a - tion pleads: Come, Lord Je - sus.

II

## SERVICE OF LIGHT
### (Dec. 24 and 25; Jan. 5 and 6; Saturday and Sunday)
**104**      Opening Sentences: Christmas–Epiphany

TEXT: *Lutheran Book of Worship,* 1978
MUSIC: John Weaver, 1985

dark - ness, and the    dark-ness has not o - ver - come it.

*Leader*

Those who dwell in the land of deep dark-ness,   on them has the light   shined.

*All*

We have be-held Christ's glo - ry, glo-ry as of the on-ly Son of the

*Leader*

Fa - ther. For to us a child is born, to us a

# SERVICE OF LIGHT
### (Evening Prayer—Saturday and Sunday)
### Opening Sentences: Lent

Be - hold, now is the ac - cept-a - ble time;

now is the day of sal - va - tion.

Turn us a - gain, O God of our sal - va - tion,

TEXT: *Lutheran Book of Worship,* 1978
MUSIC: John Weaver, 1985

# SERVICE OF LIGHT
### (Evening Prayer—Saturday and Sunday)
### Opening Sentences: Easter–Pentecost

Je - sus Christ is ris - en from the

dead.

Al - le - lu - ia,

TEXT: *Lutheran Book of Worship*, 1978
MUSIC: John Weaver, 1985

Text reprinted from *Lutheran Book of Worship*, copyright © 1978,
  by permission of Augsburg Publishing House.
Music © 1987 John Weaver.

Al - le - lu - ia, Al - le - lu - ia.

*Leader*

We are il-lu-mined by the bright-ness of his ris - ing.

*All*

Al - le - lu - ia,   Al - le - lu - ia,

Al - le - lu - ia.

*Leader*

Death has no more do - min - ion o - ver

II

*p*

32'

TEXT: English Language Liturgical Consultation
MUSIC: John Weaver, 1985

An an-gel, hold-ing a gold-en cen-ser full of in-cense, stood be-fore the al - tar. The smoke of the in-cense went up be-fore God, min-gled with the prayers of the peo - ple.

TEXT:   Based on Rev. 8:3–4
MUSIC:  John Weaver, 1987

# SERVICE OF LIGHT
### (Evening Prayer—Saturday and Sunday)
### Psalm 141

## 109

Let my prayer rise be-fore you as in-cense, the lift-ing of my hands as the eve-ning sac-ri-fice.

TEXT: Arlo D. Duba, 1980
MUSIC: John Weaver, 1985

*Verses*
*Leader*

1 I call to you, O Lord, come to me quickly;
2 Keep guard over my mouth, O Lord, watch the door of my lips;
3 Should the righteous rebuke me, let me ac - cept it as grace;
4 But my eyes are turned toward you, O Lord my God;

Hear my voice when I cry to you.
Keep my heart from slipping in - to evil.
But keep the oil of the unrighteous ever from touch-ing my head.
In you I take refuge, do not de - - - prive me of life.

Let my prayer rise be - - - - fore you as incense,
Let me not be busy with e - vil - doers;
I continually pray against their wick - ed deeds;
Keep me from the snare set for me by the evil;

The lifting of my hands as the eve - ning sacrifice.
Let me not be taken in by their sen - su - ous foods.
When they are judged they will know the truth of your Word.
Let them be ensnared, but, Lord, grant me re - lease.

## 110

# NIGHT PRAYER
## Opening Sentences (page 195)

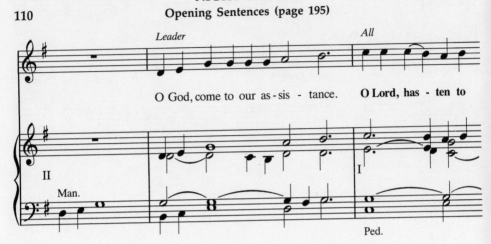

O God, come to our as - sis - tance. **O Lord, has - ten to**

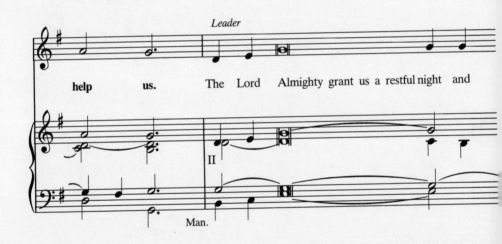

**help us.** The Lord Almighty grant us a restful night and

MUSIC: John Weaver, 1985

Music © 1987 John Weaver.

peace at the last. A - men.

*Leader*

In - to your hands, O Lord, I com-mend my spir - it;

*All*

for you have redeemed me, O Lord, O God of truth.

*Leader*

Keep us, O Lord, as the ap - ple of your eye;

TEXT: Psalms 31:5; 17:8, 15
MUSIC: John Weaver, 1985

*All* hide us under the shad - ow of your wings.

*Leader* In righ - teous - ness I shall see you;

*All* when I a - wake your pres-ence shall give me joy.

# NIGHT PRAYER
### Song of Simeon (page 203)

*Refrain*
*All*

Guide us wak-ing, O Lord, and guard us sleep-ing; that a - wake we may watch with Christ, and a - sleep rest in his peace.

*Verses*
*Leader* (free tempo)

Now, Lord, you let your ser-vant go in peace:

TEXT: Luke 2:29–32; Gloria Patri: English Language Liturgical Consultation
MUSIC: John Weaver, 1985

*All* your word has been ful-filled. *Leader* My own eyes have seen the sal-va-tion

*All* which you have prepared in the sight of ev - ery peo - ple:

*Leader* a light to re-veal you to the na-tions *All* and the glo-ry of your peo-ple

Tempo I

*(directly to Refrain)*

*(to Gloria Patri—
or as ending)*

Is - ra - el.   el.

*Gloria Patri*

Leader   All

Glory to the Fa - ther, and to the Son, **and to the Ho - ly Spir - it:**

II   I

Man.   Ped.

Leader

as it was in the beginning, is now, and will be for ev - er.

II

Man.

MUSIC: John Weaver, 1985
Music © 1987 John Weaver.

# USING MUSIC
# IN DAILY PRAYER

# SINGING PROSE PSALMS AND BIBLICAL SONGS

Prose (nonmetered) liturgical texts may be sung to a variety of psalm tones including Gregorian, Gelineau, St. Meinrad, and many others. The refrains and tones in this resource are provided for your convenience. There are eight tones and refrains (numbered 84–91), ranging from Tone 1, with its refrain "Alleluia," through Tone 8, with its refrain "Lord, You Are My Strength, Hasten to Help Me," each tone becoming progressively more somber in nature.

Each tone has its own refrain. The particular refrain assigned to a tone is appropriate to any psalm of the type for which the tone is provided. By learning the eight refrains, a congregation will be enabled to sing a familiar refrain to any psalm that may be used.

Examine the simple formula for the psalm tones, using Tone 1 (see Example I). Each tone melody is in two parts and is divided by a heavy bar line. Notice the following:

Pickup note (note head in parentheses)
Reciting note (first whole note in each part of the tone)
Two transitional notes
Final note

## Example I

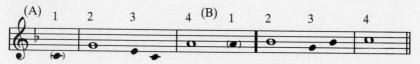

Psalm 33:1 will be used to demonstrate pointing or matching up a given text to a psalm tone (see Example II). The numbers over the text correspond to the numbers over the psalm tone.

## Example II

```
           1  2                      3        4
     (A)  Re - joice  in  the    ' Lord, you righteous;
                 2                   3        4
     (B)        Praise is fitting for ' loy - al  hearts.
```

## Instructions

1. The psalm to be sung should be divided into groups of verses after which the refrain is sung. Most often this will be in two-verse groupings.
2. Ordinarily psalm verses are in two parts. Identify each part and determine the last stressed syllable (Example II, A4 and B4). That syllable and any remaining syllables are sung to the final note of each half of the psalm tone (Example I, A4 and B4).
3. Count back two syllables from the last stressed syllable just identified and place a mark (called a "point") before that syllable (Example II, A3 and B3). This syllable and the one following it will be sung on the two transitional notes (Example I, A3 and B3).
4. When phrases begin with a stressed syllable, the pickup note in the tone is disregarded, and the reciting note accommodates that syllable as well as all syllables not already mentioned (Example III, B2).
5. Pickup syllables at the beginning of each part of the psalm verse should be sung to the pickup note of the tone and may be indicated by underlining these syllables (Example II, A1). The words of the text immediately following the pickup are sung on the reciting note (Example I, A2).

With these instructions in mind, Psalm 33:1 would be sung to Tone 1 as follows:

## Example III

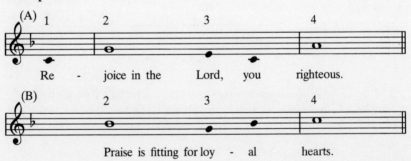

## Further instructions

6. The refrains and psalm tones should be chosen to match the spirit and theme of the psalm being sung.

7. For psalm tones such as the Lutheran and St. Meinrad (see p. 388), the above instructions apply for the most part if one disregards the instructions about the pickup notes.

8. When a psalm is to be sung, the refrain at the beginning is generally played by the organist, sung by the cantor or choir, and then sung by all.

9. The refrain texts contained in this resource may be used with the psalm tones. A sung refrain can be created by simply intoning the refrain text to the psalm tone being used. If a refrain has only one line, the last section of the psalm tone can be repeated for the refrain. Or the refrain can be intoned to the first reciting note of the psalm tone being used.

10. When chanting the biblical songs, one can easily use the same process outlined above for the pointing and singing of the psalm verses. The refrains may be sung in the same manner as outlined for the psalms above (no. 8). Music is not supplied in this resource for the refrains of the biblical songs. However, a sung refrain can be created by simply intoning the text of the refrain to the first reciting note of the psalm tone being used.

# MUSIC IN HYMNALS

HL    *The Hymnal* (1933)
HB    *The Hymnbook* (1955)
WB    *The Worshipbook* (1972)

## Morning Psalms

|  | HL | HB | WB |
|---|---|---|---|
| *Psalm 95* | | | |
| O Come and Sing Unto the Lord | 49 | 29 | 488 |
| O Come, Let Us Sing | 46– | 586– | — |
| (The *Venite*; Pss. 95:1–7; 96:9, 13) | 48* | 588 | |
| | | | |
| *Psalm 100* | | | |
| All People That on Earth Do Dwell | 1 | 24 | 288 |
| Before the Lord Jehovah's Throne | 63 | 81 | 306 |
| O Be Joyful in the Lord | 50– | 593– | — |
| *(Jubilate Deo)* | 52* | 595 | |
| O Be Joyful in the Lord! | | | 482 |
| | | | |
| *Psalm 63* | | | |
| O Lord, Our God, Most Earnestly | — | 327 | 514 |
| | | | |
| *Psalm 51* | | | |
| Create in Me a Clean Heart (Ps. 51:10–12) | — | 537 | — |
| God, Be Merciful to Me | — | 282 | — |

## Morning Hymns

| | HL | HB | WB |
|---|---|---|---|
| All Creatures of Our God and King | — | 100 | 282 |
| As the Sun Doth Daily Rise | 25 | 42 | — |
| Awake, My Soul, and with the Sun | — | 50 | — |
| Awake, My Soul, Stretch Every Nerve | 278 | 346 | — |
| Blessed Jesus, at Your Word | — | — | 309 |
| Christ, Whose Glory Fills the Skies | 26 | 47 | 332 |
| Come, My Soul, Thou Must Be Waking | 487 | 44 | 337 |

---

*Section of *The Hymnal* entitled "Ancient Hymns and Canticles"

| | HL | HB | WB |
|---|---|---|---|
| Father, We Praise Thee, Now the Night | 24, 86* | 43 | 365 |
| From All That Dwell Below the Skies | 388 | 33 | 373 |
| Heaven and Earth, and Sea and Air | 27 | 6 | 415 |
| Holy, Holy, Holy! Lord God Almighty! | 57 | 11 | 421 |
| I Sing the Mighty Power of God | 65 | 84 | 628 |
| Jesus, Sun of Righteousness | 30 | — | — |
| Joyful, Joyful, We Adore Thee | 5 | 21 | 446 |
| Light of Light, Enlighten Me | 21 | 73 | — |
| Lord, for the Mercies of the Night | — | 533 | — |
| Lord, in the Morning Thou Shalt Hear | 28 | — | — |
| Morning Has Broken | — | 464 | — |
| New Every Morning Is the Love | 31 | 45 | — |
| O Morning Star, How Fair and Bright | 321 | 415 | 521 |
| O Splendor of God's Glory Bright | 32, 84* | 46 | 529 |
| Praise the Lord: Ye Heavens, Adore Him | 10 | 3 | 554 |
| Still, Still with Thee | 107 | — | — |
| The King Shall Come When Morning Dawns | 187 | 232 | — |
| The Sun Is on the Land and Sea | 29 | — | — |
| When Morning Gilds the Skies | 3 | 41 | 637 |
| When Morning Lights the Eastern Skies | — | 49 | — |

## Hymn of Light *(Phos Hilaron)*

| | | | |
|---|---|---|---|
| Hail, Gladdening Light | 83* | — | — |
| O Gladsome Light, O Grace | 82* | 61 | 494 |

## Evening Hymns—General

| | | | |
|---|---|---|---|
| Abide with Me: Fast Falls the Eventide | 33 | 64 | 278 |
| Again, as Evening's Shadow Falls | — | 62 | — |
| All Praise to Thee, My God, This Night | 42 | 63 | 292 |
| As Now the Sun's Declining Rays | 510 | — | — |
| At Even, When the Sun Was Set | 43 | 55 | — |
| Before the Day Draws Near Its Ending | 509 | 57 | — |
| Creator of the Stars of Night | — | — | 348 |
| Ere I Sleep, for Every Favor | 511 | — | — |
| God, That Madest Earth and Heaven | 41 | 58 | 404 |
| Jesus, Kneel Beside Me | 494 | 225 | — |
| Lead, Kindly Light | 289 | 331 | — |
| Lord Jesus Christ, with Us Abide | 506 | — | — |
| Now God Be with Us, for the Night Is Closing | — | 53 | — |

|                                             | HL         | HB          | WB  |
|---------------------------------------------|------------|-------------|-----|
| Now, on Land and Sea Descending             | —          | 67          | 480 |
| Now the Day Is Over                         | 35         | 51          | —   |
| Now Woods and Fields Are Sleeping           | 505        | 66          | —   |
| O Light of Life, O Savior Dear              | 46         | —           | —   |
| On the Good and Faithful                    | —          | 52          | —   |
| Round Me Falls the Night                    | 502        | —           | —   |
| Savior, Again to Thy Dear Name We Raise     | 55         | 77          | —   |
| Savior, Breathe an Evening Blessing         | 47         | 54          | —   |
| Softly Now the Light of Day                 | 34         | 60          | —   |
| Sun of My Soul, Thou Savior Dear            | 37         | 56          | —   |
| The Day Is Past and Over                    | 44         | —           | —   |
| The Day Thou Gavest, Lord, Is Ended         | 45         | 59          | —   |
| The Radiant Morn Hath Passed Away           | 38         | —           | —   |
| The Shadows of the Evening Hours            | 36         | —           | —   |
| The Spacious Firmament on High              | 69         | 97          | 595 |
| The Sun Declines; O'er Land and Sea         | 40         | —           | —   |
| When in the Night I Meditate                | —          | 68          | —   |

### Hymns for Night Prayer

|                                             | HL         | HB          | WB  |
|---------------------------------------------|------------|-------------|-----|
| All Praise to Thee, My God, This Night      | 42         | 63          | 292 |
| Holy God, We Praise Your Name               | —          | —           | 420 |
| Lead, Kindly Light                          | 289        | 331         | —   |
| Now, on Land and Sea Descending             | —          | 67          | 480 |
| Round Me Falls the Night                    | 502        | —           | —   |

### Biblical Songs and Ancient Hymns

|                                             | HL         | HB          | WB  |
|---------------------------------------------|------------|-------------|-----|
| *Gloria in Excelsis*                        | 70*        | 572         | —   |
| Song of Creation *(Benedicite)*             | 55*        | —           | —   |
| Song of Mary *(Magnificat)*                 | 56–58*     | 596         | —   |
| Song of Simeon *(Nunc Dimittis)*            | 59–61*     | 597–600     | —   |
| Song of Zechariah *(Benedictus)*            | 53–54*     | 592         | —   |
| *Te Deum Laudamus*                          | 49*        | 589–591     | —   |
| *Te Deum Laudamus* (metrical version)       | —          | —           | 420 |

## Seasonal Hymns for Morning Prayer

*Advent*

| | HL | HB | WB |
|---|---|---|---|
| The King Shall Come When Morning Dawns | 187 | 232 | — |
| Wake, Awake, for Night Is Flying | — | — | 614 |

*Christmas*

| | | | |
|---|---|---|---|
| O Morning Star, How Fair and Bright | 321 | 415 | 521 |

*Epiphany*

| | | | |
|---|---|---|---|
| Brightest and Best of the Sons of the Morning | 136 | 175 | 318 |

*Lent*

| | | | |
|---|---|---|---|
| There's a Wideness in God's Mercy | 93 | 110 | 601 |

*Holy Week*

| | | | |
|---|---|---|---|
| Ah, Holy Jesus, How Have You Offended | 158 | 191 | 280 |

*Easter*

| | | | |
|---|---|---|---|
| Come, You Faithful, Raise the Strain | 168 | 205 | 344 |

*Ascension*

| | | | |
|---|---|---|---|
| At the Name of Jesus | — | 143 | 303 |
| The Lord Ascendeth Up on High | 172 | 212 | — |

*Pentecost*

| | | | |
|---|---|---|---|
| Holy Spirit, Truth Divine | 208 | 240 | 422 |

## Seasonal Hymns for Evening Prayer

*Advent*

| | HL | HB | WB |
|---|---|---|---|
| O Come, O Come, Emmanuel | 108 | 147 | 489 |

*Christmas*

| | | | |
|---|---|---|---|
| Of the Father's Love Begotten | 85* | 7 | 534 |

*Epiphany*

| | | | |
|---|---|---|---|
| Let All Mortal Flesh Keep Silence | 112 | 148 | 449 |

*Lent*

| | | | |
|---|---|---|---|
| Jesus, Thou Joy of Loving Hearts | 354 | 215 | 510 |

*Holy Week*

| | | | |
|---|---|---|---|
| O Sacred Head, Now Wounded | 151 | 194 | 524 |

*Easter*

| | | | |
|---|---|---|---|
| The Strife Is O'er, the Battle Done | 164 | 203 | 597 |

*Ascension*

| | | | |
|---|---|---|---|
| The Head That Once Was Crowned with Thorns | 195 | 211 | 589 |

*Pentecost*

| | | | |
|---|---|---|---|
| Come, Gracious Spirit, Heavenly Dove | 209 | — | — |
| Come, Holy Ghost, Our Souls Inspire | — | 237 | 335 |

# RESOURCES FOR MUSIC
# FOR DAILY PRAYER

*This resource list includes musical settings for only those psalms and biblical songs that are most frequently sung in daily prayer. Since the Psalter is the heart of daily prayer, it will be necessary to rely upon other sources of sung psalmody. Primary resources of psalmody and other music for daily prayer are described below. While far from exhaustive, it provides a useful collection of resources to enable daily prayer to be sung.*

## Psalms—General

*Cantor-Congregation Series.* G.I.A. Publications.
   A series of individually published pieces featuring many psalms. May be purchased individually or through subscription.
Melloh, John Allyn, and William G. Storey. *Praise God in Song: Ecumenical Daily Prayer.* G.I.A. Publications, 1979.
   This useful resource for singing daily prayer includes settings of psalms and biblical songs used most often in daily prayer. Also available are a people's edition, an organ supplement, and a cassette tape of the music.
*A Psalm Sampler.* Philadelphia: Westminster Press, 1986.
   This collection of psalms and biblical songs was prepared by the Psalter Task Force of the Office of Worship. It includes examples of many of the ways to sing the psalms.

Williams, Kenneth E. "Ways to Sing the Psalms," *Reformed Liturgy & Music,* vol. 18, no. 1 (Winter 1984), pp. 12–16. Louisville, Ky.: Office of Worship.

A survey of the varied ways psalms are being sung.

## Psalm Texts

*The Book of Common Prayer.* New York: Church Hymnal Corporation, 1977. Pp. 585–808.

This is a widely used psalm text. Although prepared for use with psalm tones, it is not pointed.

*Lutheran Book of Worship.* Minneapolis: Augsburg Publishing House, 1978. (Pew Edition, pp. 215–289.)

The psalm text is pointed for singing the psalms to the tones that are included in the book. The text is essentially the same as the one in *The Book of Common Prayer.*

*The Psalms: A New Translation for Prayer and Worship,* trans. by Gary Chamberlain. Nashville: Upper Room, 1984.

A new translation of the psalms that is inclusive in language and seeks to be faithful to the Hebrew. It is inclusive both in reference to human relations and in language about God. This is a good resource for reading the psalms. Other texts are better for singing the psalms.

*The Psalms: A New Translation for Worship.* London: Collins Liturgical Publications, 1976, 1977.

This text of the psalms is widely used in England, Ireland, and Australia. It is pointed for Anglican chant, but can be used for the Lutheran psalm tones and the St. Meinrad psalm tones by making the appropriate changes in the pointing.

*Grail Psalms: Inclusive Language Version.* G.I.A. Publications, 1983, 1986.

This edition of the popular Grail psalm texts is inclusive in reference to human relations. God language is not altered from the earlier Grail translation. The text will require pointing.

Schreck, Nancy, and Maureen Leach. *Psalms Anew: In Inclusive Language.* Winona, Minn.: St. Mary's Press, Christian Brothers Publications, 1986.

A translation of the psalms in inclusive language. It is inclusive both in reference to human relations and in language about God. It has lyrical style, and seeks to be faithful to the Hebrew text.

## Psalm Tones

Barrett, James E. *The Psalmnary: Gradual Psalms for Cantor and Congregation.* Helena, Mont.: Church Hymnary Press, 1982.

Psalm tone settings based upon Sarum (Salisbury) tones rather than Gregorian may be found in this resource. These psalms are responsorial with simple metrical refrains for the congregation to sing. The psalm text is from *The Book of Common Prayer.* This resource is oriented primarily to the Episcopalian eucharistic lectionary (Sundays and festivals) although the psalms appear in numerical order.

Frischmann, Charles, ed. *The Psalmody for the Day.* Philadelphia: Fortress Press, 1974, 1975, 1976.

Gregorian tones providing for singing the psalms appointed in the Luthern eucharistic lectionary (Sundays and festivals). Metrical refrains to be sung by the congregation are included. The psalm text is that of the *Lutheran Book of Worship.*

*Gradual Psalms—Year A; Gradual Psalms—Year B; Gradual Psalms—Year C;* and *Gradual Psalms: Holy Days and Various Occasions* (Church Hymnal Series VI). New York: Church Hymnal Corporation, 1980, 1981, 1982.

Gregorian settings, which are more traditional, are provided in this series of books for the singing of the psalms appointed in the Episcopalian eucharistic lectionary (Sundays and festivals). The psalm text is from *The Book of Common Prayer.*

Hopson, Hal H. *10 Psalms.* Hope Publishing Co., 1986.

The responsorial psalms being written by Hal H. Hopson are worthy of note. Three are included in *A Psalm Sampler,* and others will be included in the Supplemental Liturgical Resource of psalms. When this collection of ten of his responsorial psalms is used, permission is granted for reproducing the refrains for use by the congregation.

Leaver, Robin A., David Mann, David Parkes, eds. *Ways of Singing the Psalms.* London: Collins Liturgical Publications, 1984.

A valuable resource which brings together in a single source a variety of ways to sing the psalms. It includes psalm tones, chants, responsorial psalms and canons. The basic Lutheran psalm tones (no accompaniment) are among the twenty-five tones it includes. It also includes fifteen chants of Norman Warren.

*Lutheran Book of Worship.* Minneapolis: Augsburg Publishing House, 1978. (Pew Edition, pp. 290–291; Ministers Desk Edition, pp. 441–442; Accompaniment Edition, pp. 123–125.)

Of the recent efforts to make psalm tones accessible to the congregation, these are some of the easiest tones to learn. Ten tones are provided. Six are for use whenever the spirit of the psalm text calls for a bright tone (nos. 1, 3, 5, 6, 8, 9), and four are provided when the psalm text calls for a restrained tone (nos. 2, 4, 7, 10). Tones 1–5 accommodate psalms of any number of verses. When tones 6–10 are used with psalms having an uneven number of verses, the psalms are accommodated by repeating the last two segments of the tone for the last verse of the psalm. When the Lutheran psalm tones are used, the refrains in *Daily Prayer* may be employed in either of two ways. Either the antiphon melodies provided to accompany the Lutheran psalm tones may be used (provided in Pfatteicher and Messerli, *Manual on the Liturgy,* see reference below), or the last section of the psalm tone can be repeated for the refrain. In either case, the first part of a line of the refrain text is sung to the reciting tone, and the last three or four syllables are sung to the three concluding notes (if there is an extra syllable it is sung to the last note).

*Modal Psalm Tones: Organ Accompaniment.* St. Meinrad, Ind.: St. Meinrad Archabbey, 1973.

An excellent set of psalm tones, based on the Gregorian tones, prepared by the Benedictines of St. Meinrad Archabbey. Eight tones are provided, and each can accommodate stanzas of from four to six lines. A psalm text, such as the Grail text, may be pointed for use with the tones. The tones and optional accompaniment are both included. The psalm texts in the *Lutheran Book of Worship* and in *The Psalms: A New Translation for Worship* may be used with slight changes in pointing, and by dividing the texts into stanzas.

Pfatteicher, Philip H., and Carlos R. Messerli. *Manual on the Liturgy— Lutheran Book of Worship.* Minneapolis: Augsburg Publishing House, 1979.

Provides helpful suggestions for singing the psalms using the Lutheran psalm tones (pp. 82–85, 96–98). It includes a set of tones for singing the psalm antiphons (refrains) with the Lutheran psalm tones (pp. 84, 144–145). Also included are examples of pointing the refrains suggested for use with the psalms that are in the Lutheran lectionary for Sunday and festival use (pp. 138–144).

*Psalm Praise.* G.I.A. Publications, 1973.

This collection published by the Church Pastoral Aid Society in London is published in the United States by G.I.A. It provides a variety of settings for singing the psalms and biblical songs, including metrical settings such as those of Timothy Dudley-Smith. It includes chants of Norman Warren designed for antiphonal singing. These chants, structured like Anglican chant, are called "People's Chants," for they are easily sung by the congregation. They are antiphonal in nature and organized so that the congregation repeats the same melodic line, while the cantor (or choir) melodic lines vary. Since the psalm texts in *The Psalms: A New Translation for Worship* are pointed for Anglican chant, they lend themselves for use with the "People's Chants."

Smith, Geoffrey Boulton, ed. *A Responsorial Psalm Book.* London: Collins Liturgical Publications, 1986.

An excellent collection of 75 responsorial psalms and 4 canticles, with fresh musical settings, representing a wide variety of composers. The Grail text is used, although the new Grail could be substituted.

## Gelineau Psalmody

Carroll J. Robert. *Guide to Gelineau Psalmody.* G.I.A. Publications, 1979.

This booklet explains the Gelineau system of singing the psalms. Anyone wishing to learn Gelineau psalmody should study it carefully.

*The Grail/Gelineau Psalter.* G.I.A. Publications, 1963, 1972.

This is perhaps the most useful collection of Gelineau psalmody for use in daily prayer. It provides all 150 psalms (and 18 biblical songs). This particular edition of Gelineau psalms does not provide refrains. Three smaller publications, also published by G.I.A., include refrains: (1) *Twenty-four Psalms and a Canticle;* (2) *Thirty Psalms and Two Canticles;* (3) *Twenty Psalms and Three Canticles.* The inclusive-language version of the Grail psalm texts may be substituted for the texts in the earlier published volumes.

## Metrical Psalms

Anderson, Fred R. *Singing Psalms of Joy and Praise.* Philadelphia: Westminster Press, 1986.

    A collection of new metered texts for 51 of the Psalms.

*A List of Metrical Psalms Which May Be Found in Presbyterian Hymnals.* Louisville, Ky.: Office of Worship.

    Metrical psalms contained in *The Hymnal, The Hymnbook,* and *The Worshipbook* are listed.

Marier, Theodore, ed. *Hymns, Psalms and Spiritual Canticles.* Belmont, Mass.: BACS Publishing Co., 1972, 1974.

    This valuable musical resource for worship contains 20 metrical psalms by John Dunn. It contains 128 musical settings (both metrical and responsorial) for nearly 90 different psalms (or psalm portions).

*Psalter Hymnal.* CRC Publications, forthcoming.

    This new psalter-hymnal of the Christian Reformed Church contains all 150 psalms. Most texts are new versifications in contemporary English. Tunes range from Genevan to contemporary.

*Rejoice in the Lord,* ed. by Erik Routley. Wm. B. Eerdmans Publishing Co., 1985.

    This hymnal of the Reformed Church in America contains a section of 58 psalms (or psalm portions) in metrical settings, arranged numerically.

## Biblical Songs (Canticles) and Hymn of Light *(Phos Hilaron)*

    *A Psalm Sampler, The Grail/Gelineau Psalter,* the *Lutheran Book of Worship, Praise God in Song,* and *Hymns, Psalms and Spiritual Canticles,* listed above, contain settings of the Hymn of Light and the major biblical songs. See pp. 382–383 for settings that may be found in Presbyterian hymnals.

*The Book of Canticles* (Church Hymnal Series II). Church Hymnal Corporation, 1979.

    A variety of settings are provided for many of the biblical songs appearing in *Daily Prayer,* as well as Psalms 95 and 100. Much of the material in this book is now included in *The Hymnal 1982* of the Episcopal Church.

## Other Music for Daily Prayer

*Lutheran Book of Worship* (Ministers Desk Edition). Minneapolis: Augsburg Publishing House, 1978.

This service book contains full musical settings for Morning Prayer (Matins), Evening Prayer (Vespers), and Night Prayer (Compline). The setting for the opening of the Service of Light may be used for the first set of opening sentences for Saturday and Sunday evenings and the eve of major festivals in *Daily Prayer* (as an alternative to the music provided), since the texts in *Daily Prayer* are taken from the *Lutheran Book of Worship*. A setting for a thanksgiving for light (p. 82 in *Daily Prayer*, first prayer) may be found on page 60 of the *Lutheran Book of Worship*, Desk Edition. Two musical settings for the Litany, no. 40 in *Daily Prayer*, may be found in the *Lutheran Book of Worship* (Desk Ed., pp. 65–68). The Great Litany, no. 41 in *Daily Prayer*, may be sung to the setting provided in the *Lutheran Book of Worship* (Desk Ed., pp. 86–91). For information about the Great Litany and suggestions for singing it, see *Manual on the Liturgy*, listed above, pp. 299–300.

Melloh, John Allyn, and William G. Storey. *Praise God in Song: Ecumenical Daily Prayer*. G.I.A. Publications, 1979.

This is a valuable resource for a variety of musical settings for singing Morning and Evening Prayer. Settings for most of the thanksgivings for light included in *Daily Prayer* are provided in *Praise God in Song (PGS)*. The following may be found there: Ordinary days, p. 54, first prayer (*PGS* 219–221); Advent, pp. 87 and 106 (*PGS*, 230–231); Christmas and Epiphany, pp. 112 and 120 (*PGS*, 232–233); Lent, pp. 127 and 152 (*PGS*, 234–235); Easter, pp. 157 and 179 (*PGS*, 284–285); Pentecost, p. 184 (*PGS*, 236–237).

*Music from Taizé* by Jacques Berthier. G.I.A. Publications, 1978, 1980, 1981; and *Music from Taizé*, Vol. 2. G.I.A. Publications, 1982, 1983, 1984.

Music coming from the Taizé Community in France is a particularly valuable resource for musical alternatives to the beginning of morning or evening prayer, or to the hymn at the end of the service. The congregation can easily participate in this music, which may involve a cantor, or choir, and various instruments.

This music effectively conveys the spirit of sung prayer. Recordings of some of this music are available from G.I.A.

## Addresses of publishers of resources mentioned above

BACS Publishing Co., P.O. Box 167, Belmont, MA 02178

The Church Hymnal Corporation, 800 Second Avenue, New York, NY 10017

Church Hymnary Press, 1317 Sorenson Road, Helena, MT 59601

Collins Liturgical Publications, 8 Grafton Street, London, England W1X 3LA

CRC Publications, 2850 Kalamazoo Avenue S.E., Grand Rapids, MI 49560

Fortress Church Supply Stores, 2900 Queen Lane, Philadelphia, PA 19129 (or one of the branch stores, for various editions of the *Lutheran Book of Worship*)

G.I.A. Publications, 7404 South Mason Avenue, Chicago, IL 60638

Hope Publishing Co., Carol Stream, IL 60188

Office of Worship, 1044 Alta Vista Road, Louisville, KY 40205

St. Mary's Press, Christian Brothers Publications, Winona, MN 55987

St. Meinrad Archabbey, St. Meinrad, IN 47577

# DAILY
# LECTIONARY

# USING
# THE DAILY LECTIONARY

The daily lectionary which follows[21] is arranged in a two-year cycle, and provides for reading through the New Testament twice during the two-year cycle, and through the Old Testament once. It is coordinated with the church year, so that the readings are in keeping with the festivals and seasons. It is not intended for use in the principal Lord's Day service, but for services of daily prayer.

Year One begins with the First Sunday of Advent preceding odd-numbered years; Year Two begins with the First Sunday of Advent preceding even-numbered years. Thus, on the First Sunday of Advent in 1988, 1990, 1992, 1994, etc., the Lectionary for Year One is begun. On the First Sunday of Advent in 1987, 1989, 1991, 1993, etc., the Lectionary for Year Two is begun.

Three readings are provided for each day. Ordinarily the Old Testament reading and one of the New Testament readings (Epistle— Year One; Gospel—Year Two) are used in the morning, and the remaining New Testament reading is used in the evening. All three readings may be used in one service, but this is not encouraged. Traditionally, if more than one reading is used, the reading from the Old Testament is first.

When a festival interrupts the sequence of readings (or if the readings in the Common Lectionary are used for daily prayer on Sundays and festivals) the readings may be reordered by lengthening, combining, or omitting some of them to secure continuity, or to avoid repetition. Readings for "Other Festivals," for use in both years of the cycle, are listed on page 419.

This lectionary includes some readings from the Apocrypha. Within the Reformed tradition, the Apocryphal books are not recognized as part of the canon of Holy Scripture. They are not considered authoritative for doctrine, and have no greater status than other human writings.[22] Nevertheless, though they are not on a par with canonical scripture, the Apocryphal books may be instructive. Selections from the Old Testament are provided as alternatives to the readings from the Apocrypha and may be used when canonical readings are preferred, or when Apocryphal readings are not accessible.

# DAILY
# LECTIONARY

*1st Week of Advent*
**Su**  Isa. 1:1-9
    2 Peter 3:1-10
    Matt. 25:1-13
**M**  Isa. 1:10-20
    1 Thess. 1:1-10
    Luke 20:1-8
**Tu**  Isa. 1:21-31
    1 Thess. 2:1-12
    Luke 20:9-18
**W**  Isa. 2:1-4
    1 Thess. 2:13-20
    Luke 20:19-26
**Th**  Isa. 2:5-22
    1 Thess. 3:1-13
    Luke 20:27-40
**F**  Isa. 3:1–4:1
    1 Thess. 4:1-12
    Luke 20:41–21:4
**Sa**  Isa. 4:2-6
    1 Thess. 4:13-18
    Luke 21:5-19

*2nd Week of Advent*
**Su**  Isa. 5:1-7
    2 Peter 3:11-18
    Luke 7:28-35
**M**  Isa. 5:8-17

    1 Thess. 5:1-11
    Luke 21:20-28
**Tu**  Isa. 5:18-25
    1 Thess. 5:12-28
    Luke 21:29-38
**W**  Isa. 6:1-13
    2 Thess. 1:1-12
    John 7:53–8:11
**Th**  Isa. 7:1-9
    2 Thess. 2:1-12
    Luke 22:1-13
**F**  Isa. 7:10-25
    2 Thess. 2:13–3:5
    Luke 22:14-30
**Sa**  Isa. 8:1-15
    2 Thess. 3:6-18
    Luke 22:31-38

*3rd Week of Advent*
**Su**  Isa. 13:1-13
    Heb. 12:18-29
    John 3:22-30

*The readings below are interrupted after December 17 in favor of the readings identified by date in the 4th Week of Advent.*

**M**  Isa. 8:16–9:1
    2 Peter 1:1-11
    Luke 22:39-53
**Tu**  Isa. 9:2-7
    2 Peter 1:12-21
    Luke 22:54-69
**W**  Isa. 9:8-17
    2 Peter 2:1-10a
    Mark 1:1-8
**Th**  Isa. 9:18–10:4
    2 Peter 2:10b-16
    Matt. 3:1-12
**F**  Isa. 10:5-19
    2 Peter 2:17-22
    Matt. 11:2-15
**Sa**  Isa. 10:20-27
    Jude 17-25
    Luke 3:1-9

*4th Week of Advent*
**Dec**  Isa. 11:1-9
**18**  Eph. 6:10-20
    John 3:16-21
**Dec**  Isa. 11:10-16
**19**  Rev. 20:1-10
    John 5:30-47
**Dec**  Isa. 28:9-22
**20**  Rev. 20:11–21:8
    Luke 1:5-25

| Dec 21 | Isa. 29:9-24<br>Rev. 21:9-21<br>Luke 1:26-38 |
| Dec 22 | Isa. 31:1-9<br>Rev. 21:22–22:5<br>Luke 1:39-48a<br>(48b-56) |
| Dec 23 | Isa. 33:17-22<br>Rev. 22:6-11, 18-20<br>Luke 1:57-66 |
| Dec 24 | Isa. 35:1-10<br>Rev. 22:12-17, 21<br>Luke 1:67-80 |

*Christmas Eve*
Isa. 59:15b-21
Phil. 2:5-11

*Christmas Day*
Zech. 2:10-13
1 John 4:7-16
John 3:31-36

*1st Sunday after Christmas*
Isa. 62:6-7, 10-12
Heb. 2:10-18
Matt. 1:18-25

| Dec 26 | Wisd. of Sol. 4:7-15<br>*or* 2 Chron. 24:17-22<br>Acts 6:1-7<br>Acts 7:59–8:8 |
| Dec 27 | Prov. 8:22-30<br>1 John 5:1-12<br>John 13:20-35 |
| Dec 28 | Isa. 49:13-23<br>Isa. 54:1-13<br>Matt. 18:1-14 |
| Dec 29 | Isa. 12:1-6<br>Rev. 1:1-8<br>John 7:37-52 |
| Dec 30 | Isa. 25:1-9<br>Rev. 1:9-20<br>John 7:53–8:11 |
| Dec 31 | Isa. 26:1-6<br>2 Cor. 5:16–6:2<br>John 8:12-19 |

| Jan 1 | Gen. 17:1-12a, 15-16<br>Col. 2:6-12<br>John 16:23b-30 |

*2nd Sunday after Christmas*
Ecclus. 3:3-9, 14-17
*or* Deut. 33:1-5
1 John 2:12-17
John 6:41-47

| Jan 2 | Gen. 12:1-7<br>Heb. 11:1-12<br>John 6:35-42, 48-51 |
| Jan 3 | Gen. 28:10-22<br>Heb. 11:13-22<br>John 10:7-17 |
| Jan 4 | Ex. 3:1-5<br>Heb. 11:23-31<br>John 14:6-14 |
| Jan 5 | Josh. 1:1-9<br>Heb. 11:32–12:2<br>John 15:1-16 |

*Eve of Epiphany*
Isa. 66:18-23
Rom. 15:7-13

*Epiphany*
Isa. 52:7-10
Rev. 21:22-27
Matt. 12:14-21

*The readings for the dated days after the Epiphany are used only until the following Saturday evening.*

| Jan 7 | Isa. 52:3-6<br>Rev. 2:1-7<br>John 2:1-11 |
| Jan 8 | Isa. 59:15b-21<br>Rev. 2:8-17<br>John 4:46-54 |
| Jan 9 | Isa. 63:1-5<br>Rev. 2:18-29<br>John 5:1-15 |

| Jan 10 | Isa. 65:1-9<br>Rev. 3:1-6<br>John 6:1-14 |
| Jan 11 | Isa. 65:13-16<br>Rev. 3:7-13<br>John 6:15-27 |
| Jan 12 | Isa. 66:1-2, 22-23<br>Rev. 3:14-22<br>John 9:1-12, 35-38 |

*Eve of Baptism of the Lord*
Isa. 61:1-9
Gal. 3:23-29; 4:4-7

*Baptism of the Lord (1st Sunday after Epiphany) and following*
| Su | Isa. 40:1-11<br>Heb. 1:1-12<br>John 1:1-7, 19-20, 29-34 |
| M | Isa. 40:12-24<br>Eph. 1:1-14<br>Mark 1:1-13 |
| Tu | Isa. 40:25-31<br>Eph. 1:15-23<br>Mark 1:14-28 |
| W | Isa. 41:1-16<br>Eph. 2:1-10<br>Mark 1:29-45 |
| Th | Isa. 41:17-29<br>Eph. 2:11-22<br>Mark 2:1-12 |
| F | Isa. 42:(1-9) 10-17<br>Eph. 3:1-13<br>Mark 2:13-22 |
| Sa | Isa. (42:18-25)<br>43:1-13<br>Eph. 3:14-21<br>Mark 2:23–3:6 |

*Week of 2nd Sunday after Epiphany*
| Su | Isa. 43:14–44:5<br>Heb. 6:17–7:10<br>John 4:27-42 |

| M | Isa. 44:6-8, 21-23 | M | Isa. 51:17-23 | M | Isa. 63:1-6 |
|---|---|---|---|---|---|
| | Eph. 4:1-16 | | Gal. 4:1-11 | | 1 Tim. 1:1-17 |
| | Mark 3:7-19a | | Mark 7:24-37 | | Mark 11:1-11 |
| Tu | Isa. 44:9-20 | Tu | Isa. 52:1-12 | Tu | Isa. 63:7-14 |
| | Eph. 4:17-32 | | Gal. 4:12-20 | | 1 Tim. 1:18–2:8 |
| | Mark 3:19b-35 | | Mark 8:1-10 | | (9-15) |
| W | Isa. 44:24–45:7 | W | Isa. 52:13–53:12 | | Mark 11:12-26 |
| | Eph. 5:1-14 | | Gal. 4:21-31 | W | Isa. 63:15–64:9 |
| | Mark 4:1-20 | | Mark 8:11-26 | | 1 Tim. 3:1-16 |
| Th | Isa. 45:5-17 | Th | Isa. 54:1-10 (11-17) | | Mark 11:27–12:12 |
| | Eph. 5:15-33 | | Gal. 5:1-15 | Th | Isa. 65:1-12 |
| | Mark 4:21-34 | | Mark 8:27–9:1 | | 1 Tim. 4:1-16 |
| F | Isa. 45:18-25 | F | Isa. 55:1-13 | | Mark 12:13-27 |
| | Eph. 6:1-9 | | Gal. 5:16-24 | F | Isa. 65:17-25 |
| | Mark 4:35-41 | | Mark 9:2-13 | | 1 Tim. 5:(1-16) 17-22 |
| Sa | Isa. 46:1-13 | Sa | Isa. 56:1-8 | | (23-25) |
| | Eph. 6:10-24 | | Gal. 5:25–6:10 | | Mark 12:28-34 |
| | Mark 5:1-20 | | Mark 9:14-29 | Sa | Isa. 66:1-6 |
| | | | | | 1 Tim. 6:(1-5) 6-21 |
| | | | | | Mark 12:35-44 |

*Week of 3rd Sunday after*
*Epiphany*

| Su | Isa. 47:1-15 |
|---|---|
| | Heb. 10:19-31 |
| | John 5:2-18 |
| M | Isa. 48:1-11 |
| | Gal. 1:1-17 |
| | Mark 5:21-43 |
| Tu | Isa. 48:12-21 (22) |
| | Gal. 1:18–2:10 |
| | Mark 6:1-13 |
| W | Isa. 49:1-12 |
| | Gal. 2:11-21 |
| | Mark 6:13-29 |
| Th | Isa. 49:13-23 (24-26) |
| | Gal. 3:1-14 |
| | Mark 6:30-46 |
| F | Isa. 50:1-11 |
| | Gal. 3:15-22 |
| | Mark 6:47-56 |
| Sa | Isa. 51:1-8 |
| | Gal. 3:23-29 |
| | Mark 7:1-23 |

*Week of 5th Sunday after*
*Epiphany*

| Su | Isa. 57:1-13 |
|---|---|
| | Heb. 12:1-6 |
| | John 7:37-46 |
| M | Isa. 57:14-21 |
| | Gal. 6:11-18 |
| | Mark 9:30-41 |
| Tu | Isa. 58:1-12 |
| | 2 Tim. 1:1-14 |
| | Mark 9:42-50 |
| W | Isa. 59:1-21 |
| | 2 Tim. 1:15–2:13 |
| | Mark 10:1-16 |
| Th | Isa. 60:1-22 |
| | 2 Tim. 2:14-26 |
| | Mark 10:17-31 |
| F | Isa. 61:1-9 |
| | 2 Tim. 3:1-17 |
| | Mark 10:32-45 |
| Sa | Isa. 61:10–62:5 |
| | 2 Tim. 4:1-8 |
| | Mark 10:46-52 |

*Week of 7th Sunday after*
*Epiphany*

| Su | Isa. 66:7-14 |
|---|---|
| | 1 John 3:4-10 |
| | John 10:7-16 |
| M | Ruth 1:1-14 |
| | 2 Cor. 1:1-11 |
| | Matt. 5:1-12 |
| Tu | Ruth 1:15-22 |
| | 2 Cor. 1:12-22 |
| | Matt. 5:13-20 |
| W | Ruth 2:1-13 |
| | 2 Cor. 1:23–2:17 |
| | Matt. 5:21-26 |
| Th | Ruth 2:14-23 |
| | 2 Cor. 3:1-18 |
| | Matt. 5:27-37 |
| F | Ruth 3:1-18 |
| | 2 Cor. 4:1-12 |
| | Matt. 5:38-48 |
| Sa | Ruth 4:1-22 |
| | 2 Cor. 4:13–5:10 |
| | Matt. 6:1-6 |

*Week of 4th Sunday after*
*Epiphany*

| Su | Isa. 51:9-16 |
|---|---|
| | Heb. 11:8-16 |
| | John 7:14-31 |

*Week of 6th Sunday after*
*Epiphany*

| Su | Isa. 62:6-12 |
|---|---|
| | 1 John 2:3-11 |
| | John 8:12-19 |

*Week of 8th Sunday after*
*Epiphany*

| Su | Deut. 4:1-9 |
|---|---|

2 Tim. 4:1-8
John 12:1-8

**M** Deut. 4:9-14
2 Cor. 10:1-18
Matt. 6:7-15

**Tu** Deut. 4:15-24
2 Cor. 11:1-21a
Matt. 6:16-23

**W** Deut. 4:25-31
2 Cor. 11:21b-33
Matt. 6:24-34

**Th** Deut. 4:32-40
2 Cor. 12:1-10
Matt. 7:1-12

**F** Deut. 5:1-22
2 Cor. 12:11-21
Matt. 7:13-21

**Sa** Deut. 5:22-33
2 Cor. 13:1-14
Matt. 7:22-29

*Transfiguration (Last Sunday after Epiphany) and following*

**Su** Dan. 7:9-10, 13-14
2 Cor. 3:1-9
John 12:27-36a

**M** Deut. 6:1-15
Heb. 1:1-14
John 1:1-18

**Tu** Deut. 6:16-25
Heb. 2:1-10
John 1:19-28

*Lent*
*Ash Wednesday*
Jonah 3:1–4:11
Heb. 12:1-14
Luke 18:9-14

**Th** Deut. 7:6-11
Titus 1:1-16
John 1:29-34

**F** Deut. 7:12-16
Titus 2:1-15
John 1:35-42

**Sa** Deut. 7:17-26
Titus 3:1-15
John 1:43-51

*1st Week in Lent*
**Su** Jer. 9:23-24
1 Cor. 1:18-31
Mark 2:18-22

**M** Deut. 8:1-20
Heb. 2:11-18
John 2:1-12

**Tu** Deut. 9:(1-3) 4-12
Heb. 3:1-11
John 2:13-22

**W** Deut. 9:13-21
Heb. 3:12-19
John 2:23–3:15

**Th** Deut. 9:23–10:5
Heb. 4:1-10
John 3:16-21

**F** Deut. 10:12-22
Heb. 4:11-16
John 3:22-36

**Sa** Deut. 11:18-28
Heb. 5:1-10
John 4:1-26

*2nd Week in Lent*
**Su** Jer. 1:1-10
1 Cor. 3:11-23
Mark 3:31–4:9

**M** Jer. 1:11-19
Rom. 1:1-15
John 4:27-42

**Tu** Jer. 2:1-13, 29-32
Rom. 1:16-25
John 4:43-54

**W** Jer. 3:6-18
Rom. 1:(26-27)
28–2:11
John 5:1-18

**Th** Jer. 4:9-10, 19-28
Rom. 2:12-24
John 5:19-29

**F** Jer. 5:1-9
Rom. 2:25–3:18
John 5:30-47

**Sa** Jer. 5:20-31
Rom. 3:19-31
John 7:1-13

*3rd Week in Lent*
**Su** Jer. 6:9-15

1 Cor. 6:12-20
Mark 5:1-20

**M** Jer. 7:1-15
Rom. 4:1-12
John 7:14-36

**Tu** Jer. 7:21-34
Rom. 4:13-25
John 7:37-52

**W** Jer. 8:4-7, 18–9:6
Rom. 5:1-11
John 8:12-20

**Th** Jer. 10:11-24
Rom. 5:12-21
John 8:21-32

**F** Jer. 11:1-8, 14-17
Rom. 6:1-11
John 8:33-47

**Sa** Jer. 13:1-11
Rom. 6:12-23
John 8:47-59

*4th Week in Lent*
**Su** Jer. 14:1-9 (10-16)
17-22
Gal. 4:21–5:1
Mark 8:11-21

**M** Jer. 16:(1-9) 10-21
Rom. 7:1-12
John 6:1-15

**Tu** Jer. 17:19-27
Rom. 7:13-25
John 6:16-27

**W** Jer. 18:1-11
Rom. 8:1-11
John 6:27-40

**Th** Jer. 22:13-23
Rom. 8:12-27
John 6:41-51

**F** Jer. 23:1-8
Rom. 8:28-39
John 6:52-59

**Sa** Jer. 23:9-15
Rom. 9:1-18
John 6:60-71

*5th Week in Lent*
**Su** Jer. 23:16-32
1 Cor. 9:19-27
Mark 8:31–9:1

M Jer. 24:1-10
Rom. 9:19-33
John 9:1-17
Tu Jer. 25:8-17
Rom. 10:1-13
John 9:18-41
W Jer. 25:30-38
Rom. 10:14-21
John 10:1-18
Th Jer. 26:1-16 (17-24)
Rom. 11:1-12
John 10:19-42
F Jer. 29:1 (2-3) 4-14
Rom. 11:13-24
John 11:1-27
or John 12:1-10
Sa Jer. 31:27-34
Rom. 11:25-36
John 11:28-44
or John 12:37-50

*Holy Week*
*Passion/Palm Sunday*
Zech. 9:9-12*
1 Tim. 6:12-16*
or Zech. 12:9-11;
13:1, 7-9**
Matt. 21:12-17**
M Jer. 11:18-20
12:1-16 (17)
Phil. 3:1-14
John 12:9-19
Tu Jer. 15:10-21
Phil. 3:15-21
John 12:20-26
W Jer. 17:5-10, 14-17
(18)
Phil. 4:1-13
John 12:27-36

*Maundy Thursday*
Jer. 20:7-11 (12-13)
14-18
1 Cor. 10:14-17;
11:27-32
John 17:1-11 (12-26)

*Good Friday*
Wisd. of Sol. 1:16–
2:1, 12-22
or Gen. 22:1-14
1 Peter 1:10-20
John 13:36-38*
or John 19:38-42**

*Holy Saturday*
Job 19:21-27a
Heb. 4:1-16*
Rom. 8:1-11**

*Easter Week*
Su Ex. 12:1-14*
John 1:1-18*
or
Isa. 51:9-11**
Luke 24:13-35**
or John 20:19-23**
M Jonah 2:1-10
Acts 2:14, 22-32
John 14:1-14
Tu Isa. 30:18-26
Acts 2:36-41 (42-47)
John 14:15-31
W Micah 7:7-15
Acts 3:1-10
John 15:1-11
Th Ezek. 37:1-14
Acts 3:11-26
John 15:12-27
F Dan. 12:1-4, 13
Acts 4:1-12
John 16:1-15
Sa Isa. 25:1-9
Acts 4:13-21 (22-31)
John 16:16-33

*2nd Week of Easter*
Su Isa. 43:8-13
1 Peter 2:2-10
John 14:1-7
M Dan. 1:1-21

1 John 1:1-10
John 17:1-11
Tu Dan. 2:1-16
1 John 2:1-11
John 17:12-19
W Dan. 2:17-30
1 John 2:12-17
John 17:20-26
Th Dan. 2:31-49
1 John 2:18-29
Luke 3:1-14
F Dan. 3:1-18
1 John 3:1-10
Luke 3:15-22
Sa Dan. 3:19-30
1 John 3:11-18
Luke 4:1-13

*3rd Week of Easter*
Su Dan. 4:1-18
1 Peter 4:7-11
John 21:15-25
M Dan. 4:19-27
1 John 3:19–4:6
Luke 4:14-30
Tu Dan. 4:28-37
1 John 4:7-21
Luke 4:31-37
W Dan. 5:1-12
1 John 5:1-12
Luke 4:38-44
Th Dan. 5:13-30
1 John 5:13-20 (21)
Luke 5:1-11
F Dan. 6:1-15
2 John 1-13
Luke 5:12-26
Sa Dan. 6:16-28
3 John 1-15
Luke 5:27-39

*4th Week of Easter*
Su Wisd. of Sol. 1:1-15
or Gen. 18:22-33
1 Peter 5:1-11

---

*Intended for use in the morning    **Intended for use in the evening

|   | Matt. 7:15-29 | **Th** | Wisd. of Sol. 14:27– |   | Heb. 5:7-14 |
|---|---|---|---|---|---|
| **M** | Wisd. of Sol. 1:16– |   | 15:3 |   | Luke 9:37-50 |
|   | 2:11, 21-24 |   | *or* Jer. 33:1-13 |   |   |
|   | *or* Jer. 30:1-9 |   | Rom. 14:1-12 |   | *7th Week of Easter* |
|   | Col. 1:1-14 |   | Luke 8:26-39 | **Su** | Ezek. 3:16-27 |
|   | Luke 6:1-11 | **F** | Wisd. of Sol. 16:15– |   | Eph. 2:1-10 |
| **Tu** | Wisd. of Sol. 3:1-9 |   | 17:1 |   | Matt. 10:24-33, |
|   | *or* Jer. 30:10-17 |   | *or* Deut. 31:30–32:14 |   | 40-42 |
|   | Col. 1:15-23 |   | Rom. 14:13-23 | **M** | Ezek. 4:1-17 |
|   | Luke 6:12-26 |   | Luke 8:40-56 |   | Heb. 6:1-12 |
| **W** | Wisd. of Sol. 4:16— | **Sa** | Wisd. of Sol. 19:1-8, |   | Luke 9:51-62 |
|   | 5:8 |   | 18-22 | **Tu** | Ezek. 7:10-15, |
|   | *or* Jer. 30:18-22 |   | *or* Deut. 32:34-41 |   | 23b-27 |
|   | Col. 1:24–2:7 |   | (42) 43 |   | Heb. 6:13-20 |
|   | Luke 6:27-38 |   | Rom. 15:1-13 |   | Luke 10:1-17 |
| **Th** | Wisd. of Sol. 5:9-23 |   | Luke 9:1-17 | **W** | Ezek. 11:14-25 |
|   | *or* Jer. 31:1-14 |   |   |   | Heb. 7:1-17 |
|   | Col. 2:8-23 |   |   |   | Luke 10:17-24 |
|   | Luke 6:39-49 | | *6th Week of Easter* | **Th** | Ezek. 18:1-4, 19-32 |
| **F** | Wisd. of Sol. 6:12-23 | **Su** | Ecclus. 43:1-12, |   | Heb. 7:18-28 |
|   | *or* Jer. 31:15-22 |   | 27-32 |   | Luke 10:25-37 |
|   | Col. 3:1-11 |   | *or* Deut. 15:1-11 | **F** | Ezek. 34:17-31 |
|   | Luke 7:1-17 |   | 1 Tim. 3:14–4:5 |   | Heb. 8:1-13 |
| **Sa** | Wisd. of Sol. 7:1-14 |   | Matt. 13:24-34a |   | Luke 10:38-42 |
|   | *or* Jer. 31:23-25 | **M** | Deut. 8:1-10 | **Sa** | Ezek. 43:1-12 |
|   | Col. 3:12-17 |   | *or* Deut. 18:9-14 |   | Heb. 9:1-14 |
|   | Luke 7:18-28 (29-30) |   | James 1:1-15 |   | Luke 11:14-23 |
|   | 31-35 |   | Luke 9:18-27 |   |   |
|   |   | **Tu** | Deut. 8:11-20 |   |   |
|   |   |   | *or* Deut. 18:15-22 | | *Eve of Pentecost* |
| | *5th Week of Easter* |   | James 1:16-27 |   | Ex. 19:3-8a, 16-20 |
| **Su** | Wisd. of Sol. 7:22– |   | Luke 11:1-13 |   | 1 Peter 2:4-10 |
|   | 8:1 | **W** | Baruch 3:24-37 |   |   |
|   | *or* Isa. 32:1-8 |   | *or* Deut. 19:1-7 |   |   |
|   | 2 Thess. 2:13-17 |   | James 5:13-18 | | *Pentecost* |
|   | Matt. 7:7-14 |   | Luke 12:22-31 |   | Isa. 11:1-9 |
| **M** | Wisd. of Sol. 9:1, |   |   |   | 1 Cor. 2:1-13 |
|   | 7-18 | | | |   | John 14:21-29 |
|   | *or* Jer. 32:1-15 | | *Eve of Ascension* |   |   |
|   | Col. 3:18–4:18 |   | 2 Kings 2:1-15 | | *On the weekdays which* |
|   | Luke 7:36-50 |   | Rev. 5:1-14 | | *follow, the readings are taken* |
| **Tu** | Wisd. of Sol. 10:1-4 |   |   | | *from the week which* |
|   | (5-12) 13-21 | | | | *corresponds to the date of* |
|   | *or* Jer. 32:16-25 | | *Ascension Day* | | *Pentecost.* |
|   | Rom. 12:1-21 |   | Ezek. 1:1-14, 24-28b |   |   |
|   | Luke 8:1-15 |   | Heb. 2:5-18 | | |
| **W** | Wisd. of Sol. 13:1-9 |   | Matt. 28:16-20 | | *Eve of Trinity Sunday* |
|   | *or* Jer. 32:36-44 | **F** | Ezek. 1:28–3:3 |   | Ecclus. 42:15-25 |
|   | Rom. 13:1-14 |   | Heb. 4:14–5:6 |   | *or* Isa. 6:1-8 |
|   | Luke 8:16-25 |   | Luke 9:28-36 |   | Eph. 3:14-21 |
|   |   | **Sa** | Ezek. 3:4-17 |   |   |

*Trinity Sunday*
  Ecclus. 43:1-12
  (27-33)
  *or* Deut. 6:1-9
  (10-15)
  Eph. 4:1-16
  John 1:1-18

*On the weekdays which
follow, the readings are taken
from the week which
corresponds to the date of
Trinity Sunday.*

*Week following Sunday
between May 11 and May
16 inclusive, if after
Pentecost Sunday*
M   Isa. 63:7-14
    2 Tim. 1:1-14
    Luke 11:24-36
Tu  Isa. 63:15–64:9
    2 Tim. 1:15–2:13
    Luke 11:37-52
W   Isa. 65:1-12
    2 Tim. 2:14-26
    Luke 11:53–12:12
Th  Isa. 65:17-25
    2 Tim. 3:1-17
    Luke 12:13-31
F   Isa. 66:1-6
    2 Tim. 4:1-8
    Luke 12:32-48
Sa  Isa. 66:7-14
    2 Tim. 4:9-22
    Luke 12:49-59

*Week following Sunday
between May 17 and May
24 inclusive, if after
Pentecost Sunday*
M   Ruth 1:1-18
    1 Tim. 1:1-17
    Luke 13:1-9
Tu  Ruth 1:19–2:13
    1 Tim. 1:18–2:8
    Luke 13:10-17

W   Ruth 2:14-23
    1 Tim. 3:1-16
    Luke 13:18-30
Th  Ruth 3:1-18
    1 Tim. 4:1-16
    Luke 13:31-35
F   Ruth 4:1-22
    1 Tim. 5:17-22
    (23-25)
    Luke 14:1-11
Sa  Deut. 1:1-8
    1 Tim. 6:6-21
    Luke 14:12-24

*Week following Sunday
between May 24 and May
28 inclusive, if after
Pentecost Sunday*
Su  Deut. 4:1-9
    Rev. 7:1-4, 9-17
    Matt. 12:33-45
M   Deut. 4:9-14
    2 Cor. 1:1-11
    Luke 14:25-35
Tu  Deut. 4:15-24
    2 Cor. 1:12-22
    Luke 15:1-10
W   Deut. 4:25-31
    2 Cor. 1:23–2:17
    Luke 15:1-2, 11-32
Th  Deut. 4:32-40
    2 Cor. 3:1-18
    Luke 16:1-9
F   Deut. 5:1-22
    2 Cor. 4:1-12
    Luke 16:10-17 (18)
Sa  Deut. 5:22-33
    2 Cor. 4:13–5:10
    Luke 16:19-31

*Week following Sunday
between May 29 and June
4 inclusive, if after
Pentecost Sunday*
Su  Deut. 11:1-12
    Rev. 10:1-11
    Matt. 13:44-58

M   Deut. 11:13-19
    2 Cor. 5:11–6:2
    Luke 17:1-10
Tu  Deut. 12:1-12
    2 Cor. 6:3-13
    (14–7:1)
    Luke 17:11-19
W   Deut. 13:1-11
    2 Cor. 7:2-16
    Luke 17:20-37
Th  Deut. 16:18-20;
    17:14-20
    2 Cor. 8:1-16
    Luke 18:1-8
F   Deut. 26:1-11
    2 Cor. 8:16-24
    Luke 18:9-14
Sa  Deut. 29:2-15
    2 Cor. 9:1-15
    Luke 18:15-30

*Week following Sunday
between June 5 and 11
inclusive, if after Pentecost
Sunday*
Su  Deut. 29:16-29
    Rev. 12:1-12
    Matt. 15:29-39
M   Deut. 30:1-10
    2 Cor. 10:1-18
    Luke 18:31-43
Tu  Deut. 30:11-20
    2 Cor. 11:1-21a
    Luke 19:1-10
W   Deut. 31:30–32:14
    2 Cor. 11:21b-33
    Luke 19:11-27
Th  Ecclus. 44:19–45:5
    *or* S. of Sol. 1:1-3,
    9-11, 15-16a;
    2:1-3a
    2 Cor. 12:1-10
    Luke 19:28-40
F   Ecclus. 45:6-16
    *or* S. of Sol. 2:8-13;
    4:1-4a, 5-7, 9-11
    2 Cor. 12:11-21
    Luke 19:41-48

**Sa**  Ecclus. 46:1-10
*or* S. of Sol. 5:10-16,
7:1-2 (3-5) 6-7a (9);
8:6-7
2 Cor. 13:1-14
Luke 20:1-8

*Week following Sunday*
*between June 12 and 18*
*inclusive*
**Su**  Ecclus. 46:11-20
*or* Ex. 6:2-13; 7:1-6
Rev. 15:1-8
Matt. 18:1-14
**M**  1 Sam. 1:1-20
Acts 1:1-14
Luke 20:9-19
**Tu**  1 Sam. 1:21–2:11
Acts 1:15-26
Luke 20:19-26
**W**  1 Sam. 2:12-26
Acts 2:1-21
Luke 20:27-40
**Th**  1 Sam. 2:27-36
Acts 2:22-36
Luke 20:41–21:4
**F**  1 Sam. 3:1-21
Acts 2:37-47
Luke 21:5-19
**Sa**  1 Sam. 4:1b-11
Acts 4:32–5:11
Luke 21:20-28

*Week following Sunday*
*between June 19 and 25*
*inclusive*
**Su**  1 Sam. 4:12-22
James 1:1-18
Matt. 19:23-30
**M**  1 Sam. 5:1-12
Acts 5:12-26
Luke 21:29-36
**Tu**  1 Sam. 6:1-16
Acts 5:27-42
Luke 21:37–22:13
**W**  1 Sam. 7:2-17
Acts 6:1-15
Luke 22:14-23

**Th**  1 Sam. 8:1-22
Acts 6:15–7:16
Luke 22:24-30
**F**  1 Sam. 9:1-14
Acts 7:17-29
Luke 22:31-38
**Sa**  1 Sam. 9:15–10:1
Acts 7:30-43
Luke 22:39-51

*Week following Sunday*
*between June 26 and July*
*2 inclusive*
**Su**  1 Sam. 10:1-16
Rom. 4:13-25
Matt. 21:23-32
**M**  1 Sam. 10:17-27
Acts 7:44–8:1a
Luke 22:52-62
**Tu**  1 Sam. 11:1-15
Acts 8:1b-13
Luke 22:63-71
**W**  1 Sam. 12:1-6 (7-15)
16-25
Acts 8:14-25
Luke 23:1-12
**Th**  1 Sam. 13:5-18
Acts 8:26-40
Luke 23:13-25
**F**  1 Sam. 13:19–14:15
Acts 9:1-9
Luke 23:26-31
**Sa**  1 Sam. 14:16-30
Acts 9:10-19a
Luke 23:32-43

*Week following Sunday*
*between July 3 and 9*
*inclusive*
**Su**  1 Sam. 14:36-45
Rom. 5:1-11
Matt. 22:1-14
**M**  1 Sam. 15:1-3, 7-23
Acts 9:19b-31
Luke 23:44-56a
**Tu**  1 Sam. 15:24-35
Acts 9:32-43
Luke 23:56b–24:11
(12)

**W**  1 Sam. 16:1-13
Acts 10:1-16
Luke 24:13-35
**Th**  1 Sam. 16:14–17:11
Acts 10:17-33
Luke 24:36-53
**F**  1 Sam. 17:17-30
Acts 10:34-48
Mark 1:1-13
**Sa**  1 Sam. 17:31-49
Acts 11:1-18
Mark 1:14-28

*Week following Sunday*
*between July 10 and 16*
*inclusive*
**Su**  1 Sam. 17:50–18:4
Rom. 10:4-17
Matt. 23:29-39
**M**  1 Sam. 18:5-16
(17-27a) 27b-30
Acts 11:19-30
Mark 1:29-45
**Tu**  1 Sam. 19:1-18
(19-24)
Acts 12:1-17
Mark 2:1-12
**W**  1 Sam. 20:1-23
Acts 12:18-25
Mark 2:13-22
**Th**  1 Sam. 20:24-42
Acts 13:1-12
Mark 2:23–3:6
**F**  1 Sam. 21:1-15
Acts 13:13-25
Mark 3:7-19a
**Sa**  1 Sam. 21:1-23
Acts 13:26-43
Mark 3:19b-35

*Week following Sunday*
*between July 17 and 23*
*inclusive*
**Su**  1 Sam. 23:7-18
Rom. 11:33–12:2
Matt. 25:14-30
**M**  1 Sam. 24:1-22
Acts 13:44-52

Mark 4:1-20
**Tu** 1 Sam. 25:1-22
Acts 14:1-18
Mark 4:21-34
**W** 1 Sam. 25:23-44
Acts 14:19-28
Mark 4:35-41
**Th** 1 Sam. 28:3-20
Acts 15:1-11
Mark 5:1-20
**F** 1 Sam. 31:1-13
Acts 15:12-21
Mark 5:21-43
**Sa** 2 Sam. 1:1-16
Acts 15:22-35
Mark 6:1-13

*Week following Sunday*
*between July 24 and 30*
*inclusive*
**Su** 2 Sam. 1:17-27
Rom. 12:9-21
Matt. 25:31-46
**M** 2 Sam. 2:1-11
Acts 15:36–16:5
Mark 6:14-29
**Tu** 2 Sam. 3:6-21
Acts 16:6-15
Mark 6:30-46
**W** 2 Sam. 3:22-39
Acts 16:16-24
Mark 6:47-56
**Th** 2 Sam. 4:1-12
Acts 16:25-40
Mark 7:1-23
**F** 2 Sam. 5:1-12
Acts 17:1-15
Mark 7:24-37
**Sa** 2 Sam. 5:22–6:11
Acts 17:16-34
Mark 8:1-10

*Week following Sunday*
*between July 31 and Aug.*
*6 inclusive*
**Su** 2 Sam. 6:12-23
Rom. 14:7-12
John 1:43-51

**M** 2 Sam. 7:1-17
Acts 18:1-11
Mark 8:11-21
**Tu** 2 Sam. 7:18-29
Acts 18:12-28
Mark 8:22-33
**W** 2 Sam. 9:1-13
Acts 19:1-10
Mark 8:34–9:1
**Th** 2 Sam. 11:1-27
Acts 19:11-20
Mark 9:2-13
**F** 2 Sam. 12:1-14
Acts 19:21-41
Mark 9:14-29
**Sa** 2 Sam. 12:15-31
Acts 20:1-16
Mark 9:30-41

*Week following Sunday*
*between Aug. 7 and 13*
*inclusive*
**Su** 2 Sam. 13:1-22
Rom. 15:1-13
John 3:22-36
**M** 2 Sam. 13:23-39
Acts 20:17-38
Mark 9:42-50
**Tu** 2 Sam. 14:1-20
Acts 21:1-14
Mark 10:1-16
**W** 2 Sam. 14:21-33
Acts 21:15-26
Mark 10:17-31
**Th** 2 Sam. 15:1-18
Acts 21:27-36
Mark 10:32-45
**F** 2 Sam. 15:19-37
Acts 21:37–22:16
Mark 10:46-52
**Sa** 2 Sam. 16:1-23
Acts 22:17-29
Mark 11:1-11

*Week following Sunday*
*between Aug. 14 and 20*
*inclusive*
**Su** 2 Sam. 17:1-23

Gal. 3:6-14
John 5:30-47
**M** 2 Sam. 17:24–18:8
Acts 22:30–23:11
Mark 11:12-26
**Tu** 2 Sam. 18:9-18
Acts 23:12-24
Mark 11:27–12:12
**W** 2 Sam. 18:19-33
Acts 23:23-35
Mark 12:13-27
**Th** 2 Sam. 19:1-23
Acts 24:1-23
Mark 12:28-34
**F** 2 Sam. 19:24-43
Acts 24:24–25:12
Mark 12:35-44
**Sa** 2 Sam. 23:1-7, 13-17
Acts 25:13-27
Mark 13:1-13

*Week following Sunday*
*between Aug. 21 and 27*
*inclusive*
**Su** 2 Sam. 24:1-2, 10-25
Gal. 3:23–4:7
John 8:12-20
**M** 1 Kings 1:(1-4) 5-31
Acts 26:1-23
Mark 13:14-27
**Tu** 1 Kings 1:32–2:4
(5-46a) 46b
Acts 26:24–27:8
Mark 13:28-37
**W** 1 Kings 3:1-15
Acts 27:9-26
Mark 14:1-11
**Th** 1 Kings 3:16-28
Acts 27:27-44
Mark 14:12-26
**F** 1 Kings 5:1–6:1, 7
Acts 28:1-16
Mark 14:27-42
**Sa** 1 Kings 7:51–8:21
Acts 28:17-31
Mark 14:43-52

*Week following Sunday between Aug. 28 and Sept. 3 inclusive*

**Su** 1 Kings 8:22-30
(31-40)
1 Tim. 4:7b-16
John 8:47-59

**M** 2 Chron. 6:32–7:7
James 2:1-13
Mark 14:53-65

**Tu** 1 Kings 8:65–9:9
James 2:14-26
Mark 14:66-72

**W** 1 Kings 9:24–10:13
James 3:1-12
Mark 15:1-11

**Th** 1 Kings 11:1-13
James 3:13–4:12
Mark 15:12-21

**F** 1 Kings 11:26-43
James 4:13–5:6
Mark 15:22-32

**Sa** 1 Kings 12:1-20
James 5:7-20
Mark 15:33-39

*Week following Sunday between Sept. 4 and 10 inclusive*

**Su** 1 Kings 12:21-33
Acts 4:18-31
John 10:31-42

**M** 1 Kings 13:1-10
Phil. 1:1-11
Mark 15:40-47

**Tu** 1 Kings 16:23-34
Phil. 1:12-30
Mark 16:1-8 (9-20)

**W** 1 Kings 17:1-24
Phil. 2:1-11
Matt. 2:1-12

**Th** 1 Kings 18:1-19
Phil. 2:12-30
Matt. 2:13-23

**F** 1 Kings 18:20-40
Phil. 3:1-16
Matt. 3:1-12

**Sa** 1 Kings 18:41–19:8
Phil. 3:17–4:7
Matt. 3:13-17

*Week following Sunday between Sept. 11 and 17 inclusive*

**Su** 1 Kings 19:8-21
Acts 5:34-42
John 11:45-57

**M** 1 Kings 21:1-16
1 Cor. 1:1-19
Matt. 4:1-11

**Tu** 1 Kings 21:17-29
1 Cor. 1:20-31
Matt. 4:12-17

**W** 1 Kings 22:1-28
1 Cor. 2:1-13
Matt. 4:18-25

**Th** 1 Kings 22:29-45
1 Cor. 2:14–3:15
Matt. 5:1-10

**F** 2 Kings 1:2-17
1 Cor. 3:16-23
Matt. 5:11-16

**Sa** 2 Kings 2:1-18
1 Cor. 4:1-7
Matt. 5:17-20

*Week following Sunday between Sept. 18 and 24 inclusive*

**Su** 2 Kings 4:8-37
Acts 9:10-31
Luke 3:7-18

**M** 2 Kings 5:1-19
1 Cor. 4:8-21
Matt. 5:21-26

**Tu** 2 Kings 5:19-27
1 Cor. 5:1-8
Matt. 5:27-37

**W** 2 Kings 6:1-23
1 Cor. 5:9–6:11
Matt. 5:38-48

**Th** 2 Kings 9:1-16
1 Cor. 6:12-20
Matt. 6:1-6, 16-18

**F** 2 Kings 9:17-37
1 Cor. 7:1-9
Matt. 6:7-15

**Sa** 2 Kings 11:1-20a
1 Cor. 7:10-24
Matt. 6:19-24

*Week following Sunday between Sept. 25 and Oct. 1 inclusive*

**Su** 2 Kings 17:1-18
Acts 9:36-43
Luke 5:1-11

**M** 2 Kings 17:24-41
1 Cor. 7:25-31
Matt. 6:25-34

**Tu** 2 Chron. 29:1-3; 30:1
(2-9) 10-27
1 Cor. 7:32-40
Matt. 7:1-12

**W** 2 Kings 18:9-25
1 Cor. 8:1-13
Matt. 7:13-21

**Th** 2 Kings 18:28-37
1 Cor. 9:1-15
Matt. 7:22-29

**F** 2 Kings 19:1-20
1 Cor. 9:16-27
Matt. 8:1-17

**Sa** 2 Kings 19:21-36
1 Cor. 10:1-13
Matt. 8:18-27

*Week following Sunday between Oct. 2 and 8 inclusive*

**Su** 2 Kings 20:1-21
Acts 12:1-17
Luke 7:11-17

**M** 2 Kings 21:1-18
1 Cor. 10:14–11:1
Matt. 8:28-34

**Tu** 2 Kings 22:1-13
1 Cor. 11:2 (3-16)
17-22
Matt. 9:1-8

**W** 2 Kings 22:14–23:3
1 Cor. 11:23-34
Matt. 9:9-17

**Th** 2 Kings 23:4-25
1 Cor. 12:1-11
Matt. 9:18-26

**F** 2 Kings 23:36–24:17
1 Cor. 12:12-26
Matt. 9:27-34

**Sa** Jer. 35:1-19

1 Cor. 12:27–13:3
Matt. 9:35–10:4

*Week following Sunday
between Oct. 9 and 15
inclusive*
Su  Jer. 36:1-10
    Acts 14:8-18
    Luke 7:36-50
M   Jer. 36:11-26
    1 Cor. 13:(1-3) 4-13
    Matt. 10:5-15
Tu  Jer. 36:27–37:2
    1 Cor. 14:1-12
    Matt. 10:16-23
W   Jer. 37:3-21
    1 Cor. 14:13-25
    Matt. 10:24-33
Th  Jer. 38:1-13
    1 Cor. 14:26-33a
      (33b-36) 37-40
    Matt. 10:34-42
F   Jer. 38:14-28
    1 Cor. 15:1-11
    Matt. 11:1-6
Sa  Jer. 52:1-34
    1 Cor. 15:12-29
    Matt. 11:7-15

*Week following Sunday
between Oct. 16 and 22
inclusive*
Su  Jer. 29:1, 4-14
    *or* Jer. 39:11–40:6
    Acts 16:6-15
    Luke 10:1-12, 17-20
M   Jer. 44:1-14
    *or* Jer. 29:1, 4-14
    1 Cor. 15:30-41
    Matt. 11:16-24
Tu  Lam. 1:1-5 (6-9)
      10-12
    *or* Jer. 40:7–41:3
    1 Cor. 15:41-50
    Matt. 11:25-30
W   Lam. 2:8-15
    *or* Jer. 41:4-18
    1 Cor. 15:51-58

Matt. 12:1-14
Th  Ezra 1:1-11
    *or* Jer. 42:1-22
    1 Cor. 16:1-9
    Matt. 12:15-21
F   Ezra 3:1-13
    *or* Jer. 43:1-13
    1 Cor. 16:10-24
    Matt. 12:22-32
Sa  Ezra 4:7, 11-24
    *or* Jer. 44:1-14
    Philemon 1-25
    Matt. 12:33-42

*Week following Sunday
between Oct. 23 and 29
inclusive*
Su  Hag. 1:1–2:9
    *or* Jer. 44:15-30
    Acts 18:24–19:7
    Luke 10:25-37
M   Zech. 1:7-17
    *or* Jer. 45:1-5
    Rev. 1:4-20
    Matt. 12:43-50
Tu  Ezra 5:1-17
    *or* Lam. 1:1-5 (6-9)
      10-12
    Rev. 4:1-11
    Matt. 13:1-9
W   Ezra 6:1-22
    *or* Lam. 2:8-15
    Rev. 5:1-10
    Matt. 13:10-17
Th  Neh. 1:1-11
    *or* Lam. 2:16-22
    Rev. 5:11–6:11
    Matt. 13:18-23
F   Neh. 2:1-20
    *or* Lam. 4:1-22
    Rev. 6:12–7:4
    Matt. 13:24-30
Sa  Neh. 4:1-23
    *or* Lam. 5:1-22
    Rev. 7:(4-8) 9-17
    Matt. 13:31-35

*Week following Sunday
between Oct. 30 and Nov.
5 inclusive*
Su  Neh. 5:1-9
    *or* Ezra 1:1-11
    Acts 20:7-12
    Luke 12:22-31
M   Neh. 6:1-19
    *or* Ezra 3:1-13
    Rev. 10:1-11
    Matt. 13:36-43
Tu  Neh. 12:27-31a,
      42b-47
    *or* Ezra 4:7, 11-24
    Rev. 11:1-19
    Matt. 13:44-52
W   Neh. 13:4-22
    *or* Hag. 1:1–2:9
    Rev. 12:1-12
    Matt. 13:53-58
Th  Ezra 7:(1-10) 11-26
    *or* Zech. 1:7-17
    Rev. 14:1-13
    Matt. 14:1-12
F   Ezra 7:27-28; 8:21-36
    *or* Ezra 5:1-17
    Rev. 15:1-8
    Matt. 14:13-21
Sa  Ezra 9:1-15
    *or* Ezra 6:1-22
    Rev. 17:1-14
    Matt. 14:22-36

*Week following Sunday
between Nov. 6 and 12
inclusive*
Su  Ezra 10:1-17
    *or* Neh 1:1-11
    Acts 24:10-21
    Luke 14:12-24
M   Neh. 9:1-15 (16-25)
    *or* Neh. 2:1-20
    Rev. 18:1-8
    Matt. 15:1-20
Tu  Neh. 9:26-38
    *or* Neh. 4:1-23
    Rev. 18:9-20
    Matt. 15:21-28
W   Neh. 7:73b–8:3, 5-18
    *or* Neh. 5:1-19

Rev. 18:21-24
Matt. 15:29-39
**Th** 1 Macc. 1:1-28
*or* Neh. 6:1-19
Rev. 19:1-10
Matt. 16:1-12
**F** 1 Macc. 1:41-63
*or* Neh. 12:27-31a,
42b-47
Rev. 19:11-16
Matt. 16:13-20
**Sa** 1 Macc. 2:1-28
*or* Neh. 13:4-22
Rev. 20:1-6
Matt. 16:21-28

*Week following Sunday*
*between Nov. 13 and 19*
*inclusive*
**Su** 1 Macc. 2:29-43
(44-48)
*or* Ezra 7:(1-10)
11-26
Acts 28:14b-23
Luke 16:1-13
**M** 1 Macc. 2:49-70

*or* Ezra 7:27-28;
8:21-36
Rev. 20:7-15
Matt. 17:1-13
**Tu** 1 Macc. 3:1-24
*or* Ezra 9:1-15
Rev. 21:1-8
Matt. 17:14-21
**W** 1 Macc. 3:25-41
*or* Ezra 10:1-17
Rev. 21:9-21
Matt. 17:22-27
**Th** 1 Macc. 3:42-60
*or* Neh. 9:1-15
(16-25)
Rev. 21:22–22:5
Matt. 18:1-9
**F** 1 Macc. 4:1-25
*or* Neh. 9:26-38
Rev. 22:6-13
Matt. 18:10-20
**Sa** 1 Macc. 4:36-59
*or* Neh. 7:73b–8:3,
5-18
Rev. 22:14-21
Matt. 18:21-35

*Christ the King (Sunday*
*between Nov. 20 and 26)*
*and following*
**Su** Isa. 19:19-25
Rom. 15:5-13
Luke 19:11-27
**M** Joel 3:1-2, 9-17
1 Peter 1:1-12
Matt. 19:1-12
**Tu** Nahum 1:1-13
1 Peter 1:13-25
Matt. 19:13-22
**W** Obad. 15-21
1 Peter 2:1-10
Matt. 19:23-30
**Th** Zeph. 3:1-13
1 Peter 2:11-25
Matt. 20:1-16
**F** Isa. 24:14-23
1 Peter 3:13–4:6
Matt. 20:17-28
**Sa** Micah 7:11-20
1 Peter 4:7-19
Matt. 20:29-34

## YEAR TWO

*1st Week of Advent*
**Su** Amos 1:1-5, 13–2:8
1 Thess. 5:1-11
Luke 21:5-19
**M** Amos 2:6-16
2 Peter 1:1-11
Matt. 21:1-11
**Tu** Amos 3:1-11
2 Peter 1:12-21
Matt. 21:12-22
**W** Amos 3:12–4:5
2 Peter 3:1-10
Matt. 21:23-32
**Th** Amos 4:6-13
2 Peter 3:11-18
Matt. 21:33-46

**F** Amos 5:1-17
Jude 1-16
Matt. 22:1-14
**Sa** Amos 5:18-27
Jude 17-25
Matt. 22:15-22

*2nd Week of Advent*
**Su** Amos 6:1-14
2 Thess. 1:5-12
Luke 1:57-68
**M** Amos 7:1-9
Rev. 1:1-8
Matt. 22:23-33
**Tu** Amos 7:10-17

Rev. 1:9-16
Matt. 22:34-46
**W** Amos 8:1-14
Rev. 1:17–2:7
Matt. 23:1-12
**Th** Amos 9:1-10
Rev. 2:8-17
Matt. 23:13-26
**F** Hag. 1:1-15
Rev. 2:18-29
Matt. 23:27-39
**Sa** Hag. 2:1-9
Rev. 3:1-6
Matt. 24:1-14

*3rd Week of Advent*
**Su** Amos 9:11-15
  2 Thess. 2:1-3, 13-17
  John 5:30-47

*The readings below are interrupted after December 17 in favor of the readings identified by date in the 4th Week of Advent.*

**M** Zech. 1:7-17
  Rev. 3:7-13
  Matt. 24:15-31
**Tu** Zech. 2:1-13
  Rev. 3:14-22
  Matt. 24:32-44
**W** Zech. 3:1-10
  Rev. 4:1-8
  Matt. 24:45-51
**Th** Zech. 4:1-14
  Rev. 4:9–5:5
  Matt. 25:1-13
**F** Zech. 7:8–8:8
  Rev. 5:6-14
  Matt. 25:14-30
**Sa** Zech. 8:9-17
  Rev. 6:1-17
  Matt. 25:31-46

*4th Week of Advent*
**Dec** Gen. 3:8-15
**18** Rev. 12:1-10
  John 3:16-21
**Dec** Zeph. 3:14-20
**19** Titus 1:1-16
  Luke 1:1-25
**Dec** 1 Sam. 2:1b-10
**20** Titus 2:1-10
  Luke 1:26-38
**Dec** 2 Sam. 7:1-17
**21** Titus 2:11–3:8a
  Luke 1:39-48a (48b-56)
**Dec** 2 Sam. 7:18-29
**22** Gal. 3:1-14
  Luke 1:57-66

**Dec** Jer. 31:10-14
**23** Gal. 3:15-22
  Luke 1:67-80
  *or* Matt. 1:1-17
**Dec** Isa. 60:1-6
**24** Gal. 3:23–4:7
  Matt. 1:18-25

*Christmas Eve*
  Isa. 59:15b-21
  Phil. 2:5-11

*Christmas Day*
  Micah 4:1-5; 5:2-4
  1 John 4:7-16
  John 3:31-36

*1st Sunday after Christmas*
  1 Sam. 1:1-2, 7b-28
  Col. 1:9-20
  Luke 2:22-40
**Dec** Wisd. of Sol. 4:7-15
**26** *or* 2 Chron. 24:17-22
  Acts 6:1-7
  Acts 7:59–8:8
**Dec** Prov. 8:22-30
**27** 1 John 5:1-12
  John 13:20-35
**Dec** Isa. 49:13-23
**28** Isa. 54:1-13
  Matt. 18:1-14
**Dec** 2 Sam. 23:13-17b
**29** 2 John 1-13
  John 2:1-11
**Dec** 1 Kings 17:17-24
**30** 3 John 1-15
  John 4:46-54
**Dec** 1 Kings 3:5-14
**31** James 4:13-17; 5:7-11
  John 5:1-15
**Jan** Isa. 62:1-5, 10-12
**1** Rev. 19:11-16
  Matt. 1:18-25

*2nd Sunday after Christmas*
  1 Kings 3:5-14
  Col. 3:12-17
  John 6:41-47
**Jan** 1 Kings 19:1-8
**2** Eph. 4:1-16
  John 6:1-14
**Jan** 1 Kings 19:9-18
**3** Eph. 4:17-32
  John 6:15-27
**Jan** Josh. 3:14–4:7
**4** Eph. 5:1-20
  John 9:1-12, 35-38
**Jan** Jonah 2:2-9
**5** Eph. 6:10-20
  John 11:17-27, 38-44

*Eve of Epiphany*
  Isa. 66:18-23
  Rom. 15:7-13

*Epiphany*
**Jan** Isa. 49:1-7
**6** Rev. 21:22-27
  Matt. 12:14-21

*The readings for the dated days after the Epiphany are used only until the following Saturday evening.*

**Jan** Deut. 8:1-3
**7** Col. 1:1-14
  John 6:30-33, 48-51
**Jan** Ex. 17:1-7
**8** Col. 1:15-23
  John 7:37-52
**Jan** Isa. 45:14-19
**9** Col. 1:24–2:7
  John 8:12-19
**Jan** Jer. 23:1-8
**10** Col. 2:8-23
  John 10:7-17
**Jan** Isa. 55:3-9
**11** Col. 3:1-17
  John 14:6-14

Jan Gen. 49:1-2, 8-12
12 Col. 3:18–4:6
John 15:1-16


Eve of Baptism of the Lord
Isa. 61:1-9
Gal. 3:23-29; 4:4-7


Baptism of the Lord (1st
Sunday after Epiphany)
and following
Su Gen. 1:1–2:3
Eph. 1:3-14
John 1:29-34
M Gen. 2:4-9 (10-15)
16-25
Heb. 1:1-14
John 1:1-18
Tu Gen. 3:1-24
Heb. 2:1-10
John 1:19-28
W Gen. 4:1-16
Heb. 2:11-18
John 1:(29-34) 35-42
Th Gen. 4:17-26
Heb. 3:1-11
John 1:43-51
F Gen. 6:1-8
Heb. 3:12-19
John 2:1-12
Sa Gen. 6:9-22
Heb. 4:1-13
John 2:13-22


Week of 2nd Sunday after
Epiphany
Su Gen. 7:1-10, 17-23
Eph. 4:1-16
Mark 3:7-19
M Gen. 8:6-22
Heb. 4:14–5:6
John 2:23–3:15
Tu Gen. 9:1-17
Heb. 5:7-14
John 3:16-21
W Gen. 9:18-29
Heb. 6:1-12

John 3:22-36
Th Gen. 11:1-9
Heb. 6:13-20
John 4:1-15
F Gen. 11:27–12:8
Heb. 7:1-17
John 4:16-26
Sa Gen. 12:9–13:1
Heb. 7:18-28
John 4:27-42


Week of 3rd Sunday after
Epiphany
Su Gen. 13:2-18
Gal. 2:1-10
Mark 7:31-37
M Gen. 14:(1-7) 8-24
Heb. 8:1-13
John 4:43-54
Tu Gen. 15:1-11, 17-21
Heb. 9:1-14
John 5:1-18
W Gen. 16:1-14
Heb. 9:15-28
John 5:19-29
Th Gen. 16:15–17:14
Heb. 10:1-10
John 5:30-47
F Gen. 17:15-27
Heb. 10:11-25
John 6:1-15
Sa Gen. 18:1-16
Heb. 10:26-39
John 6:16-27


Week of 4th Sunday after
Epiphany
Su Gen. 18:16-33
Gal. 5:13-25
Mark 8:22-30
M Gen. 19:1-17 (18-23)
24-29
Heb. 11:1-12
John 6:27-40
Tu Gen. 21:1-21
Heb. 11:13-22
John 6:41-51
W Gen. 22:1-18

Heb. 11:23-31
John 6:52-59
Th Gen. 23:1-20
Heb. 11:32–12:2
John 6:50-71
F Gen. 24:1-27
Heb. 12:3-11
John 7:1-13
Sa Gen. 24:28-38, 49-51
Heb. 12:12-29
John 7:14-36


Week of 5th Sunday after
Epiphany
Su Gen. 24:50-67
2 Tim. 2:14-21
Mark 10:13-22
M Gen. 25:19-34
Heb. 13:1-16
John 7:37-52
Tu Gen. 26:1-6, 12-33
Heb. 13:17-25
John 7:53–8:11
W Gen. 27:1-29
Rom. 12:1-8
John 8:12-20
Th Gen. 27:30-45
Rom. 12:9-21
John 8:21-32
F Gen. 27:46–28:4,
10-22
Rom. 13:1-14
John 8:33-47
Sa Gen. 29:1-20
Rom. 14:1-23
John 8:47-59


Week of 6th Sunday after
Epiphany
Su Gen. 29:20-35
1 Tim. 3:14–4:10
Mark 10:23-31
M Gen. 30:1-24
1 John 1:1-10
John 9:1-17
Tu Gen. 31:1-24
1 John 2:1-11
John 9:18-41
W Gen. 31:25-50
1 John 2:12-17

|  | John 10:1-18 |  | John 13:1-20 |  | Mark 1:1-13 |
|----|----|----|----|----|----|
| Th | Gen. 32:3-21 | Th | Prov. 21:30–22:6 | Tu | Gen. 37:12-24 |
|  | 1 John 2:18-29 |  | 2 Tim. 4:1-8 |  | 1 Cor. 1:20-31 |
|  | John 10:19-30 |  | John 13:21-30 |  | Mark 1:14-28 |
| F | Gen. 32:22–33:17 | F | Prov. 23:19-21, | W | Gen. 37:25-36 |
|  | 1 John 3:1-10 |  | 29–24:2 |  | 1 Cor. 2:1-13 |
|  | John 10:31-42 |  | 2 Tim. 4:9-22 |  | Mark 1:29-45 |
| Sa | Gen. 35:1-20 |  | John 13:31-38 | Th | Gen. 39:1-23 |
|  | 1 John 3:11-18 | Sa | Prov. 25:15-28 |  | 1 Cor. 2:14–3:15 |
|  | John 11:1-16 |  | Phil. 1:1-11 |  | Mark 2:1-12 |
|  |  |  | John 18:1-14 | F | Gen. 40:1-23 |
|  |  |  |  |  | 1 Cor. 3:16-23 |
|  |  |  |  |  | Mark 2:13-22 |

*Week of 7th Sunday after Epiphany*

|  |  |  | *Transfiguration (Last* | Sa | Gen. 41:1-13 |
|----|----|----|----|----|----|
| Su | Prov. 1:20-33 |  | *Sunday after Epiphany)* |  | 1 Cor. 4:1-7 |
|  | 2 Cor. 5:11-21 |  | *and following* |  | Mark 2:23–3:6 |
|  | Mark 10:35-45 | Su | Mal. 4:1-6 |  |  |
| M | Prov. 3:11-20 |  | 2 Cor. 3:7-18 |  |  |
|  | 1 John 3:18–4:6 |  | Luke 9:18-27 |  | *2nd Week in Lent* |
|  | John 11:17-29 | M | Prov. 27:1-6, 10-12 | Su | Gen. 41:14-45 |
| Tu | Prov. 4:1-27 |  | Phil. 2:1-13 |  | Rom. 6:3-14 |
|  | 1 John 4:7-21 |  | John 18:15-18, 25-27 |  | John 5:19-24 |
|  | John 11:30-44 | Tu | Prov. 30:1-4, 24-33 | M | Gen. 41:46-57 |
| W | Prov. 6:1-19 |  | Phil. 3:1-11 |  | 1 Cor. 4:8-20 (21) |
|  | 1 John 5:1-12 |  | John 18:28-38 |  | Mark 3:7-19a |
|  | John 11:45-54 |  |  | Tu | Gen. 42:1-17 |
| Th | Prov. 7:1-27 |  |  |  | 1 Cor. 5:1-8 |
|  | 1 John 5:13-21 | *Lent* |  |  | Mark 3:19b-35 |
|  | John 11:55–12:8 | *Ash Wednesday* |  | W | Gen. 42:18-28 |
| F | Prov. 8:1-21 |  | Amos 5:6-15 |  | 1 Cor. 5:9–6:11 |
|  | Philemon 1-25 |  | Heb. 12:1-14 |  | Mark 4:1-20 |
|  | John 12:9-19 |  | Luke 18:9-14 | Th | Gen. 42:29-38 |
| Sa | Prov. 8:22-36 | Th | Hab. 3:1-10 (11-15) |  | 1 Cor. 6:12-20 |
|  | 2 Tim. 1:1-14 |  | 16-18 |  | Mark 4:21-34 |
|  | John 12:20-26 |  | Phil. 3:12-21 | F | Gen. 43:1-15 |
|  |  |  | John 17:1-8 |  | 1 Cor. 7:1-9 |
|  |  | F | Ezek. 18:1-4, 25-32 |  | Mark 4:35-41 |

*Week of 8th Sunday after Epiphany*

|  |  |  | Phil. 4:1-9 | Sa | Gen. 43:16-34 |
|----|----|----|----|----|----|
|  |  |  | John 17:9-19 |  | 1 Cor. 7:10-24 |
| Su | Prov. 9:1-12 | Sa | Ezek. 39:21-29 |  | Mark 5:1-20 |
|  | 2 Cor. 9:6b-15 |  | Phil. 4:10-20 |  |  |
|  | Mark 10:46-52 |  | John 17:20-26 |  |  |
| M | Prov. 10:1-12 |  |  |  | *3rd Week in Lent* |
|  | 2 Tim. 1:15–2:13 |  |  | Su | Gen. 44:1-17 |
|  | John 12:27-36a | *1st Week in Lent* |  |  | Rom. 8:1-10 |
| Tu | Prov. 15:16-33 | S | Dan. 9:3-10 |  | John 5:25-29 |
|  | 2 Tim. 2:14-26 |  | Heb. 2:10-18 | M | Gen. 44:18-34 |
|  | John 12:36b-50 |  | John 12:44-50 |  | 1 Cor. 7:25-31 |
| W | Prov. 17:1-20 | M | Gen. 37:1-11 |  | Mark 5:21-43 |
|  | 2 Tim. 3:1-17 |  | 1 Cor. 1:1-19 | Tu | Gen. 45:1-15 |

|     |                      |     |                     |
|-----|----------------------|-----|---------------------|
|     | 1 Cor. 7:32-40       |     | 1 Cor. 14:1-19      |
|     | Mark 6:1-13          |     | Mark 9:30-41        |
| W   | Gen. 45:16-28        | Tu  | Ex. 5:1–6:1         |
|     | 1 Cor. 8:1-13        |     | 1 Cor. 14:20-33a,   |
|     | Mark 6:13-29         |     | 39-40               |
| Th  | Gen. 46:1-7, 28-34   |     | Mark 9:42-50        |
|     | 1 Cor. 9:1-15        | W   | Ex. 7:8-24          |
|     | Mark 6:30-46         |     | 2 Cor. 2:14–3:6     |
| F   | Gen. 47:1-26         |     | Mark 10:1-16        |
|     | 1 Cor. 9:16-27       | Th  | Ex. 7:25–8:19       |
|     | Mark 6:47-56         |     | 2 Cor. 3:7-18       |
| Sa  | Gen. 47:27–48:7      |     | Mark 10:17-31       |
|     | 1 Cor. 10:1-13       | F   | Ex. 9:13-35         |
|     | Mark 7:1-23          |     | 2 Cor. 4:1-12       |
|     |                      |     | Mark 10:32-45       |
|     |                      | Sa  | Ex. 10:21–11:8      |

*4th Week in Lent*

| Su | Gen. 48:8-22 |
|----|--------------|
|    | Rom. 8:11-25 |
|    | John 6:27-40 |
| M  | Gen. 49:1-28 |
|    | 1 Cor. 10:14–11:1 |
|    | Mark 7:24-37 |
| Tu | Gen. 49:29–50:14 |
|    | 1 Cor. 11:2-34 |
|    | Mark 8:1-10 |
| W  | Gen. 50:15-26 |
|    | 1 Cor. 12:1-11 |
|    | Mark 8:11-26 |
| Th | Ex. 1:6-22 |
|    | 1 Cor. 12:12-26 |
|    | Mark 8:27–9:1 |
| F  | Ex. 2:1-22 |
|    | 1 Cor. 12:27–13:3 |
|    | Mark 9:2-13 |
| Sa | Ex. 2:23–3:15 |
|    | 1 Cor. 13:1-13 |
|    | Mark 9:14-29 |

2 Cor. 4:13-18
Mark 10:46-52

*Holy Week*
*Passion/Palm Sunday*
Zech. 9:9-12*
1 Tim. 6:12-16*
*or*
Zech. 12:9-11; 13:1,
7-9**
Luke 19:41-48**

| M  | Lam. 1:1-2, 6-12 |
|----|------------------|
|    | 2 Cor. 1:1-7     |
|    | Mark 11:12-25    |
| Tu | Lam. 1:17-22     |
|    | 2 Cor. 1:8-22    |
|    | Mark 11:27-33    |
| W  | Lam. 2:1-9       |
|    | 2 Cor. 1:23–2:11 |
|    | Mark 12:1-11     |

*Good Friday*
Lam. 3:1-9, 19-33
1 Peter 1:10-20
John 13:36-38*
*or* John 19:38-42**

*Holy Saturday*
Lam. 3:37-58
Heb. 4:1-16*
Rom. 8:1-11**

*Easter Week*

| Su | Ex. 12:1-14*       |
|----|--------------------|
|    | John 1:1-18*       |
|    | *or*               |
|    | Isa. 51:9-11**     |
|    | Luke 24:13-35**    |
|    | *or* John 20:19-23** |
| M  | Ex. 12:14-27       |
|    | 1 Cor. 15:1-11     |
|    | Mark 16:1-8        |
| Tu | Ex. 12:28-39       |
|    | 1 Cor. 15:12-28    |
|    | Mark 16:9-20       |
| W  | Ex. 12:40-51       |
|    | 1 Cor. 15:(29) 30-41 |
|    | Matt. 28:1-16      |
| Th | Ex. 13:3-10        |
|    | 1 Cor. 15:41-50    |
|    | Matt. 28:16-20     |
| F  | Ex. 13:1-2, 11-16  |
|    | 1 Cor. 15:51-58    |
|    | Luke 24:1-12       |
| Sa | Ex. 13:17–14:4     |
|    | 2 Cor. 4:16–5:10   |
|    | Mark 12:18-27      |

*5th Week in Lent*

| Su | Ex. 3:16–4:12         |
|----|-----------------------|
|    | Rom. 12:1-21          |
|    | John 8:46-59          |
| M  | Ex. 4:10-20 (21-26)   |
|    | 27-31                 |

*Maundy Thursday*
Lam. 2:10-18
1 Cor. 10:14-17;
11:27-32
Mark 14:12-25

*2nd Week of Easter*

| Su | Ex. 14:5-22    |
|----|----------------|
|    | 1 John 1:1-7   |
|    | John 14:1-7    |
| M  | Ex. 14:21-31   |
|    | 1 Peter 1:1-12 |

---

*Intended for use in the morning      **Intended for use in the evening

John 14:(1-7) 8-17
Tu   Ex. 15:1-21
    1 Peter 1:13-25
    John 14:18-31
W   Ex. 15:22–16:10
    1 Peter 2:1-10
    John 15:1-11
Th   Ex. 16:10-22
    1 Peter 2:11–3:12
    John 15:12-27
F   Ex. 16:23-36
    1 Peter 3:13–4:6
    John 16:1-15
Sa   Ex. 17:1-16
    1 Peter 4:7-19
    John 16:16-33

*3rd Week of Easter*
Su   Ex 18:1-12
    1 John 2:7-17
    Mark 16:9-20
M   Ex. 18:13-27
    1 Peter 5:1-14
    Matt. (1:1-17) 3:1-6
Tu   Ex. 19:1-16
    Col. 1:1-14
    Matt. 3:7-12
W   Ex. 19:16-25
    Col. 1:15-23
    Matt. 3:13-17
Th   Ex. 20:1-21
    Col. 1:24–2:7
    Matt. 4:1-11
F   Ex. 24:1-18
    Col. 2:8-23
    Matt. 4:12-17
Sa   Ex. 25:1-22
    Col. 3:1-17
    Matt. 4:18-25

*4th Week of Easter*
Su   Ex. 28:1-4, 30-38
    1 John 2:18-29
    Mark 6:30-44
M   Ex. 32:1-20
    Col. 3:18–4:6 (7-18)
    Matt. 5:1-10

Tu   Ex. 32:21-34
    1 Thess. 1:1-10
    Matt. 5:11-16
W   Ex. 33:1-23
    1 Thess. 2:1-12
    Matt. 5:17-20
Th   Ex. 34:1-17
    1 Thess. 2:13-20
    Matt. 5:21-26
F   Ex. 34:18-35
    1 Thess. 3:1-13
    Matt. 5:27-37
Sa   Ex. 40:18-38
    1 Thess. 4:1-12
    Matt. 5:38-48

*5th Week of Easter*
Su   Lev. 8:1-13, 30-36
    Heb. 12:1-14
    Luke 4:16-30
M   Lev. 16:1-19
    1 Thess. 4:13-18
    Matt. 6:1-6, 16-18
Tu   Lev. 16:20-34
    1 Thess. 5:1-11
    Matt. 6:7-15
W   Lev. 19:1-18
    1 Thess. 5:12-28
    Matt. 6:19-24
Th   Lev. 19:26-37
    2 Thess. 1:1-12
    Matt. 6:25-34
F   Lev. 23:1-22
    2 Thess. 2:1-17
    Matt. 7:1-12
Sa   Lev. 23:23-44
    2 Thess. 3:1-18
    Matt. 7:13-21

*6th Week of Easter*
Su   Lev. 25:1-17
    James 1:2-8, 16-18
    Luke 12:13-21
M   Lev. 25:35-55
    Col. 1:9-14
    Matt. 13:1-16
Tu   Lev. 26:1-20

    1 Tim. 2:1-6
    Matt. 13:18-23
W   Lev. 26:27-42
    Eph. 1:1-10
    Matt. 22:41-46

*Eve of Ascension*
    2 Kings 2:1-15
    Rev. 5:1-14

*Ascension Day*
    Dan. 7:9-14
    Heb. 2:5-18
    Matt. 28:16-20
F   1 Sam. 2:1-10
    Eph. 2:1-10
    Matt. 7:22-27
Sa   Num. 11:16-17, 24-29
    Eph. 2:11-22
    Matt. 7:28–8:4

*7th Week of Easter*
Su   Ex. 3:1-12
    Heb. 12:18-29
    Luke 10:17-24
M   Josh. 1:1-9
    Eph. 3:1-13
    Matt. 8:5-17
Tu   1 Sam. 16:1-13a
    Eph. 3:14-21
    Matt. 8:18-27
W   Isa. 4:2-6
    Eph. 4:1-16
    Matt. 8:28-34
Th   Zech. 4:1-14
    Eph. 4:17-32
    Matt. 9:1-8
F   Jer. 31:27-34
    Eph. 5:1-32
    Matt. 9:9-17
Sa   Ezek. 36:22-27
    Eph. 6:1-24
    Matt. 9:18-26

*Eve of Pentecost*
 Ex. 19:3-8a, 16-20
 1 Peter 2:4-10


*Pentecost*
 Deut. 16:9-12
 Acts 4:18-21, 23-33
 John 4:19-26


*On the weekdays which
follow, the readings are taken
from the week which
corresponds to the date of
Pentecost.*


*Eve of Trinity Sunday*
 Ecclus. 42:15-25
 *or* Isa. 6:1-8
 Eph. 3:14-21


*Trinity Sunday*
 Job 38:1-11; 42:1-5
 Rev. 19:4-16
 John 1:29-34


*On the weekdays which
follow, the readings are taken
from the week which
corresponds to the date of
Trinity Sunday.*


*Week following Sunday
 between May 11 and May
 16 inclusive, if after
 Pentecost Sunday*
M   Ezek. 33:1-11
    1 John 1:1-10
    Matt. 9:27-34
Tu  Ezek. 33:21-33
    1 John 2:1-11
    Matt. 9:35–10:4
W   Ezek. 34:1-16
    1 John 2:12-17
    Matt. 10:5-15
Th  Ezek. 37:21b-28
    1 John 2:18-29

         Matt. 10:16-23
F    Ezek. 39:21-29
     1 John 3:1-10
     Matt. 10:24-33
Sa   Ezek. 47:1-12
     1 John 3:11-18
     Matt. 10:34-42

*Week following Sunday
 between May 17 and May
 23 inclusive, if after
 Pentecost Sunday*
M    Prov. 3:11-20
     1 John 3:18–4:6
     Matt. 11:1-6
Tu   Prov. 4:1-27
     1 John 4:7-21
     Matt. 11:7-15
W    Prov. 6:1-19
     1 John 5:1-12
     Matt. 11:16-24
Th   Prov. 7:1-27
     1 John 5:13-21
     Matt. 11:25-30
F    Prov. 8:1-21
     2 John 1-13
     Matt. 12:1-14
Sa   Prov. 8:22-36
     3 John 1-15
     Matt. 12:15-21


*Week following Sunday
 between May 24 and 28
 inclusive, if after Pentecost
 Sunday*
Su   Prov. 9:1-12
     Acts 8:14-25
     Luke 10:25-28, 38-42
M    Prov. 10:1-12
     1 Tim. 1:1-17
     Matt. 12:22-32
Tu   Prov. 15:16-33
     1 Tim. 1:18–2:15
     Matt. 12:33-42
W    Prov. 17:1-20
     1 Tim. 3:1-16
     Matt. 12:43-50
Th   Prov. 21:30–22:6

         1 Tim. 4:1-16
         Matt. 13:24-30
F    Prov. 23:19-21,
        29–24:2
     1 Tim. 5:17-22
        (23-25)
     Matt. 13:31-35
Sa   Prov. 25:15-28
     1 Tim. 6:6-21
     Matt. 13:36-43


*Week following Sunday
 between May 29 and June
 4 inclusive, if after
 Pentecost Sunday*
Su   Eccl. 1:1-11
     Acts 8:26-40
     Luke 11:1-13
M    Eccl. 2:1-15
     Gal. 1:1-17
     Matt. 13:44-52
Tu   Eccl. 2:16-26
     Gal. 1:18–2:10
     Matt. 13:53-58
W    Eccl. 3:1-15
     Gal. 2:11-21
     Matt. 14:1-12
Th   Eccl. 3:16–4:3
     Gal. 3:1-14
     Matt. 14:13-21
F    Eccl. 5:1-7
     Gal. 3:15-22
     Matt. 14:22-36
Sa   Eccl. 5:8-20
     Gal. 3:23–4:11
     Matt. 15:1-20


*Week following Sunday
 between June 5 and 11
 inclusive, if after Pentecost
 Sunday*
Su   Eccl. 6:1-12
     Acts 10:9-23
     Luke 12:32-40
M    Eccl. 7:1-14
     Gal. 4:12-20
     Matt. 15:21-28
Tu   Eccl. 8:14–9:10

Gal. 4:21-31
Matt. 15:29-39
**W** Eccl. 9:11-18
Gal. 5:1-15
Matt. 16:1-12
**Th** Eccl. 11:1-8
Gal. 5:16-24
Matt. 16:13-20
**F** Eccl. 11:9–12:14
Gal. 5:25–6:10
Matt. 16:21-28
**Sa** Num. 3:1-13
Gal. 6:11-18
Matt. 17:1-13

*Week following Sunday*
*between June 12 and 18*
*inclusive*
**Su** Num. 6:22-27
Acts 13:1-12
Luke 12:41-48
**M** Num. 9:15-23;
10:29-36
Rom. 1:1-15
Matt. 17:14-21
**Tu** Num. 11:1-23
Rom. 1:16-25
Matt. 17:22-27
**W** Num. 11:24-33
(34-35)
Rom. 1:28–2:11
Matt. 18:1-9
**Th** Num. 12:1-16
Rom. 2:12-24
Matt. 18:10-20
**F** Num. 13:1-3, 21-30
Rom. 2:25–3:8
Matt. 18:21-35
**Sa** Num. 13:31–14:25
Rom. 3:9-20
Matt. 19:1-12

*Week following Sunday*
*between June 19 and 25*
*inclusive*
**Su** Num. 14:26-45
Acts 15:1-12
Luke 12:49-56

**M** Num. 16:1-19
Rom. 3:21-31
Matt. 19:13-22
**Tu** Num. 16:20-35
Rom. 4:1-12
Matt. 19:23-30
**W** Num. 16:36-50
Rom. 4:13-25
Matt. 20:1-16
**Th** Num. 17:1-11
Rom. 5:1-11
Matt. 20:17-28
**F** Num. 20:1-13
Rom. 5:12-21
Matt. 20:29-34
**Sa** Num. 20:14-29
Rom. 6:1-11
Matt. 21:1-11

*Week following Sunday*
*between June 26 and July*
*2 inclusive*
**Su** Num. 21:4-9, 21-35
Acts 17:(12-21) 23-24
Luke 13:10-17
**M** Num. 22:1-21
Rom. 6:12-23
Matt. 21:12-22
**Tu** Num. 22:21-38
Rom. 7:1-12
Matt. 21:23-32
**W** Num. 22:41–23:12
Rom. 7:13-25
Matt. 21:33-46
**Th** Num. 23:11-26
Rom. 8:1-11
Matt. 22:1-14
**F** Num. 24:1-13
Rom. 8:12-17
Matt. 22:15-22
**Sa** Num. 24:12-25
Rom. 8:18-25
Matt. 22:23-40

*Week following Sunday*
*between July 3 and 9*
*inclusive*
**Su** Num. 27:12-23

Acts 19:11-20
Mark 1:14-20
**M** Num. 32:1-6, 16-27
Rom. 8:26-30
Matt. 23:1-12
**Tu** Num. 35:1-3, 9-15,
30-34
Rom. 8:31-39
Matt. 23:13-26
**W** Deut. 1:1-18
Rom. 9:1-18
Matt. 23:27-39
**Th** Deut. 3:18-28
Rom. 9:19-33
Matt. 24:1-14
**F** Deut. 31:7-13, 24–
32:4
Rom. 10:1-13
Matt. 24:15-31
**Sa** Deut. 34:1-12
Rom. 10:14-21
Matt. 24:32-51

*Week following Sunday*
*between July 10 and 16*
*inclusive*
**Su** Josh. 1:1-18
Acts 21:3-15
Mark 1:21-27
**M** Josh. 2:1-14
Rom. 11:1-12
Matt. 25:1-13
**Tu** Josh. 2:15-24
Rom. 11:13-24
Matt. 25:14-30
**W** Josh. 3:1-13
Rom. 11:25-36
Matt. 25:31-46
**Th** Josh. 3:14–4:7
Rom. 12:1-8
Matt. 26:1-16
**F** Josh. 4:19–5:1, 10-15
Rom. 12:9-21
Matt. 26:17-25
**Sa** Josh. 6:1-14
Rom. 13:1-7
Matt. 26:26-35

*Week following Sunday
between July 17 and 23
inclusive*

Su   Josh. 6:15-27
     Acts 22:30–23:11
     Mark 2:1-12
M    Josh. 7:1-13
     Rom. 13:8-14
     Matt. 26:36-46
Tu   Josh. 8:1-22
     Rom. 14:1-12
     Matt. 26:47-56
W    Josh. 8:30-35
     Rom. 14:13-23
     Matt. 26:57-68
Th   Josh. 9:3-21
     Rom. 15:1-13
     Matt. 26:69-75
F    Josh. 9:22–10:15
     Rom. 15:14-24
     Matt. 27:1-10
Sa   Josh. 23:1-16
     Rom. 15:25-33
     Matt. 27:11-23

*Week following Sunday
between July 31 and Aug.
6 inclusive*

Su   Judg. 6:1-24
     2 Cor. 9:6-15
     Mark 3:20-30
M    Judg. 6:25-40
     Acts 2:37-47
     John 1:1-18
Tu   Judg. 7:1-18
     Acts 3:1-11
     John 1:19-28
W    Judg. 7:19–8:12
     Acts 3:12-26
     John 1:29-42
Th   Judg. 8:22-35
     Acts 4:1-12
     John 1:43-51
F    Judg. 9:1-16, 19-21
     Acts 4:13-31
     John 2:1-12
Sa   Judg. 9:22-25, 50-57
     Acts 4:32–5:11
     John 2:13-25

*Week following Sunday
between Aug. 14 and 20
inclusive*

Su   Judg. 16:15-31
     2 Cor. 13:1-11
     Mark 5:25-34
M    Judg. 17:1-13
     Acts 7:44–8:1a
     John 5:19-29
Tu   Judg. 18:1-15
     Acts 8:1-13
     John 5:30-47
W    Judg. 18:16-31
     Acts 8:14-25
     John 6:1-15
Th   Job 1:1-22
     Acts 8:26-40
     John 6:16-27
F    Job 2:1-13
     Acts 9:1-9
     John 6:27-40
Sa   Job 3:1-26
     Acts 9:10-19a
     John 6:41-51

*Week following Sunday
between July 24 and 30
inclusive*

Su   Josh. 24:1-15
     Acts 28:23-31
     Mark 2:23-28
M    Josh. 24:16-33
     Rom. 16:1-16
     Matt. 27:34-31
Tu   Judg. 2:1-5, 11-23
     Rom. 16:17-27
     Matt. 27:32-44
W    Judg. 3:12-30
     Acts 1:1-14
     Matt. 27:45-54
Th   Judg. 4:4-23
     Acts 1:15-26
     Matt. 27:55-66
F    Judg. 5:1-18
     Acts 2:1-21
     Matt. 28:1-10
Sa   Judg. 5:19-31
     Acts 2:22-36
     Matt. 28:11-20

*Week following Sunday
between Aug. 7 and 13
inclusive*

Su   Judg. 11:1-11, 29-40
     2 Cor. 11:21b-31
     Mark 4:35-41
M    Judg. 12:1-7
     Acts 5:12-26
     John 3:1-21
Tu   Judg. 13:1-15
     Acts 5:27-42
     John 3:22-36
W    Judg. 13:15-24
     Acts 6:1-15
     John 4:1-26
Th   Judg. 14:1-19
     Acts 6:15–7:16
     John 4:27-42
F    Judg. 14:20–15:20
     Acts 7:17-29
     John 4:43-54
Sa   Judg. 16:1-14
     Acts 7:30-43
     John 5:1-18

*Week following Sunday
between Aug. 21 and 27
inclusive*

Su   Job 4:1-6, 12-21
     Rev. 4:1-11
     Mark 6:1-6a
M    Job 4:1; 5:1-11,
       17-21, 26-27
     Acts 9:19b-31
     John 6:52-59
Tu   Job 6:1-4, 8-15, 21
     Acts 9:32-43
     John 6:60-71
W    Job 6:1; 7:1-21
     Acts 10:1-16
     John 7:1-13
Th   Job 8:1-10, 20-22
     Acts 10:17-33
     John 7:14-36
F    Job 9:1-15, 32-35
     Acts 10:34-48
     John 7:37-52
Sa   Job 9:1; 10:1-9, 16-22
     Acts 11:1-18

John 8:12-20

Su    Job 11:1-9, 13-20
      Rev. 5:1-14
      Matt. 5:1-12
M     Job 12:1-6, 13-25
      Acts 11:19-30
      John 8:21-32
Tu    Job 12:1; 13:3-17,
      21-27
      Acts 12:1-17
      John 8:33-47
W     Job 12:1; 14:1-22
      Acts 12:18-25
      John 8:47-59
Th    Job 16:16-22; 17:1,
      13-16
      Acts 13:1-12
      John 9:1-17
F     Job 19:1-7, 14-27
      Acts 13:13-25
      John 9:18-41
Sa    Job 22:1-4, 21–23:7
      Acts 13:26-43
      John 10:1-18


*Week following Sunday
between Sept. 4 and 10
inclusive*
Su    Job 25:1-6; 27:1-6
      Rev. 14:1-7, 13
      Matt. 5:13-20
M     Job 32:1-10, 19–33:1,
      19-28
      Acts 13:44-52
      John 10:19-30
Tu    Job 29:1-20
      Acts 14:1-18
      John 10:31-42
W     Job 29:1; 30:1-2,
      16-31
      Acts 14:19-28
      John 11:1-16
Th    Job 29:1; 31:1-23
      Acts 15:1-11

      John 11:17-29
F     Job 29:1; 31:24-40
      Acts 15:12-21
      John 11:30-44
Sa    Job 38:1-17
      Acts 15:22-35
      John 11:45-54


*Week following Sunday
between Sept. 11 and 17
inclusive*
Su    Job 38:1, 18-41
      Rev. 18:1-8
      Matt. 5:21-26
M     Job 40:1-24
      Acts 15:36–16:5
      John 11:55–12:8
Tu    Job 40:1; 41:1-11
      Acts 16:6-15
      John 12:9-19
W     Job 42:1-17
      Acts 16:16-24
      John 12:20-26
Th    Job 28:1-28
      Acts 16:25-40
      John 12:27-36a
F     Esth. 1:1-4, 10-19
      Acts 17:1-15
      John 12:36b-43
Sa    Esth. 2:5-8, 15-23
      Acts 17:16-34
      John 12:44-50


*Week following Sunday
between Sept. 18 and 24
inclusive*
Su    Esth. 3:1–4:3
      James 1:19-27
      Matt. 6:1-6, 16-18
M     Esth. 4:4-17
      Acts 18:1-11
      Luke (1:1-4) 3:1-14
Tu    Esth. 5:1-14
      Acts 18:12-28
      Luke 3:15-22
W     Esth. 6:1-14
      Acts 19:1-10
      Luke 4:1-13

Th    Esth. 7:1-10
      Acts 19:11-20
      Luke 4:14-30
F     Esth. 8:1-8, 15-17
      Acts 19:21-41
      Luke 4:31-37
Sa    Esth. 9:1-32
      Acts 20:1-16
      Luke 4:38-44


*Week following Sunday
between Sept. 25 and Oct.
1 inclusive*
Su    Hos. 1:1–2:1
      James 3:1-13
      Matt. 13:44-52
M     Hos. 2:2-15
      Acts 20:17-38
      Luke 5:1-11
Tu    Hos. 2:16-23
      Acts 21:1-14
      Luke 5:12-26
W     Hos. 3:1-5
      Acts 21:15-26
      Luke 5:27-39
Th    Hos. 4:1-10
      Acts 21:27-36
      Luke 6:1-11
F     Hos. 4:11-19
      Acts 21:37–22:16
      Luke 6:12-26
Sa    Hos. 5:1-7
      Acts 22:17-29
      Luke 6:27-38


*Week following Sunday
between Oct. 2 and 8
inclusive*
Su    Hos. 5:8–6:6
      1 Cor. 2:6-16
      Matt. 14:1-12
M     Hos. 6:7–7:7
      Acts 22:30–23:11
      Luke 6:39-49
Tu    Hos. 7:8-16
      Acts 23:12-24
      Luke 7:1-17
W     Hos. 8:1-14

Acts 23:23-35
Luke 7:18-35
**Th** Hos. 9:1-9
Acts 24:1-23
Luke 7:36-50
**F** Hos. 9:10-17
Acts 24:24–25:12
Luke 8:1-15
**Sa** Hos. 10:1-15
Acts 25:13-27
Luke 8:16-25

*Week following Sunday
between Oct. 9 and 15
inclusive*
**Su** Hos. 11:1-11
1 Cor. 4:9-16
Matt. 15:21-28
**M** Hos. 11:12–12:1
Acts 26:1-23
Luke 8:26-39
**Tu** Hos. 12:2-14
Acts 26:24–27:8
Luke 8:40-56
**W** Hos. 13:1-3
Acts 27:9-26
Luke 9:1-17
**Th** Hos. 13:4-8
Acts 27:27-44
Luke 9:18-27
**F** Hos. 13:9-16
Acts 28:1-16
Luke 9:28-36
**Sa** Hos. 14:1-9
Acts 28:17-31
Luke 9:37-50

*Week following Sunday
between Oct. 16 and 22
inclusive*
**Su** Ecclus. 4:1-10
*or Micah 1:1-9*
1 Cor. 10:1-13
Matt. 16:13-20
**M** Ecclus. 4:20–5:7
*or Micah 2:1-13*
Rev. 7:1-8
Luke 9:51-62

**Tu** Ecclus. 6:5-17
*or Micah 3:1-8*
Rev. 7:9-17
Luke 10:1-16
**W** Ecclus. 7:4-14
*or Micah 3:9–4:5*
Rev. 8:1-13
Luke 10:17-24
**Th** Ecclus. 10:1-18
*or Micah 5:1-4, 10-15*
Rev. 9:1-12
Luke 10:25-37
**F** Ecclus. 11:2-20
*or Micah 6:1-8*
Rev. 9:13-21
Luke 10:38-42
**Sa** Ecclus. 15:9-20
*or Micah 7:1-7*
Rev. 10:1-11
Luke 11:1-13

*Week following Sunday
between Oct. 23 and 29
inclusive*
**Su** Ecclus. 18:19-33
*or Jonah 1:1-17a*
1 Cor. 10:15-24
Matt. 18:15-20
**M** Ecclus. 19:4-17
*or Jonah 1:17–2:10*
Rev. 11:1-14
Luke 11:14-26
**Tu** Ecclus. 24:1-12
*or Jonah 3:1–4:11*
Rev. 11:14-19
Luke 11:27-36
**W** Ecclus. 28:14-26
*or Nahum 1:1-14*
Rev. 12:1-6
Luke 11:37-52
**Th** Ecclus. 31:12-18,
25–32:2
*or Nahum 1:15–2:12*
Rev. 12:7-17
Luke 11:53–12:12
**F** Ecclus. 34:1-8, 18-22
*or Nahum 2:13–3:7*
Rev. 13:1-10
Luke 12:13-31

**Sa** Ecclus. 35:1-17
*or Nahum 3:8-19*
Rev. 13:11-18
Luke 12:32-48

*Week following Sunday
between Oct. 30 and Nov.
5 inclusive*
**Su** Ecclus. 36:1-17
*or Zeph. 1:1-6*
1 Cor. 12:27–13:13
Matt. 18:21-35
**M** Ecclus. 38:24-34
*or Zeph. 1:7-13*
Rev. 14:1-13
Luke 12:49-59
**Tu** Ecclus. 43:1-22
*or Zeph. 1:14-18*
Rev. 14:14–15:8
Luke 13:1-9
**W** Ecclus. 43:23-33
*or Zeph. 2:1-15*
Rev. 16:1-11
Luke 13:10-17
**Th** Ecclus. 44:1-15
*or Zeph. 3:1-7*
Rev. 16:12-21
Luke 13:18-30
**F** Ecclus. 50:1, 11-24
*or Zeph. 3:8-13*
Rev. 17:1-18
Luke 13:31-35
**Sa** Ecclus. 51:1-12
*or Zeph. 3:14-20*
Rev. 18:1-14
Luke 14:1-11

*Week following Sunday
between Nov. 6 and 12
inclusive*
**Su** Ecclus. 51:13-22
*or Joel 1:1-13*
1 Cor. 14:1-12
Matt. 20:1-16
**M** Joel 1:1-13
*or Joel 1:15–2:2*
Rev. 18:15-24
Luke 14:12-24

| | | | | | |
|---|---|---|---|---|---|
| **Tu** | Joel 1:15–2:2 (3-11) | | Phil. 3:13–4:1 | | *Christ the King (Sunday* |
| | *or* Joel 2:3-11 | | Matt. 23:13-24 | | *between Nov. 20 and 26)* |
| | Rev. 19:1-10 | **M** | Hab. 2:1-4, 9-20 | | *and following* |
| | Luke 14:25-35 | | James 2:14-26 | **Su** | Zech. 9:9-16 |
| **W** | Joel 2:12-19 | | Luke 16:19-31 | | 1 Peter 3:13-22 |
| | Rev. 19:11-21 | **Tu** | Hab. 3:1-10 (11-15) | | Matt. 21:1-13 |
| | Luke 15:1-10 | | 16-18 | **M** | Zech. 10:1-12 |
| **Th** | Joel 2:21-27 | | James 3:1-12 | | Gal. 6:1-10 |
| | James 1:1-15 | | Luke 17:1-10 | | Luke 18:15-30 |
| | Luke 15:1-2, 11-32 | **W** | Mal. 1:1, 6-14 | **Tu** | Zech. 11:4-17 |
| **F** | Joel 2:28–3:8 | | James 3:13–4:12 | | 1 Cor. 3:10-23 |
| | James 1:16-27 | | Luke 17:11-19 | | Luke 18:31-43 |
| | Luke 16:1-9 | **Th** | Mal. 2:1-16 | **W** | Zech. 12:1-10 |
| **Sa** | Joel 3:9-17 | | James 4:13–5:6 | | Eph. 1:3-14 |
| | James 2:1-13 | | Luke 17:20-37 | | Luke 19:1-10 |
| | Luke 16:10-17 (18) | **F** | Mal. 3:1-12 | **Th** | Zech. 13:1-9 |
| | | | James 5:7-12 | | Eph. 1:15-23 |
| | | | Luke 18:1-8 | | Luke 19:11-27 |
| | *Week following Sunday* | **Sa** | Mal. 3:13–4:6 | **F** | Zech. 14:1-11 |
| | *between Nov. 13 and 19* | | James 5:13-20 | | Rom. 15:7-13 |
| | *inclusive* | | Luke 18:9-14 | | Luke 19:28-40 |
| **Su** | Hab. 1:1-4 (5-11) | | | **Sa** | Zech. 14:12-21 |
| | 12–2:1 | | | | Phil. 2:1-11 |
| | | | | | Luke 19:41-48 |

## OTHER FESTIVALS

*The Presentation—Feb. 2*
Mal. 3:1-4
Heb. 2:14-18
Luke 2:22-40

*The Annunciation—*
*March 25*
Isa. 7:10-14
1 Tim. 3:16
*or* Heb. 10:5-10
Luke 1:26-38

*The Visitation—May 31*
Isa. 11:1-5
*or* 1 Sam. 2:1-10
Rom. 12:9-16b
Luke 1:39-47

*Birth of John the Baptist—*
*June 24*
Mal. 3:1-4
*or* Isa. 40:1-11
Luke 1:5-23, 57-67
(68-80)*
Matt. 11:2-19**

*Holy Cross—Sept. 14*
Num. 21:4b-9
*or* Isa. 45:21-25
1 Cor. 1:18-24
John 3:13-17
*or* John 12:20-33

*All Saints' Day—Nov. 1*
Isa. 26:1-4, 8-9,
12-13, 19-21
Rev. 21:9-11, 22-27
(22:1-5)
*or* Heb. 11:32–12:2
Matt. 5:1-12

*Day of Thanksgiving*
Deut. 8:1-10
Phil. 4:6-20
*or* 1 Tim. 2:1-4
Luke 17:11-19

---

*Intended for use in the morning       **Intended for use in the evening

# NOTES

1. John Calvin, Preface to *Commentary on the Psalms*.

2. For a thorough discussion of the history of daily prayer see Robert Taft, *The Liturgy of the Hours in East and West: The Origins of the Divine Office and Its Meaning for Today* (Collegeville, Minn.: Liturgical Press, 1986). Other helpful accounts of the background of daily prayer are included in: Marion J. Hatchett, *Sanctifying Life, Time and Space* (New York: Seabury Press, 1976); and idem, *Commentary on the American Prayer Book* (New York: Seabury Press, 1980), pp. 89–153.

3. Hughes Oliphant Old, *Praying with the Bible* (Philadelphia: Geneva Press, 1980), p. 78.

4. Hughes Oliphant Old, "Daily Prayer in the Reformed Church of Strasbourg, 1525–1530," *Worship*, vol. 52, no. 2 (March 1978), pp. 121ff.

5. John Calvin, *Institutes of the Christian Religion* 3.20.50.

6. Hughes Oliphant Old, loc. cit. (see note 4, above), pp. 126–127.

7. Ford Lewis Battles, ed., *The Piety of John Calvin* (Grand Rapids: Baker Book House, 1978), pp. 137ff.

8. John Calvin, *Institutes of the Christian Religion*, 3.20.32.

9. Millar Patrick, ed., *The Scottish Collects from the Scottish Metrical Psalter of 1595* (Edinburgh: Church of Scotland Committee on Publications, n.d.), pp. 3–8.

10. It will be helpful to those who use this resource to be familiar with other resources for daily prayer. The most important are: *Christian Prayer: The Liturgy of the Hours* (New York: Catholic Book Publishing Co., 1976); *Praise God: Common Prayer at Taizé* (New York: Oxford University Press, 1977); *Lutheran Book of Worship*, Ministers Desk Edition (Minneapolis: Augsburg Publishing House, 1978); *The Book of Common Prayer* (New York: Seabury Press, 1977). A useful edition of the Orthodox daily office is *A Prayerbook* (Cambridge, N.Y.: New Skete, 1976). Another daily office in the Eastern

tradition is: *Byzantine Daily Worship* (Allendale, N.J.: Alleluia Press, 1969).

11. A Supplemental Liturgical Resource is projected that will provide a variety of musical settings for singing the psalms and biblical songs.

12. Massey H. Shepherd, Jr., *The Psalms in Christian Worship: A Practical Guide* (Minneapolis: Augsburg Publishing House, 1976) is a helpful overview of the history of the use of psalms in Jewish and Christian worship.

13. In many psalters prepared for liturgical use, the numbering of the psalms is taken from the Greek Septuagint. This numbering differs from that in the Hebrew text and the Bibles we use. The result is that in these psalters, many of the psalms have a different number from what we are accustomed to. For example, Psalm 23 in our Bibles is Psalm 22 in the Greek Septuagint. The following comparative numbering of the two systems will be helpful when different numbering is encountered:

| Greek Septuagint | Hebrew |
| --- | --- |
| 1–8 | 1–8 |
| 9 | 9–10 |
| 10–112 | 11–113 |
| 113 | 114–115 |
| 114–115 | 116 |
| 116–145 | 117–146 |
| 146–147 | 147 |
| 148–150 | 148–150 |

Furthermore, when using the psalm text in some liturgical psalters, one will find variations in the numbering of the verses of the psalms from that in the Bible. This altered versification is for musical reasons. The versification in this book conforms to that in the Bible. Consequently, the verse numbers of a psalm noted in this resource may not always match those in a liturgical psalter.

14. See John Folkening, *Handbells in the Liturgical Service* (St. Louis: Concordia Publishing House, 1984).

15. A variety of incense resins and self-starting charcoal may be purchased from some church supply houses such as Fortress Church Supply Stores.

16. Millar Patrick, op. cit. (see note 9, above).

17. Two useful resources for such readings are: John W. Doberstein, ed., *Minister's Prayer Book* (Philadelphia: Fortress Press, 1986); and Reuben P. Job and Norman Shawchuck, *A Guide to Prayer for Ministers and Other Servants* (Nashville: The Upper Room, 1983).

18. Philip H. Pfatteicher and Carlos R. Messerli, *Manual on the Liturgy— Lutheran Book of Worship* (Minneapolis: Augsburg Publishing House, 1979), p. 300.

19. A treasury of prayers is being developed by the Office of Worship. This resource will be a collection of prayers suitable for daily prayer, representative of the centuries of Christian history and of the variety of liturgical and ethnic traditions. It is anticipated that it will be available in 1988.

20. *A Manual of Eastern Orthodox Prayers* (Crestwood, N.Y.: St. Vladimir's Seminary Press, 1983), p. 11.

21. This lectionary is from *The Book of Common Prayer* and the *Lutheran Book of Worship*, the Lutheran version being a slight revision of the lectionary in *The Book of Common Prayer*. The lectionary included in this resource incorporates most of the revisions in the Lutheran version.

22. The Second Helvetic Confession, ch. 1; and the Westminster Confession of Faith, ch. 1, para. 3.

# SOURCES
# OF THE LITURGICAL TEXTS

The texts contained in this volume are both new and old. Many have been written for this resource. Other texts are broadly representative of ecumenical traditions in both West and East, and are drawn from ancient sources as well as contemporary. To enable users to appreciate the breadth of this resource, sources are identified for texts whose source is not noted with the text itself. These abbreviations are used in the source notes.

ASB  *The Alternative Service Book 1980.* Church of England.

BAS  *The Book of Alternative Services of the Anglican Church of Canada*, 1985.

BCP  *The Book of Common Prayer.* Episcopal Church, U.S.A., 1979.

BCW  *The Book of Common Worship.* Presbyterian, U.S.A. The edition (1906, 1932, or 1946) is identified in the source notes.

BL  *Bless the Lord*, William G. Storey, ed. Ave Maria Press, 1974.

EAS  *Authorized Services.* Episcopal Church, U.S.A., 1973.

ELLC English Language Liturgical Consultation

LBW  *Lutheran Book of Worship.* Lutheran, U.S.A., 1978.

LH  *The Liturgy of the Hours.* According to the Roman rite. English translation prepared by the International Committee on English in the Liturgy, Inc., 1975.

LPC  *A Liturgical Psalter for the Christian Year* by Massey H. Shepherd, Jr., 1976.

PGS  *Praise God in Song.* G.I.A. Publications, Inc., 1979.

PH  *Praise Him: A Prayerbook for Today's Christians*, William G. Storey. Ave Maria Press, 1973.

RS  *The Sacramentary.* Roman Catholic, 1974.

SMP  *Scottish Metrical Psalter.* Church of Scotland, 1595.

TAZ  Daily Office of the Community of Taizé. France, 1971.

WBK  *The Worshipbook—Services and Hymns.* Presbyterian, U.S.A., 1972.

Abbreviations for Bible translations are:

JB   *The Jerusalem Bible*
NAB *The New American Bible*
NEB *The New English Bible*
PHL J.B. Phillips, *The New Testament in Modern English*
RSV *Revised Standard Version*
TEV *The Bible in Today's English Version*

## Opening Sentences (pp. 51–186)

*From RSV:* Isa. 53:5; Matt. 2:2; Luke 12:37; 1 Cor. 15:56. *Altered:* Ps. 69:16; Ps. 85:11–12; Ps. 96:3; Ps. 96:11, 13; Isa. 7:14; Isa. 9:6; Isa. 55:12; Zech. 9:9; Zech. 14:5–7; Matt. 6:13; Luke 1:28, 30–31, 35; Luke 2:14; John 1:1–3; John 1:9; John 1:14; John 13:34–35; Acts 1:8; Heb. 2:9; Heb. 4:14, 16; 1 Peter 1:3; Rev. 6:9–10; Rev. 22:5.

*From TEV:* Ps. 5:2–3; Isa. 40:3. *Altered:* Deut. 32:11; Ps. 74:16–17; Isa. 40:30–31; Lam. 3:22; Amos 5:8; Matt. 26:41, 45; Mark 11:25; Luke 23:53, 56; Acts 5:32; Rom. 5:1–2; Rom. 6:4; Rom. 6:8–9; Rom. 8:31, 39; Rom. 13:11–13; 1 Cor. 15:51–52, 54, 57; 2 Cor. 1:4–5; Eph. 1:6–8; Phil. 2:12–13; Heb. 12:2; Rev. 22:12–13.

*From NEB:* Ps. 86:9–10. *Altered:* Isa. 40:3; Luke 19:41; Rom. 11:33, 36.

*Based on more than one version of scripture:* Ps. 32:1–2 (RSV, TEV, Grail); Ps. 32:6–7 (RSV, TEV, NEB); Ps. 34:3 (RSV, TEV); Ps. 51:6–7 (RSV, BCP, Grail); Ps. 63:1, 3–4 (TEV, Grail); Ps. 85:10–11 (RSV, TEV, NEB); Ps. 86:5–6 (RSV, TEV, NEB); Ps. 86:12–13 (RSV, TEV, Grail); Ps. 130:1–4 (RSV, Grail); Ps. 139:11–12 (RSV, TEV, JB); Ps. 143:10 (RSV, TEV); Isa. 26:9, 19 (RSV, NEB); Isa. 33:2 (TEV, NEB); Isa. 60:1, 3, 6 (RSV, TEV); Isa. 64:8–9c (RSV, TEV); Jer. 31:15 (RSV, TEV); Dan. 2:22–23; Matt. 21:5, 9 (RSV, TEV); Matt. 21:12–13 (RSV, TEV); Matt. 21:15–16 (RSV, TEV); Matt. 21:22 (RSV, TEV, NEB); Matt. 26:1–2 (RSV, TEV); Matt. 26:21–22 (RSV, TEV); Luke 23:33–34 (RSV, TEV); Rom. 5:6, 8 (RSV, TEV, PHL); Eph. 1:34 (RSV, TEV); Phil. 1:6, 9–10 (RSV, TEV, NEB); Col. 3:16–17 (TEV, RSV); 1 John 1:5, 7 (RSV, TEV); Rev. 21:23–24 (RSV, TEV, NEB, JB).

*From JB:* John 1:4–5. Altered.

*From LPC:* Isa. 45:8.

*Opening sentences for Sat. and Sun. evenings*—Ordinary Days: "Jesus Christ is the light . . ."; Advent: "The Spirit and the church cry out . . ."; Christmas and Epiphany: "The people who walked . . ."; Lent: "Behold, now is the accepted time . . ."; Easter and Pentecost: "Jesus Christ is risen . . ."; are from LBW. Those for Christmas–Epiphany are altered.

*Opening sentences* for Christmas evening prayer, "Today Christ is born . . . ," are based on the antiphon for the Song of Mary for Christmas Day in the

LH. The opening sentences for Epiphany morning prayer, "Today the church is joined . . . ," are based on the antiphon for the Song of Zechariah for Epiphany in the LH. The opening sentences for morning prayer for Epiphany (for Baptism of the Lord), "Sealed with the sign . . . ," are adapted from the antiphon for the Song of Zechariah for Baptism of the Lord in TAZ. The opening sentences for evening prayer for Epiphany, "This is a holy day . . . ," are based on the antiphon for the Song of Mary in the LH.

From the psalter in the BCP and LBW: Ps. 51:10–11; Ps. 51:14. Altered: Ps. 51:1–2; Ps. 51:9, 12; Ps. 103:8.

The sentence for evening prayer for Friday evening of Easter, "Christ is risen from the dead . . . ," is based on an antiphon sung in the Eastern Byzantine Easter liturgy.

## Thanksgivings for Light—in Service of Light (pp. 51–186)

Ordinary days—Sunday: The thanksgiving for light from the Apostolic Constitutions is a translation from LBW, altered. The Jewish berakah of the evening is based on traditional and Reformed texts.

Ordinary days—Saturday: The first thanksgiving for light is from LBW, altered. The thanksgiving for light from the Apostolic Tradition is based on translations in LBW and Lucien Deiss, Springtime of the Liturgy.

Other: The thanksgivings for light for Advent, Christmas–Epiphany, Lent, Easter, and Pentecost were written by John Allyn Melloh, S.M., and are from PGS. Those for Advent, Christmas–Epiphany, and Easter are altered.

## Prayers Concluding Thanksgivings and Intercessions (pp. 51–186)

From LH: Ordinary days—Tues. morning, second prayer (alt.); Advent—Sun. morning (alt.); Thurs. evening (alt.); Fri. morning (alt.); Fri. evening (alt.); Sat. morning (based on two prayers); Christmas morning; Lent—Wed. morning, for other days (alt.); Good Friday morning (alt.); Easter—Sun. morning (alt.); Sun. evening (alt.); Sat. morning, 1st prayer (alt.); Pentecost morning (alt.).

From TAZ: Advent—Sat. evening (adapted); Christmas evening, Dec. 24, 25, Sat. and Sun. (alt.); Christmas evening, Dec. 26–Jan. 4 (alt.); Epiphany morning (alt.), and Ascension Day (alt.).

From BL: Epiphany, evening Jan. 7 through following Sunday (alt.).

From BCP: Ash Wednesday morning (second prayer).

## Dismissals (pp. 51–186)

From RSV: Rom. 15:13 (adapted); 1 Tim. 1:17 (adapted); 2 Peter 3:18 (adapted). From TEV: Phil. 4:7 (adapted); Phil. 4:9 (adapted); Phil. 4:23 (alt.); 2 Thess. 3:16 (adapted); 1 Tim. 6:21 (adapted).

## Midday Prayer (pp. 189–194)

*Prayers of the People: From BCP:* first prayer, "Eternal God, send . . ."; sixth prayer, "Almighty Savior . . ."; seventh prayer, "Blessed Savior. . . ." *From WBK:* second prayer, "New every morning. . . ." *From LH:* eighth prayer, "God of mercy . . ." *From LBW:* fourth prayer, "Eternal God, you call. . . ."


## Night Prayer (pp. 195–203)

*Prayers of Confession:* The first prayer, "Merciful God, we confess . . . ," is a revision of a prayer from BCW (1946) and BCP. The second prayer, "Eternal God, in whom . . . ," is a revision of a prayer from BCW (1906, 1932, 1946). The third prayer, "I confess to God Almighty . . . ," is adapted from the penitential rite in the RS. The fourth prayer, "May the almighty and merciful God . . . ," is a revision of a prayer in BCW (1946).

*Scripture Readings. From RSV:* Matt. 11:28–30; John 14:27; 1 Thess. 5:9–10; 1 Thess. 5:23 (alt.); Heb. 13:20–21 (alt.); Rev. 22:3c–5 (alt.). *From TEV:* Deut. 6:4–7. *From NEB:* Rom. 8:38–39. *Based on RSV and NEB:* Jer. 14:9.

*Prayers.* The versicles are from Ps. 31:5 and Ps. 17:8, 15. Lines 3 and 4, "Keep me as . . . ," are traditional for night prayer. The sources of the collects are as follows: "O Lord, support . . . ," is attributed to John Henry Newman. "O God, you have designed . . ." is from WBK. "Keep watch, dear Lord . . ." is from BCP and derives from the writings of St. Augustine of Hippo. "O God, who appointed . . ." is revised from BCW (1946). "Lord God, send peaceful . . ." is from the liturgy for night prayer of the Roman Catholic Church. "Visit our dwellings . . ." is a traditional prayer for night prayer; the text is from LBW. "Gracious Lord, we give . . ." is from LBW. "Eternal God, the hours . . ." is from EAS. "Be our light . . ." dates from at least the ninth century and is taken from BCP. "Be present, O merciful God . . ." dates from at least the sixth century and is taken from BCP. "Lord, fill this night . . ." and "Lord, give our bodies . . ." are from the Roman rite for night prayer in LH.


## Psalm Prayers (pp. 207–254)

Many of the psalm prayers were prepared by the daily prayer task force. Sources of other psalm prayers are as follows.

*Based on prayers in the SMP (1595):* Ps. 15, first prayer; Ps. 17, second prayer; Ps. 23, third prayer; Ps. 25, Lent; Ps. 27, second prayer; Ps. 32, second prayer; Ps. 43; Ps. 46, second prayer; Ps. 89:1–18; Ps. 93, second prayer; Ps. 95; Ps. 97, second prayer; Ps. 98, Christmas; Ps. 105; Ps. 113, Easter; 119:73–80; Ps. 145, first prayer; 147:12–20, first prayer.

*Based on psalm prayers from LH:* In many instances alterations of LH prayers that were incorporated in LBW are reflected in those used in this book. Ps. 2; Ps. 5, second prayer; Ps. 6, first prayer; Ps. 9, Easter; Ps. 12, first prayer; Ps. 16, Advent; Ps. 18:1–20; Ps. 22; Ps. 23, first prayer; Ps. 34; Ps. 40, first prayer; Ps. 50; Ps. 62, second prayer; Ps. 66, first prayer; Ps. 67, Advent; Ps. 80; Ps. 89:19–52; Ps. 92; Ps. 100, Epiphany; Ps. 107; Ps. 115; Ps. 118, Easter; Ps. 122, Advent; Ps. 124; Ps. 138, second prayer; Ps. 147:1–11, Lent; Ps. 148, second prayer; Ps. 149, Advent.

*Adapted from LBW:* Ps. 3; Ps. 7; Ps. 8; Ps. 15, second prayer; Ps. 17, first prayer; Ps. 25, Advent; Ps. 26; Ps. 28; Ps. 29, Baptism of the Lord; Ps. 42, second prayer; Ps. 45; Ps. 46, first prayer; Ps. 47, Easter; Ps. 54; Ps. 67, first prayer; Ps. 72, first prayer; Ps. 82; Ps. 85, Advent; Ps. 94; Ps. 96, Christmas; Ps. 97, first prayer; Ps. 98, Easter; Ps. 99, Easter; Ps. 102, Lent; Ps. 117, Easter; Ps. 126, Lent; Ps. 130, Advent and Lent; Ps. 134; Ps. 136; Ps. 141, first prayer; Ps. 142; Ps. 145, Advent; and the prayer for Pss. 145; 147:1–11; and 148 suggested for use during Christmas–Epiphany.

*Adapted from the Eastern rite:* Ps. 33, Pentecost; and the prayer suggested for Pss. 146; 147:12–20; 149; 150 for use during Christmas–Epiphany.

*Adapted from BL:* Ps. 96, Easter.

*Adapted from PH:* Ps. 146, Advent.


## Biblical Songs and Ancient Hymns (pp. 260–278)

Song of Zechariah; Song of Mary; "We Praise You, O God"; "Glory to God"; and Song of Simeon are ecumenically agreed texts prepared by the English Language Liturgical Consultation (ELLC). The refrain for the Song of Simeon is the traditional antiphon for the Song of Simeon for night prayer.

"O Radiant Light" *(Phos Hilaron)* is a translation by William G. Storey.

Song of Miriam and Moses; Song of Thanksgiving; "Seek the Lord"; The New Jerusalem; A Song of Praise; A Song of Penitence; A Song to the Lamb; Song of the Redeemed; and Christ Our Passover are from BCP. All are altered.

Song of David is from NAB and is altered.

A Song for Pentecost; Christ, the Head of All Creation; "Jesus Christ Is Lord"; The Beatitudes; and Christ the Servant are from RSV and are altered.

A Song of Love is based on the RSV and NEB.

"Holy, Holy, Holy Is the Lord" is from TEV and is altered.

"Worthy Is the Lamb" is based on the RSV and TEV texts.


## Prayers of Thanksgiving and Intercession (pp. 279–319)

The Litany (no. 40), based on litanies from the Eastern liturgies, is drawn from translations in BCP and LBW. The concluding collect is an altered version of the Collect for Peace in the BCP, and dates from at least the eighth century.

The Great Litany (no. 41) is a classic Christian prayer that has ancient roots. A version of it appeared in BCW (1946). The text in this resource is based on texts in BCP, ASB, BAS, and BCW (1946). The "Jesus, Lamb of God" incorporated into the litany is the ecumenically agreed text of the ELLC.

The Advent Litany (no. 45) is comprised of the "O Antiphons" which, since the Middle Ages, have been sung before and after the *Magnificat* in evening prayer during the final days of Advent.

The litanies for Christmas, morning and evening (nos. 47, 49); Epiphany (nos. 51, 53); Lent (nos. 57, 59); morning prayer for Good Friday and Holy Saturday (no. 62); evening prayer for Holy Saturday (no. 64); and Ascension Day, morning and evening (no. 69), are revisions of litanies used in TAZ. The "Jesus, Lamb of God" incorporated into the litanies for Other Days in Lent/Evening Prayer 2; Good Friday and Holy Saturday/Morning Prayer; and Holy Saturday/Evening Prayer is the ecumenically agreed text of the ELLC.

## Grace at Meals (pp. 320–322)

"Give us grateful hearts . . ." is from BCP.

"Lord Jesus, be our holy guest . . ." is from BCW (1906, 1932, 1946), and was written by Henry van Dyke. Altered.

The fourth-century prayer is from the *Apostolic Constitutions*, c. A.D. 380.

# ACKNOWLEDGMENTS

Material from the following sources is gratefully acknowledged and is used by permission. Adaptations are by permission of copyright holders. Every effort has been made to determine the ownership of all texts and music used in this resource and to make proper arrangements for their use. The publisher regrets any oversight that may have occurred and will gladly make proper acknowledgment in future editions if brought to the publisher's attention.

Scripture quotations from the Revised Standard Version of the Bible are copyrighted 1946, 1952, © 1971, 1973 by the Division of Christian Education of the National Council of the Churches of Christ in the U.S.A.

Scripture quotations from The New English Bible are copyrighted © 1961, 1970 by The Delegates of the Oxford University Press and The Syndics of the Cambridge University Press.

Scripture quotations from The Bible in Today's English Version are copyrighted © 1976 by the American Bible Society.

Scripture quotation from The Jerusalem Bible is copyrighted © 1966, 1967, and 1968 by Darton, Longman & Todd Ltd and Doubleday & Company, Inc.

Scripture quotation from The New American Bible is copyrighted © 1970 by the Confraternity of Christian Doctrine, Washington, D.C. All rights reserved.

Song of Zechariah; Song of Mary; "We Praise You, O God," "Glory to God," "Jesus, Lamb of God," "Glory to the Father," and Song of Simeon texts copyright © English Language Liturgical Consultation (ELLC) 1987. All rights reserved.

"O Radiant Light" (Phos Hilaron), by William G. Storey, is from Praise God in Song, and is used with his permission. Thanksgivings for light by John Allyn Melloh, S.M., for Advent (pp. 87, 106), Christmas–Epiphany (pp. 112, 120), Lent (pp. 127, 152), Easter (pp. 157, 179), and Pentecost (p. 184) are from *Praise God in Song*, copyright © 1979 by G.I.A. Publications, Inc., Chicago, Illinois. All rights reserved.

*The Book of Common Worship*, copyright © 1932 and 1946 by The Board of Christian Education of the Presbyterian Church in the United States of America. Used by permission of The Westminster Press.

*The Worshipbook—Services*, copyright © MCMLXX by The Westminster Press.

The Song of Miriam and Moses; Song of Thanksgiving; "Seek the Lord"; The New Jerusalem; A Song of Praise; A Song of Penitence; A Song to the Lamb; The Song of the Redeemed; Christ Our Passover, and various prayers from *The Book of Common Prayer*, 1977.

Opening sentences as noted on pp. 425–426, thanksgivings for light noted on p. 426, prayers in Night Prayer noted on p. 427, and musical setting for the Lord's Prayer, from the *Lutheran Book of Worship*, copyright © 1978. Used by permission of Augsburg Publishing House.

English translation of prayers noted on pp. 425–427, and psalm prayers noted on p. 428, from *The Liturgy of the Hours* © 1974, International Committee on English in the Liturgy, Inc., are used by permission of the International Commission on English in the Liturgy. All rights reserved. Psalm prayers from *The Liturgy of the Hours* (Pss. 9; 12; 16; 22; 23; 40; 62; 66; 115; 138; 149), adapted for the *Lutheran Book of Worship*, copyright © 1978, are also used by permission of Augsburg Publishing House.

English translation of the *Confiteor*, the prayer of confession in Night Prayer, "I confess to God . . ." (p. 196), from *The Roman Missal* © 1973, International Committee on English in the Liturgy, Inc. All rights reserved.

Psalm prayer for Ps. 96 (Easter), prayer "Eternal Light . . ." (p. 123), and adaptations of antiphons from the Liturgy of the Hours: "Today the church is . . ." (p. 117), and "This is a holy day . . ." (pp. 120, 123), from *Bless the Lord! A Prayerbook for Advent, Christmas, Lent and Eastertide,* © 1974 by Ave Maria Press, Notre Dame, Indiana. All rights reserved.

Psalm prayer for Ps. 146 (Advent), and Pentecost litany (no. 72), from *Praise Him! A Prayerbook for Today's Christian,* © 1973 by Ave Maria Press, Notre Dame, Indiana. All rights reserved.

Prayer "Eternal God, the hours . . . ," from *Authorized Services*, copyright © 1973 by the Church Hymnal Corporation. Used by permission.

Text of Isa. 45:8 (pp. 93–94) is a translation from *A Liturgical Psalter for the Christian Year*, copyrighted © 1976 by Massey H. Shepherd, Jr. All rights reserved.

Translation of the prayer "Blessed are you, Lord . . ." (no. 78), from *Early Christian Prayers,* ed. by A. Hamman, O.F.M., tr. by Walter Mitchel, is copyrighted © 1961 by Longmans, Green & Co., Ltd.

Texts based upon the Daily Office of the Community of Taizé, from *Praise God: Common Prayer at Taizé.* Copyright © 1975 by Les Presses de Taizé. Published by Oxford University Press, 1977. Reprinted by permission of Oxford University Press, Inc.

Text of thanksgiving for light from *The Apostolic Tradition* (pp. 82–83) is based in part on a translation in *Springtime of the Liturgy* by Lucien Deiss, tr. by Matthew J. O'Connell, copyright © 1979 by The Order of St. Benedict, Inc. Published by The Liturgical Press, Collegeville, Minnesota. All rights reserved. Used with permission.

# INDEX OF BIBLICAL SONGS
# AND ANCIENT HYMNS

*Numbers refer to texts on pages 260ff.*
*Italic numbers refer to musical settings on pages 325ff.*

# GENERAL INDEX

*Unless otherwise noted, numbers refer to pages.*